European Integration

Annual of European and Global Studies

An annual collection of the best research on European and global themes, the *Annual of European and Global Studies* publishes issues with a specific focus, each addressing critical developments and controversies in the field.

Published volumes:
Religion and Politics: European and Global Perspectives
Edited by Johann P. Arnason and Ireneusz Paweł Karolewski

African, American and European Trajectories of Modernity: Past Oppression, Future Justice?
Edited by Peter Wagner

Social Transformations and Revolutions: Reflections and Analyses
Edited by Johann P. Arnason and Marek Hrubec

European Integration: Historical Trajectories, Geopolitical Contexts
Edited by Johann P. Arnason

https://edinburghuniversitypress.com/series-annual-of-european-and-global-studies.html

Annual of European and Global Studies

European Integration

Historical Trajectories, Geopolitical Contexts

Edited by Johann P. Arnason

EDINBURGH
University Press

Edinburgh University Press is one of the leading university presses in the UK. We publish academic books and journals in our selected subject areas across the humanities and social sciences, combining cutting-edge scholarship with high editorial and production values to produce academic works of lasting importance. For more information visit our website: edinburghuniversitypress.com

Edinburgh University Press Ltd
TheTun–HolyroodRoad
12(2f) Jackson's Entry
Edinburgh EH8 8PJ

First published in hardback by Edinburgh University Press 2019

Typeset in 11.5/13.5 Minion Pro by
IDSUK (DataConnection) Ltd

A CIP record for this book is available from the British Library

ISBN 978 1 4744 5589 3 (hardback)
ISBN 978 1 4744 5590 9 (paperback)
ISBN 978 1 4744 5591 6 (webready PDF)
ISBN 978 1 4744 5592 3 (epub)

Contents

Contributors

Johann P. Arnason is Professor Emeritus of Sociology at La Trobe University, Melbourne, and an associate of the Department of Historical Sociology, Faculty of Human Studies, Charles University, Prague. His research interests centre on historical sociology, with particular emphasis on the comparative analysis of civilisations. Publications include: *Civilizations in Dispute*, Brill 2003; *Axial Civilizations and World History* (ed., with S. N. Eisenstadt and Björn Wittrock), Brill 2005; *Anthropology and Civilizational Analysis* (ed., with Chris Hann), SUNY Press 2018.

Paul Blokker is Associate Professor, Department of Sociology and Business Law, University of Bologna, and research coordinator at the Institute of Sociological Studies, Charles University, Prague. His recent publications include: *Sociological Constitutionalism* (ed., with Chris Thornhill), Cambridge University Press 2017, and *Constitutional Acceleration within the European Union and Beyond* (ed.), Routledge 2017.

Natalie J. Doyle is Senior Lecturer in the School of Languages, Literature, Cultures and Linguistics, Monash University, Melbourne. She has written on the contemporary crisis of the European Union and political radicalisation in the name of Islam. Recent publications include: *Marcel Gauchet and the Loss of Common Purpose*, Lexington Books 2018, and *(Il)liberal Europe: Islamophobia, Modernity and Radicalization* (ed., with Irfan Ahmad), Routledge 2018.

Chris Hann is a British anthropologist and Director of the Max Planck Institute for Social Anthropology in Halle. He has written on economic anthropology, religion, the long-term history of Eurasia, and post-socialist transformations. His publications include *Economic Anthropology: History, Ethnography, Critique* (with Keith Hart), Cambridge

University Press 2011, *Anthropology and Civilizational Analysis* (ed., with Johann P. Arnason), SUNY Press 2018, and *Repatriating Polanyi: Market Society in the Visegrad States,* Central University Press, 2019.

Toby E. Huff is a Research Associate at Harvard University in the Department of Astronomy, and a Designated Campus Scholar at the University of Arizona. He has lectured in Europe, Asia and the Middle East. His book, *The Rise of Early Modern Science: Islam, China and the West,* was issued in a third edition by Cambridge University Press in 2017. He edited a collection of Benjamin Nelson's essays, *On the Roads to Modernity: Conscience, Science and Civilizations,* Lexington Books 1981, reprinted with a new Introduction in 2012. Other publications include *Intellectual Curiosity and the Scientific Revolution: A Global Perspective,* Cambridge University Press 2011, and *Max Weber and Islam* (ed., with Wolfgang Schluchter), Transaction Books 1999. His current project is titled *The Hidden Structure of Modernity: Bringing Law Back In.*

Ireneusz Paweł Karolewski holds the Chair of Political Science at the Willy Brandt Centre for German and European Studies at the University of Wroclaw, and has been editor of the *Annual of European and Global Studies* since its foundation. His main areas of research are modern political theory, collective identity and nationalism in Europe. His recent publications include *European Identity Revisited,* Routledge 2016, *Civic Resources and the Future of the European Union,* Routledge 2012, and *Citizenship and Collective Identity in Europe,* Routledge 2010.

Helmut Kuzmics was, until his retirement in 2013, Professor of Sociology at the University of Graz. He has written on the historical sociology of state and nation formation, the sociology of war, the sociology of emotions, the work of Norbert Elias, and the Habsburg Monarchy. His publications include *Emotion, Habitus und erster Weltkrieg* (with Sabine Haring), Vandenhoeck and Ruprecht 2013, *Theorizing Emotions: Sociological Explorations and Applications,* Campus 2009, and *Authority, State and National Character* (with Roland Axtmann), Ashgate 2007.

Dennis Smith is Emeritus Professor of Sociology at Loughborough University. His work has ranged from Victorian cities such as Birmingham and Sheffield to postwar ex-colonies of the British empire, especially apartheid-ridden South Africa and Burma under military dictatorship. He has also written on social theorists such as Zygmunt Bauman, Norbert

Elias and Barrington Moore, and edited *Sociological Review* and *Current Sociology*. His most recent book, *Civilized Rebels*, Routledge 2018, focuses on four prisoners: Oscar Wilde, Jean Améry, Nelson Mandela and Aung San Suu Kyi. He is currently writing about Brexit, the European Union and the West.

Bo Stråth is Emeritus Professor of Nordic, European and World History at the University of Helsinki. He also taught contemporary history at the European University Institute in Florence. He has written widely on modernity and Europe in the world from a historical perspective. His most recent books are *Europe's Utopias of Peace*, Bloomsbury 2018, and *European Modernity: A Global Approach* (with Peter Wagner), Bloomsbury 2017.

Acknowledgements

Thanks are due to my fellow editors of the *Annual*, Ireneusz Paweł Karolewski and Peter Wagner; also to the Centre of Global Studies, Czech Academy of Sciences, and especially its director, Marek Hrubec, for supporting this project, and to Marie Hlavičková for invaluable technical assistance.

Introduction: Perspectives on European Unity and Diversity

Johann P. Arnason

QUESTIONS REGARDING EUROPEAN integration, its background and its prospects have already been raised in this *Annual*, and the discussion will continue in a later issue. Volume 5 was devoted to migrations and borders, which will not be covered in the present volume; the next one will deal at length with relations between North and South within and beyond Europe, not addressed here, and in particular with the dynamics of debt and crisis. The chapters below are selective explorations of historical, regional and substantive aspects. Historical perspectives are briefly outlined as a way of contextualising recent trends; regional approaches focus on cases often seen as peripheral and therefore less present in mainstream debates than are the core countries of the European Union (EU); substantive analyses highlight problems arising in the most recent or current phases. The Brexit upset, unfolding as this is written and likely to cause further trouble, is noted in connection with broader developments.

Integrative processes of various kinds were at work in Europe long before the postwar project of unification, and the latter can be understood only in light of earlier constellations and transformations. At the same time, it should be emphasised that integrative moves were always accompanied by divisions and intertwined with counter-trends. If we reflect on Europe from a long-term perspective, four different periodisations and temporalities must be considered. There is, first, the whole trajectory of Europe as a historical formation. All of that experience is, in one way or another, relevant to questions of present and future importance. There is, notoriously, no consensus on the dating of European beginnings (the present writer has identified some ten different answers to that question). This is not the place to pursue the controversy; the view adopted here, though neither explained in detail nor essential to most of the papers, is that it makes most sense to regard

Europe as emerging from the transformation of the Roman world: that is, from the fourth to the ninth centuries CE. One major reason for taking that line is that – contrary to modernist orthodoxy – European nation-forming processes can be traced back to this epoch (for a strong but neglected formulation of this thesis, see Zientara 1997). The story begins with the co-emergence of two divergent but interconnected Europes, Western Christian and Byzantine, and the former's road to dominance was a long-drawn-out one.

A second historical frame of reference is the European experience and interpretive patterning of modernity. Early modernity is widely recognised and extensively studied as a historical epoch, and the fifteenth and sixteenth centuries are mostly taken to mark its onset. Historical research has also shown that the emergence of modernity is not to be understood as an exclusively European breakthrough followed by diffusion. At least some of the trends taken to define the new epoch appeared in various parts of Eurasia, notably in Islamic empires and in East Asia; but due to a concatenation of circumstances (to use Weber's terms), the mutation took a more expansive and transformative turn in Europe than elsewhere, and this episode is therefore more easily equated with the formation of a new civilisation (it should be underlined that none of the terms used here implies a value judgement).

The trajectory of modernity, including the multiple interactions of Europe with other regions, culminated in the short twentieth century, from 1914 to 1991. This periodisation is now very widely accepted by historians; both its beginning and its end are more visible in Europe than elsewhere, but their global ramifications are indisputable. On the other hand, there are weighty reasons to construct a longer twentieth century, not so much as a separate frame but as a useful complement to the short one. The expanded period then ends with the great recession of the early present century; the beginning is less obvious but the years around 1880 are a plausible choice. They saw the breakthrough of the second industrial revolution, the German take-off to great power status, the final acceleration of Western colonial expansion, and the polarisation of power blocs within Europe. Both the long and the short versions are of major importance for the fourth and final chronological framework: the history of the postwar integrative push, embodied in the institutions of the EU, and of its often unforeseen ramifications.

Within the limited space of this volume, there can be no balanced coverage of all these historical dimensions. The majority of the chapters deal with aspects of European integration in the specific sense indicated in the preceding paragraph. But there are some references to long- and middle-term developments, and it may be useful to outline the approaches in debate on those levels. Interpretations of the European trajectory can draw on the legacy of civilisational analysis, strongly rooted in classical sociology from Weber and Mauss to Elias and Eisenstadt, but it should be noted that this background does not exclude major differences. Three chapters published here (by Chris Hann, Toby Huff and the present writer) reflect civilisational points of view and illustrate their diversity. One line of analysis stresses basic continuities (not unchanging foundations) of Europe as a civilisation. Another version casts doubt on the idea of Europe as a civilisational unit in time and space, but insists on the application of civilisational concepts to European history. As noted above, the transformation of the Roman world gave rise to three civilisations; the one most relevant to later European destinies is commonly known as Western Christendom, but it may be mentioned that a recent major work (Baschet 2018) refers to it as feudal civilisation. Its relationships with the two other cultural worlds have been described as inter-civilisational encounters. And if the conception of modernity as a new civilisation is accepted, European history in the second millennium CE is marked by a major rupture. Finally, a third variation on civilisational themes broadens the geocultural and geopolitical focus, envisaging the Eurasian macro-region as a civilisational zone. The spatial enlargement then allows a temporal extension, taking into account the very long-term interaction of regions and centres.

Another way of contextualising the *longue durée* and the successive turns of European paths is linked to visions of world history or global history. These terms are not always synonymous, and when they are distinguished, there is no agreement on the defining points; to be brief, world history stresses the plurality of cultural worlds and historical trajectories, without necessarily foregrounding their interconnections, while global history places a stronger emphasis on globalising processes, while leaving scope for disagreement on their origins and patterns. In any case, analyses in this vein tend to view both the formation of Europe and its subsequent transformations as results of complex interregional processes, and to remain sceptical about conceptual schemes (including civilisational ones) applied to unfolding chains of events.

Although discussion of postwar integration does not necessitate explicit references to world horizons or global contexts, it would not seem far-fetched to suggest that the chapters dealing with that field have affinities with the approach just outlined. They all treat the present state of European integration as a pattern in process, to be understood in relation to historical contexts and dynamics, not as a definite achievement to be theorised in terms of strong models. Theories of European integration had a certain appeal when the situation seemed conducive to visions of further progress. The rival models applied in this spirit are reminiscent of basic sociological paradigms: there are functionalist, institutionalist and actor-centred explanations. Strong theories of society, with corresponding explanatory ambitions, came under radical criticism during the reorientation of sociological discourse in the 1970s and 1980s. Objections were raised against the overemphasis on normative integration, and more generally against systemic images of society, based on unrealistic assumptions about coherence. Michael Mann's observation that 'societies are much *messier* than our theories of them' (Mann 1983: 4) sums up a broader current of thought. The notions thus questioned were often associated with idealised visions of the nation-state. It may be suggested that the strong theories of European integration were shifting their focus from the nation-state to a larger domain, and attempting to find more solid ground for interpretations that had become less tenable in their original context.

Alan Milward, whose key contribution will be discussed in the third and fifth chapters, had good reason to note a victory of history over theory (Milward 2000). Some revival of theorising was apparent in the first years of this century, when enlargement and deeper integration seemed to go hand in hand and foreshadow further progress. But as a result of the financial crisis and its fallout, a return to history is obviously on the agenda. If we look for scholarly responses to this turn, Adam Tooze's remarkable analysis of the crisis (Tooze 2018) is so far the most salient example. As he shows, the integrative institutions and procedures of the EU are partial patterns, superimposed on a geopolitical and geo-economic field of tensions. The member states of the Union act and function within a global capitalist economy with increasingly visible symptoms of instability; they also relate to global power structures where the interplay of China, Russia and the USA is of decisive importance. Divergences and conflicting strategies within the Union affected responses to the crisis. These internal disputes oppose the Western European core states to the East Central European ones, and northern and southern parts of the Union, as well as – so far less openly – the two most important member countries, France and Germany. The Brexit controversy has opened up a new conflict zone. In addition, dissonances between key institutions of the Union came to the fore when the crisis called for counter-measures. The European Council remains the most important power centre but its relationship to other instances is not unproblematic. All these considerations add up to a strong case for restoring historical approaches to their proper place.

To conclude, it should be noted that although the above remarks distinguish between civilisational and macro-historical perspectives, there is no reason to leave it there and assume that the two orientations are mutually exclusive. Rather, the task is to build bridges between them, and such efforts need not start from scratch. To mention only one example, the great historian Marshall Hodgson – increasingly recognised as a pioneering scholar – outlined a programme for world history; its main focus was to be on the interrelations of societies and on the large-scale units emerging from them. Among the latter, Hodgson regarded regions and civilisations as particularly significant. The idea of civilisations in the plural referred to 'certain limited but very important aspects of civilized life' (Hodgson 1993: 13). These aspects are roughly identical to the 'civilisational dimension of societies' singled out by Eisenstadt: the intertwining of cultural visions of the world with institutional patterns.

It should also be noted that this way of situating civilisations is closely linked to a critique of Eurocentrism. In that regard, as in many others, Hodgson was ahead of his time; in light of later debates, his arguments can now be taken further and given more precise aims. Eurocentrism is neither an inbuilt and unchanging feature of European thought, nor a medieval legacy carried over into modern times (as Brague 2009 and other authors have argued, medieval Western Christendom was more aware of centres and origins located elsewhere than later accounts liked to admit). Nor can it be shown that a whole set of basic notions must be discarded in order to break with Eurocentrism. The concepts of nation, state, society and civilisation – as well as many others – have an ambiguous history of overstressed European backgrounds and corrections in light of other historical experiences. The issue can be clarified in historical terms. Early modern European perceptions and interpretations of other cultures were remarkably open to expanding horizons (for a particularly instructive analysis of this phase, see Osterhammel 2013). A marked turn to Eurocentrism came later, around and after 1800, and was obviously linked to the global growth of European power; but in the most complex and ambitious cases, such as in Hegel's philosophy of history, it also involved efforts to rethink European traditions in ways that would bolster their claims to primacy in a more manifestly multicultural world. The nineteenth century was the Eurocentric period par excellence; the twentieth-century record is a good deal more mixed, not only because of the global redistribution of power, but also in regard to developments in European thought. Eurocentrism was questioned, although less continuously and comprehensively than we might now wish, but the break with Eurocentric modes of thought is, in any case, bound to be a long-term and many-sided effort, not reducible to a pre-programmed conversion. And progress has not been straightforward. Important critical insights can be found in the work of authors more commonly associated with Eurocentric views (Max Weber is the most obvious case in point; for further discussion of his work, see Arnason 2019).

Regional dynamics and divisions

Both civilisational and world or global historical approaches to the European experience must take note of its regional frameworks. Historical regions are still an under-researched theme, and that applies even more to contrasts and parallels between regional divisions in Europe and in other parts of the world. But available scholarship in this field leaves no doubt about the particular salience of regional factors in European history. Their part in the present troubles of the EU has not gone unnoticed. Since the chapters in this volume can deal only very selectively with this aspect, a brief overview is in order.

Around the turn of the century, when Euro-optimism was at its peak, European integration was widely seen as a Western European project destined to encompass and upgrade the long- under-developed eastern periphery of the continent and not confined to pre-established eastern borders. Recent developments cast doubt on the coherence and solidity of the Western foundations. Most spectacularly, the Brexit saga has reproblematised the relationship between Britain and the continental core of the EU. The claim to reaffirm sovereign status and separate destiny has prompted reflections on the historical background. Brendan Simms (2017) has written a detailed and persuasive account of European connections, decisively important at critical junctures in British history. His suggestion that the internal structure of the UK might serve as a model for reform of the EU is less convincing. Rather, the lesson to be drawn from the impact of Brexit on divisions within the UK and relations with its Irish neighbour is that the Isles (as Davies 1999 calls them, in explicit rejection of the all-British view) are a historical region unto themselves, marked by internal tensions, and that their present geopolitical makeup may not be a final destination.

Moving eastwards, the Nordic countries obviously matter less for the prospects of the Union than the UK does. But their record of involvement and detachment is an instructive case of national divergences within a region. The states in question constitute a clearly demarcated region, with affinities, connections and cooperative relations all conducive to strong unity. But their attitudes and experiences in relation to the integrative process differ markedly. For Finland, membership of the EU, including the eurozone, was an obvious solution to problems caused by the collapse of the politically constraining but economically important Soviet neighbour. At the other extreme, Norway's repeated rejection of membership exemplifies the most reserved view of the EU and the greatest distance between political elites and public opinion on this issue. In between, Danish and Swedish versions of European engagement have been marked by exemptions and special options, each in its own ways, with Denmark having a longer and more chequered history of participation.

East Central Europe (now more commonly but less precisely known as Central and Eastern Europe) presents a different picture. This is a region that has recently acquired a clearer profile due to divergences within the EU; doubts about both its historical reality and its political relevance had previously been rife. The case for long-term regional dynamics can go back to medieval state formation, early modern imperial divisions and experiences of post-imperial states in the aftermath of World War II. However, the brief but catastrophic Nazi conquest and the much longer Soviet domination were widely believed to have obliterated East Central Europe as a distinctive region. Visions of a regional identity, to be remembered as a cultural resource rather than restored, tended to focus on a broader notion of Central Europe (often with open questions about the inclusion of Germany). The countries in question entered the EU in the early phase of eastern enlargement and on similar terms; later developments led to a certain convergence of their objections to EU policies. This has been most obvious in regard to the refugee crisis and the ensuing plans for relocation. To explain this in terms of xenophobia pure and simple, as is often done in the West, is about as enlightening as the 'dormitive virtue explanations' held up to ridicule in textbooks of logic. More specific factors should be acknowledged. The experience of multiethnic societies in late Habsburg and interwar times has left negative traces in collective memory and is seen as a reminder of destabilising threats. This can be regretted but not ignored. The fact that opinion turns against Muslim immigrants without any direct contact with them is less relevant than is often claimed: East Central Europeans watch events on the Western side through the inherently sensationalising medium of television, which results in vastly exaggerated notions of the problems caused by Muslim immigration, and they combine with other predisposing factors.

That said, there is some evidence for unified regional resistance to EU policies (not opposition to the Union as such), and this gives rise to exaggerated Western perceptions of a 'V4' regional bloc. Closer examination reveals significant contrasts between the countries thus described. Polish and Hungarian nationalisms have different connotations, not least because of the very divergent experiences of the two states in recent history. The Czech Republic has so far seen no nationalist turn comparable to those of its neighbours. Slovakia, the only V4 country without historical memories of separate statehood, is an atypical case: it is second to none in the strength of its nationalist attitudes and the invocation of 'Christian values' by otherwise different political subjects, but it is also the only state in the region to join the eurozone and has declared its aspirations to join the more rapidly integrating core if a two-track EU takes more formal shape.

Southeastern Europe is a well-established geopolitical and geocultural category, and numerous histories of that region have been written (for the most recent example, see Calic 2018). But it is so far the clearest case of a region not present as such in the context of European integration. Relations with the EU have had a fragmenting effect. Romania and Bulgaria were late recruits to eastern enlargement; Greece stands apart, both because of longer membership and as a result of its unique crisis; the two ex-Yugoslav member states, Slovenia and Croatia, are not closely associated, and the former is in many ways more aligned with East Central Europe.

It remains to consider an area that looms large in contemporary debate on the problems and unintended consequences of European integration: the European South. To begin with, it should be noted that we are not dealing with a historically defined and continuously researched region (and there is no suggestion of a regional bloc). For one thing, it would be difficult to draw an eastern border: should Southeastern Europe be included, or only Greece, or even the east coast of the Mediterranean? The area that has figured prominently in regional studies is not Southern Europe but a broader one: the Mediterranean. It is the subject of the most celebrated and influential regional study ever written (Braudel 1986), and that work took in northern and southern shores, as well as western and eastern extremities, at a time when religious and civilisational divisions within this space were particularly pronounced. Braudel's analysis has met with criticism, and a productive debate on unity and diversity in the Mediterranean world is still going on. In any case, the nineteenth and early twentieth centuries saw a radical change in the structure of the region, through European colonisation of the southern shore, followed by more erratic ventures at the eastern end. Twentieth-century decolonisation then made it more difficult than before to think of the Mediterranean as a region.

If we think of the South most discussed in relation to the EU's current predicament – that is, the northern shore of the Mediterranean – a geopolitical perspective must include both sides of the Adriatic, irrespective of formal membership (it should not be forgotten that the Yugoslav collapse, unfolding beyond the Union's borders, entailed its most spectacular foreign policy failure, largely due to disagreements between core states). From that point of view, some aspects of the historical background are worth noting. In the first half of the twentieth century, the area was particularly marked by civil wars. It was also, partly in that connection, characterised by a strong and distinctive Communist presence. The cases in point included the first Communist state to revolt against Soviet domination (Yugoslavia from 1948), the strongest and most autonomous Communist movement on the western side of the Iron Curtain (Italy), but also unsuccessful Communist bids for power, from Greece after World War II to the much more muted attempt in Portugal in 1974–5. In the post-1989 phase, the southern European countries have been the most affected by the disruptive consequences of economic integration (that connection was already of some importance for the Yugoslav crisis).

There is one further twist to the question of the South: the possibility of South-orientated strategies interfering with relations between core states, especially France and Germany. As Wolf Lepenies shows in a recent book (2016), French visions of reinforcement through influence on or allies in the South have a long history, reappeared in recent initiatives, and should not be written off as obsolete. But they have found expression in two different projects: a Latin zone and a Mediterranean horizon of integration. The Latin option, more in evidence after World War II, proved unrealistic because there were no adequate geopolitical or geo-economic underpinnings for the claim to a special cultural relationship with Italy and Spain. The first massive bid to gain mastery over the Mediterranean was Napoleon's abortive invasion of Egypt; but the most fateful move on this front was the attempt to complete the conquest of Algeria through full incorporation into France, ultimately leading to a conflict that combined the characteristics of civil and colonial war. This particularly painful road to decolonisation did not put an end to Mediterranean visions; they resurfaced in Sarkozy's 2007 plan for a Mediterranean Union, thwarted by opposition from other EU states, especially Germany. It remains to be seen what might still be tried in response to declining French strength within the Union.

Summary of chapters

The chapters in this volume can be roughly divided into three groups. The first three deal with historical trajectories and comparisons. Toby Huff reconstructs the high medieval transformation of Western Christendom, the matrix of the cultural world later known as Europe, with particular emphasis on the legal revolution. This process changed basic sociocultural frameworks and gave rise to new institutions, including the universities that paved the way for the scientific revolution. By linking this background to the much later process of European integration, Huff is not following the well-known line of argument that the shared religious culture of Western Europe was a first step towards unification, followed – with long and troubled intervals – by the Enlightenment and then by the project of European integration. His thesis is that medieval transformations created deep structures of modernity, thus enabling later and more far-reaching breakthroughs. Johann P. Arnason focuses on recent historical background and argues that the conflicts and catastrophes of the twentieth century should be understood in terms of a civilisational crisis, rather than the frequently used metaphor of a European civil war. The latter approach is misleading in several respects. On this view, the Cold War and the division of Europe are best seen as a continuation of the crisis in different forms due to a changed environment. To grasp European integration in this context is to stress its dependence on specific circumstances, the ambiguous logic of its progress, and its uncertain prospects in a changing global setting. Finally, Helmut Kuzmics discusses contrasts and parallels between the EU and the Habsburg empire. The latter is sometimes described as a precursor to the EU; in both cases, attempts to build a multinational state faced multiple problems, including some of their own making. Kuzmics takes a closer look at the Habsburg experience and the lessons it might hold for the strategists of European integration. Although the composite Habsburg state underwent major transformations, the core structures of statehood were much stronger than those of the EU; they nevertheless developed in a way that obstructed decision-making in critical situations. At the same time, the imperial centre confronted national forces and nationalist demands on several levels: movements aspiring to autonomy within the Austrian domains, the Hungarian state recognised as a sovereign partner, and a pan-German current boosted by the inescapable alliance with Germany.

The second group of chapters engages with various aspects of the present situation. Dennis Smith takes the unfinished Brexit crisis as an occasion to reflect on past vicissitudes, as well as underlying dilemmas and antinomies of European integration. Reviewing the prehistory, postwar progress and present troubles of the Union, he applies basic distinctions of social theory, not least the concepts of system integration and social integration, to clarify the trends at work; this helps to distinguish between the institutional dynamics and what another author has called the informal politics of the EU. He also suggests historical analogies, including court society as described by Norbert Elias, and draws on literary models to describe the social and political actors and episodes that have marked the unfolding story. Paul Blokker discusses the sustained efforts to establish a constitutional framework for European integration; this is the most ambitious expression of a more general legalistic trend, but also the level where it becomes most problematic and provokes resistance. Blokker analyses the constitutionalising and judicialising processes of the last decades (with particular emphasis on the growing role of courts in the institutional edifice of the Union), their historical roots, their impact on political life, and the varying supportive and critical interpretations responding to them. He concludes that the disputed relationship between legal regulation and political imperatives is a crucial aspect of the EU's present crisis. Finally, Natalie Doyle deals with questions regarding the presence of Islam in Europe and ideological controversies around that issue. She stresses the multifaceted interaction of Islamic communities with the European environment, including exposure to economic conditions shaped by neo-liberalism, as well as different strategies of adaptation and alternative self-definition. The phenomenon of 'co-radicalisation', the mutual reinforcement of extremisms on both sides, noted especially by French researchers, should be seen in this context. Doyle criticises both those who condemn European societies as intrinsically intolerant and the attempts to equate radical Islam with European totalitarian ideologies.

The last section explores some regional perspectives. Ireneusz Paweł Karolewski considers the increasingly difficult relationship between the EU and the Central and Eastern European (CEE) states, with particular reference to Poland. Analysing the disputes between Brussels and Warsaw in detail and on the basis of ongoing exchanges, he shows that the most visible conflicts – concerning the rule of law and the responses to migration – are aspects of a broad divergence. The Polish deviation from dominant conceptions of European integration should not be mistaken for opposition to the Union as such, but the ambition to change its course is closely linked to the domestic policies of the ruling party. A very different regional constellation is described in Bo Stråth's chapter on Scandinavia and Europe. Here, the changing and currently diverse attitudes to Europe are more prominent than any signs of coordinated dissent. As Stråth shows, Scandinavia (in the broad sense, including Denmark and Finland) has a long history of complex relationships with continental Europe, and this experience has left layers of cultural memory that can still prove relevant to political issues. In the postwar phase, the countries in question were latecomers to European integration, and that turn combined in ambiguous ways with the decline of the Social Democratic hegemony that had been characteristic of a whole epoch. Both opponents and supporters of Social Democracy expected European connections to open up new opportunities. Chris Hann proposes a more macro-regional approach. As he sees it, conflicts between incompatible visions of Europe's historical experience and desirable future are a major factor of the present crisis. He suggests that a broader perspective, enlarged to include the Eurasian world to which the European 'pseudo-continent' historically and geographically belongs, might enable more balanced views of problems and possibilities. There is no short-term prospect of Eurasian integration but much could be done to promote more constructive relationships. Hann adds that the geopolitical and geocultural broadening of horizons should be accompanied by a historical one, leading to better understanding of the diverse but not mutually closed civilisational legacies of Eurasia.

References

Arnason, J. P. (2019, forthcoming), 'From Occidental Rationalism to Multiple Modernities', in E. Hanke, L. Scaff and S. Whimster (eds), *The Oxford Handbook of Max Weber*, Oxford: Oxford University Press.

Baschet, J. (2018), *La Civilisation féodale: De l'an mil à la colonisation de l'Amérique*, Paris: Flammarion.

Brague, R. (2009), *Eccentric Culture: A Theory of Western Civilization*, South Bend, IN: St Augustine's Press.

Braudel, F. (1986), *The Mediterranean and the Mediterranean World in the Age of Philip II*, tr. S. Reynolds, London: Fontana.

Calic, M.-J. (2018), *Südosteuropa: Weltgeschichte einer Region*, Munich: C. H. Beck.

Davies, N. (1999), *The Isles*, London: Macmillan.

Hodgson, M. (1993), *Rethinking World History: Essays on Europe, Islam and World History*, Cambridge: Cambridge University Press.

Lepenies, W. (2016), *Die Macht am Mittelmeer: Französische Träume von einem anderen Europa*, Munich: C. H. Beck.

Mann, M. (1983), *Sources of Social Power*, vol. 1, Cambridge: Cambridge University Press.

Milward, A. (2000), *The European Rescue of the Nation-State*, London: Routledge.

Osterhammel, J. (2013), *Die Entzauberung Asiens: Europa und die asiatischen Reiche im 18. Jahrhundert*, Munich: C. H. Beck.

Simms, B. (2017), *Britain's Europe: A Thousand Years of Conflict and Cooperation*, London: Penguin.

Tooze, A. (2018), *Crashed: How a Decade of Financial Crises Changed the World*, London: Allen Lane.

Zientara, B. (1997), *Frühzeit der europäischen Nationen: Die Entstehung von National-bewusstsein im nachkarolingischen Europa*, Osnabrück: fibre.

2

Europe as a Civilisation and the Hidden Structure of Modernity

Toby E. Huff

Introduction

IT IS NOT SURPRISING that the international economic meltdown from 2007 to 2009 precipitated a corresponding crisis of belief in the future of the European Union. From an economic policy point of view, such a reaction is justified, yet in the longer view, it would seem that the naysaying about the foundational principles of the EU are overdone. In that longer view, the many crises decried in the current moment (Castells 2017; Stiglitz 2016) seem minor in comparison to the severely fractured state of the continent during its many religious conflicts, revolutions, fascist takeovers, depression-level economic downturns and transnational wars. Moreover, despite the structural flaws created in the founding of the EU, Europeans of the past have indeed created unique sociocultural, political, economic and legal innovations. These have put Europe in a position of high regard that, historically considered, was not equalled in other civilisational areas of the world such as the Middle East, Africa, East and Southeast Asia.

No doubt a great deal of this malaise has been precipitated by the general cultural shift asserting the 'decline of the West' (among others, Robertson 1986; Goldstone 2002), claiming that there is nothing unique about 'the West' (Conrad 2012), that its Enlightenment either did not happen or also happened in the non-West, and that 'the great divergence' only happened in the mid- to late nineteenth century (Pomeranz 2000; challenged by Vries 2013, 2015).

In contrast to those views, I shall argue that when Europe as a whole is seen against its historical background and as a unique civilisational formation, one discovers that Europeans collectively, from the Middle Ages onward, invented a great many sociocultural, political and economic innovations that paved the way for human development for centuries to come. A not insignificant part of that was the scientific revolution and the institutional structures sustaining it. In a singularly important sense, Europeans invented what I shall call the hidden structure of modernity, the proof of which can be seen in the founding of the USA, even in the European-derived 'template' for political and economic success that emerged, often independently, in many of the earliest British–American colonies (Kuperman 2009: 287). These same structures and legal assumptions lie at the foundation of the EU and give it a deeper historical legacy than would be detected by those focusing only on the present.

Civilisational constructs

The term 'Western civilisation' has long been a commonly used identifier but the idea of 'Europe as a civilisation' needs articulation. This requires both a serviceable definition of a 'civilisation' and a historically and conceptually rich sketch of the formation of the European traditions.

As an anchoring point for discussing a civilisation-in-the-making, I start with the long-neglected 'Note on the Notion of Civilization', published in 1913 by Emile Durkheim and Marcel Mauss (1971). It is useful to point out that these two authors developed their new conception of a civilisation on the eve of World War I, at the end of a long period of peace and harmony in Europe. As several recent authors of books on the causes of World War I have pointed out, many European commentators at the time could hardly believe that the European powers would go to war and that the harmony would end (for example, Clark 2012).

In their short essay, Durkheim and Mauss hit upon three seminal ideas indispensable for a viable *civilisational analysis*. Other writers attempting civilisational analysis tend to follow the pattern established by anthropologists and ethnographers, who mainly try to identify any distinctive cultural group, ancient or modern, and call that group a 'civilisation' without utilising the deeper analytic insights of Durkheim and Mauss. What Durkheim and Mauss noticed was that

> social phenomena that are not strictly attached to a determinate social organism do exist; they extend into areas that reach beyond the national territory or they develop over periods of time that exceed the history of a single society. They have a life which is in some ways supranational. (1971: 810).

Here the defining criterion is a *transnational* or supranational emergence that goes beyond the original group that generated the symbolic capital. Consequently, the authors claim that '*A civilization constitutes a kind of moral milieu encompassing a certain number of nations, each national culture being only a particular form of the whole*' (Durkheim and Mauss 1971: 811).

This is, of course, what Europe has increasingly become: a composite of many nation-states with deep religious, legal and cultural foundations. Moreover, Durkheim and Mauss observed that not all social phenomena have the same ability to be transported, to be *universalised* to other social or national groups. They laid out a major task, still unfulfilled, which is to explain on what this 'unequal coefficient of expansion and internationalization' depends. Put differently, this idea of a 'coefficient of expansion' possessed by some social phenomena suggests the striking process of universalisation, without which civilisations and civilisational phenomena, in our sense, would not exist. Hence, it is important to consider the degree to which the universalisation of elements of civilisational complexes has been a voluntary process in contrast to an imposition by an expanding empire. From today's perspective, we know that even those civilisational complexes that have the ability to be assimilated over time and over vast stretches of territory also have their limits; and yet certain of these phenomena, whether they be described as aspects of 'Westernisation' or 'globalisation', seem to have still more potential to expand voluntarily around the globe.

In Benjamin Nelson's reformulation of these seminal ideas, civilisations are composed of 'the governing cultural heritages of 2+n societies, territories [or] areas which generally enjoy or have enjoyed a certain proximity' to each other (Nelson 1973: 82).

Furthermore, what gives a civilisation in this sense an identity is the existence of a set of shared civilisation-wide symbolic structures, such as religious and logical commitments, as well as practical legal processes that enable the smooth functioning of economic as well as political processes. Sometimes Nelson referred to these cultural phenomena, especially in the sociopsychological realm, as the 'directive structures' that shape human thought, action and emotion (Nelson 1981: 17–33).

However, one could also refer to these internationalising and globalising transformations as contributions to 'world culture' and 'world polity'. Considered in this light, there have already been moves in this direction, attempting to describe and understand the *construction of world culture* as elements of the Western tradition that became firmly established in the emerging global polity (Boli and Thomas 1999; Drori et al. 2003).

Although the scholars working on this research programme have not articulated an appropriate civilisational context, and have seriously truncated the historical time frame needed to unravel these developments, they are aware of the need to 'study the origins, expansion, and characteristics of the world polity', to understand how these cultural elements evolved out of Western civilisation and served to create a 'coherent world culture, society, and set of institutions that might plausibly influence nation [states]'. Furthermore, they are keen to explore 'in which substantive areas [of] world society norms [have] been clearly worked out, codified, and institutionalized' (Schofer and McEneaney 2003: 47). It remains to be seen how this agenda could be fulfilled without paying much more attention to the early legal and logical foundations of international law that underlie virtually all international business and diplomatic negotiations worldwide.

Beyond that, it is evident that, though the proponents of this research programme refer to 'world culture', they point out that the participants recorded in the datasets of international organisations come 'mainly from Europe and North America' (Boli 2001: 6261). This suggests that, in fact, *this* 'world culture' is basically internationalised European culture among countries that have historically been part of 'Europe overseas'. The task of studying the spread of European (or global culture) to *non*-Western civilisational areas, to China, the Islamic world, Russia, Central Asia and the Indian subcontinent, has hardly begun.

That said, it is evident that serious scholars with highly sophisticated methodological techniques have lent considerable currency to this effort of exploring how transnational phenomena expand across the world.

Beginnings and cultural landmarks

In an effort to identify the unique cultural and intellectual strands that most defined the European essence that crystallised in the twelfth-century Renaissance and thereafter, historians have suggested that there were three critical components: Greek philosophy, Roman law and Christian theology (Nelson 1981; Grant 2001). When one considers the impact on Europe of such Greek thinkers as Socrates, Plato and the whole Aristotelian corpus (along with Euclid), there is little doubt that this legacy decisively shaped Western consciousness from that time to the present. It is also clear that the naturalistic legacy of Aristotle was radically different from the Chinese and Indian worlds, while its reception in the Muslim world took a very different course (Huff 2017: 81–110).

When it comes to defining the Christian and religious component of European civilisation, the task becomes much more complex and, indeed, contentious. In large part, this is because Christianity was born in the context of a Greek-speaking civilisation that was, at the same time, being redefined by Roman culture and the Latin language. None of this was true during the rise of Islam, which, for better or worse, was spared that kind of cultural amalgamation (Huff 2000).

In later Western Christendom, however, the origins and defining essence of Christianity became a matter of major contention from the time of the Papal crusades in southern France until the Reformation. Moreover, classic analysts of the Christian Middle Ages, above all Johan Huizinga, pointed to the 'undisciplined religious exuberance of daily life', along with 'the endless multiplication of religious images, paintings, convents and religious orders, festivals and holy days' that prevailed, and which many believers thought corrupted and perverted 'the essence of Christianity' (Ozment 1993: 33). The proliferation of monastic convents and mendicant orders by the thousands across Europe from about 1100 on (Bartlett 1993: Ch. 10) gave the impression that such 'otherworldly' and 'exaggerated devotion' was the ideal image of Christianity. By the time of Martin Luther, Huldrych Zwingli, Calvin and others, it was evident that, whatever the origins of the Church had been, both the Church hierarchy and local priestly establishment had been corrupted, requiring major reform. In Protestant cities, officials and magistrates enacted ordinances abolishing 'Catholic practices such as fasting, penance, veneration of saints, indulgences, masses for the dead, the giving of alms to Mendicants and friars and numerous festivals and holidays' (Berman 2003: 64; Ozment 1993).

In this context, it is evident that there was a major religious and cultural shift toward what Max Weber called a new religious 'ethos' that was far more concerned with 'innerworldly' activities devoted to transforming the mundane world (Weber 1958; Gorski 2003; Berman 2003). Without ascribing too much to that cultural and psychological shift, there are good reasons for thinking that the Reformation inspired reforms that did have an impact on social organisation and economic activity very like what Weber surmised (Becker and Woessman 2009).

While it is important to acknowledge this level of the spiritual and motivational side of Western Christendom, there are equally deep structures and transformations that emerged prior to the Reformation and which gave Western civilisation indelible structures of identity that became permanent parts of Western consciousness and practical action, yet have rarely been noted.

I shall attempt to identify this hidden structure of modernity by focusing on what I shall call the multiple revolutions – legal, political and economic – of the Middle Ages. I shall place special stress on Europe's unique institutional arrangements that are deeply rooted in its singular legal history. Unfortunately, many scholars who have written with great insight and authority about this period have entirely neglected the unique legal history of Europe and its centrality to all the developments of that era (as seen in Bisson 2009; Moore 2000; Mitterauer 2010). It is this particular institutional history that gave Europe the foundations on which the EU could be founded, centuries later.

The revolution of the Middle Ages

Any broad evaluation of the social, legal and political development of Western Europe that took place in the twelfth and thirteenth centuries will show that it witnessed sweeping legal reforms, indeed, a *revolutionary reconstruction*, of all the realms and divisions of law – feudal law, manorial law, urban law, commercial law and royal law – and therewith the reconstitution of medieval European society (Berman 1983). It is also true that neither Islamic law nor Chinese law passed through an equivalent radical transformation (Huff 2017: 219–35). Consequently, neither of those systems of law ever recognised the broad variety of competing *legal jurisdictions* found in Europe. For example, religious, commercial, urban, public and professional jurisdictions were recognised throughout Europe.

At the centre of this development one finds the legal and political principle of treating *collective actors* as a *whole body* – a corporation (*universitas* is the common medieval Latin term but there were others). The emergence of corporate actors was unquestionably revolutionary in that the legal theory that made them possible created a variety of new forms and powers of association that were distinctly European. This singular legal transformation laid the foundations for the rise and autonomous development of universities and stabilised the pursuit of modern science, while laying the foundations for the rise of constitutionalism and parliamentary democracy. Beyond that, it articulated the very concept of what we know as due process of law along with the idea of elective representation in all forms of corporate bodies. These became foundational a principles for the legal autonomy of cities and towns, and a broad array of additional legal forms unique to the West.

That legal theory of corporations brings in its train organisational principles establishing such political ideas as constitutional government, consent in political decision-making, the right of political and legal representation, the powers of adjudication and jurisdiction, and even the power of autonomous legislation. Aside from the scientific revolution itself, and perhaps the Reformation, no other revolution has been as pregnant with new social and political implications as the legal revolution of the European Middle Ages. By laying out the conceptual foundations for new institutional forms in legal thought, it prepared the way for the two other revolutions – the scientific and the economic. But more than that, the rise of this collective form of legally defined social organisation led directly to the formation of joint-stock companies in the commercial arena; and this, as we shall see, had momentous consequences for political and economic development in the new world.

Consider for a moment what this idea of *autonomous legislation* means. It means that some public body – some corporate entity, some group of citizens – is capable of composing and promulgating new laws that transcend Biblical injunctions, customary law, Quranic legal prescriptions, or even edicts issued by an emperor in China. That power of autonomous legislation did not exist either in Chinese or Islamic law of the early modern period, whereas such autonomous law-creation was in fact a power shared by a variety of legally autonomous groups throughout Europe and Europe-overseas.

Some phases of development

Around 1000 CE commerce began to revive in southern Europe and then to spread northward. This was conjoined with the rise of commercial fairs and the emergence of cities and towns. But there was also a profound wave of economic growth in the Hanseatic cites in the north centred on Hamburg, Germany, and which expanded south and eastward at the same time (Bartlett 1993: 292ff.). First, however, we need to focus on some earlier, far-reaching intellectual developments.

As we may recall, back in the early 6th century CE the Emperor Justinian told his legal experts to trim down radically and consolidate the existing Roman legal code, and especially to prune away the unending commentary of judges and scholars. The end result was the Roman *Corpus Juris Civilis* – the Roman Civil Law – that Justinian put into effect across the empire in 534 CE (Schiavone 2012; Brundage 2008a; Hoeflich and Grabher 2008). However, the code did not fare well in the western empire because it was collapsing. Consequently, with the collapse of the western portion of the Roman empire (after 476), the *Corpus Juris Civilis* was lost, not to be recovered until about 1070 CE. But when it was found and recovered, it jolted legal scholars into action.

At first the scholars did not fully understand it, though they imagined that they were inheritors of a 'Holy Roman Empire' based on these newly discovered protocols. The task of the commentators known as the Glossators was to write marginal commentaries and perhaps standardise the grammar, while explaining the new conceptual terminology. At the same time, a scholar and monk by the name of Gratian took it upon himself to rethink the whole amorphous body of laws then known to him, and to create what he called a *Harmony of Discordant Canons* – first issued in about 1140. Here the word *canons* simply means 'rules', but especially rules that had been adopted by the Christian Church. In a very short period of time, this became a standard legal text used all across Europe, though the Church never officially promulgated it.

What Gratian had done was to collect legal texts from Church councils, Papal letters, the writings of Church Fathers, passages from the Bible, and a host of secular sources such as Roman and German law. His great effort was designed to point out the contradictions in these legal rules, to remove them, and to find the underlying legal principles that ought to prevail.

All of this is an example of what Max Weber (and many other scholars) called the *rationalisation* process: that is, the process by which legal rules and procedures were made more coherent, consistent and rationally explicable.

By 1200, these legal scholars had become a distinct literate class of specialists; they had mastered the Roman legal corpus, and in a great many ways had modified, systematised and transformed it into a new *legal science*, which was now to be taught for the first time in universities across Europe. The initial leading centre of this new science of law was at the university in Bologna. These legal scholars were known as the civilians: that is, the ones who taught the new science focused largely on secular issues and everyday social and economic causes. Furthermore, these legal specialists were a *community of scholars and students*, most of whom came from outside town and even outside Italy. They could move on a moment's notice to another town where social, legal and economic conditions might be better (Hyde 1972). Hence it was in the circle of these early legal scholars that we find some of the earliest seed-beds of the universities, a budding community of scholars who were free to move around, as they were not confined to a particular diocese or parish.

With these developments, Europeans had a new legal science based on original texts, all of which became what legal historians call the *ius commune*, the common law of Europe that began to spread from south to north, to Germany, Britain and Scandinavia. Moreover, law students across Europe now had to learn both the Canon Law and Civil Law because, first, the Church universal had courts all across Europe, and second, lawyers specialising in the Civil Law might be called upon to defend a case in an ecclesiastical court.

It is worth stressing at this point that, despite the many ethnic and religious groups that existed across Western Europe at this time, scholars had made a major advance in creating an underlining legal structure that, however varied its reception in different proto-states and ethnic enclaves, was in fact a fundamental social architecture that was to endure through all its later modifications and succeeding centuries. At the time of the Reformation, it was just this juridical structure that the Reformers used to establish the legal standing of their religiously tinged political and social norms (Berman 2003: 31ff.; Ozment 1993: 87–148).

Here then we have the first and second legs of this medieval revolution. First we have a new legal science that was being taught in the free-floating schools (later universities) and applied across Europe in both secular and ecclesiastical courts. To the degree that this legal system established new institutional foundations for the emerging European civilisation, it was legal scholars in the schools who underwrote this development.

Second, the medieval legists recognised the legal rights of collective actors: that is, legally autonomous entities, sometimes called 'fictive personalities'. Among these, we find cities and towns, charitable organisations, and professional associations of doctors and lawyers, as well as merchant guilds – all of which could create their own rules and regulations. These new entities were treated as collective individuals and they had a whole new bundle of rights: the right to own property, to sue and be sued, to issue their own regulations and ordinances – that is, to act as legislative entities. Such entities had the right to be represented by attorneys in courts, and before the king's court regarding taxation (Post 1964: 214–21).

Furthermore, these entities were said to be governed by the principle 'what concerns all should be considered and approved by all' – a Roman maxim (Berman 1983: 221) – and the harbinger of 'election by consent'.

This idea of election by consent was to become a central operating principle for all such collective enterprises, including the soon-to-emerge joint-stock companies.

While today we think of corporations as primarily significant for commercial enterprises, their original impact was in the sphere of public law, where their presence radically transformed the whole basis of political, constitutional and economic life in Europe, for it was the presence of these new entities that established the foundations for parliamentary democracy. Indeed, the first European parliament was founded in 1188 in Spain, quickly followed by a dozen or more regional parliaments across Europe: in Spain, then in Portugal, Sicily, southern France, Paris in 1298, then the Estates General in 1302 (van Zanden et al. 2012). Indeed, the effort to establish constitutional regimes in which the people were deemed to have a legitimate voice was a great struggle carried on broadly across Europe from the Middle Ages onward with the final culmination in the revolutionary new political thought of Scotland, Holland, France and then England in the sixteenth and seventeenth centuries (Skinner 1979; Gorski 2001).

Third, the canonists and civilians established new principles of due process of law that applied to all individuals who were involved in legal proceedings. By the end of the twelfth century, this new system had been formally articulated as the *ordo iudiciarius* (the system of legal procedures) (Pennington 1998; Brundage 2008a, 2008b; Hartmann and Pennington 2016). According to this legal doctrine (which was established in court cases and Papal decretals), every trial must involve a plaintiff and a defendant, advocates for those two parties, the appearance of witnesses, and the presence of court recorders such as clerks, proctors and notaries who record the names of those present at the trial and what each person said; if written evidence were presented, it too would be redacted into the court record. This became established legal procedure by the end of the twelfth century – all worked out by legal scholars usually attached to the schools and emerging universities. Such formal legal procedures did not exist in Islamic or Chinese law then or later (Huff 2017: Chs 3, 4 and 7).

In addition, the procedures established the right of any accused person to be notified of a complaint, the right to appear in court and testify, and, above all, to be represented by a legal expert. By 1200, it was firmly established that anyone appearing in a court could elect to have legal assistance and was well advised to do so. But if they did not do so, they were forewarned, as one writer put it in 1169: 'If someone is brash enough to presume to rely on his own devices even though he is inexperienced and does not wish to have an advocate, let him do so. Everyone is free to muck up his own case' (Brundage 2008a: 152).

Here, then, we have the outline and details of due process of law, assumed to be universal, that must be applied in all legal proceedings – all set out by the end of the twelfth century, with full implementation occurring in later centuries (Langbein 2003: 152).

But – fourth – this process went even further toward the establishment of additional legal principles that applied to prince and pope alike. The most important case establishing that these principles applied to the prince as well as to the ordinary citizen concerned King Henry of Luxemburg and Robert of Naples. In 1311, King Henry moved to be crowned Emperor of the Holy Roman Empire, and in doing so, intended to displace Robert of Naples and his kingdom. In the process, Henry condemned King Robert, declaring him to be a traitor and an outlaw to the empire. Pope Clement V did not agree with these declarations and tried to mediate between the two parties (Pennington 1998).

Luckily – or unluckily – Henry died (in 1313) before he could move to displace Robert forcefully, but Pope Clement V stepped forward with legal opinions curtailing such presumptuous condemnation of an adversary. The Pope solicited opinions from the best legal scholars and all of them averred that the right of self-defence, both physical and legal, was a right granted by natural law and it could not be taken away. Hence King Henry's rulings were without merit and were annulled. Furthermore, Pope Clement went on to issue several more legislative rulings, clearly stating what due process of law entails and how it must not be abridged. In his final ruling, indeed a constitutional document called *Saepe contingit*, he established these principles, which of necessity must be upheld by the Prince. Legal scholars have concurred that this legal ruling of the very early fourteenth century was 'the most important single piece of medieval legislation in the history of summary judicial procedure' (Kuttner 1964: 427).

In sum, by the opening of the fourteenth century, European law had established legal principles restricting the actions of prince and pope. The principle that the pope too is subject to natural law and may not abridge a defendant's right of self-defence was established in a notorious case involving the Medici and the attempt of the Pazzi family to eliminate them violently. The result was that Pope Sixtus IV (who had condemned Lorenzo de Medici without a trial) had to back down while acknowledging that, just as Adam in the Bible had to respond to God's summons to judgement, so too 'neither Pope nor Prince could dispense with this part of the judicial process because no one can ignore a precept of divine law' (Pennington 1993: 188; Martines 2003). In other words, the earlier legal principles that restricted the actions of the prince applied in the same way to the pope. Neither he nor the prince could issue summary judgements without actually holding a trial. Here again, we find unique European contributions to international legal development and, above all, the idea of *legal* restraints on the highest officials.

In recounting this legal history, I do not suggest that the people of Florence in the fifteenth century were particularly law-abiding – they most definitely were not. Nevertheless, a precedent had been established and future rulers who wished to be regarded as lawful occupants of elective or appointed office had to abide by such rules. It took time for the rule of law as we understand it to become widely and deeply established; nevertheless, the institutional apparatus had been constructed, and civil and ecclesiastical courts had been established all across Western Europe. Let us also not forget that the lords of England forced King John of England to submit to the Magna Carta (in 1215), which, likewise, restricted his sovereign powers and required the establishment of a jury system for legal proceedings.

Law, commerce and self-government

As suggested earlier, the revolution of the Middle Ages was indeed a society- or civilisation-wide transformation. This new legal regime had powerful implications for every aspect of social, political and economic action. In that context, I need to say something about the impact on ordinary business transactions. Of course, the spread of the new legal science, both canon and civil, was uneven across Western Europe, but the trend and result are clear.

It is imperative for those engaged in business dealings to have a secure sense of their rights of ownership, the possibility of regulating trade, and the availability of legal officials who can authoritatively adjudicate business conflicts. As legal scholars know, the very foundations of business transactions establish what are sometimes tedious conceptions that spell out property rights, along with broad guidelines for the kinds of transactions that can be carried out, the limits of individual and collective action and responsibility, what happens to collective assets when people die, and so on.

What happens, for example, if a business partner dies? Islamic law dictates that if any partner dies or withdraws, the enterprise completely dissolves (Udovitch 1970; Kuran 2012), whereas European business partnerships and corporations live on with lives of their own.

Moreover, economic historians have shown that during this same period of time, the twelfth and thirteenth centuries, and especially in Holland and the Low Countries, villages and urban conclaves were forming in which people were acting collectively to self-govern, to regulate collectively owned grazing grounds known as 'the commons', and to regulate grinding mills, riverways and other assets that were considered jointly owned by the community. Such communities formed their own judicial bodies, bought, sold and rented property, and hired clerks, even an occasional police officer and other agents who worked for the collective public enterprise (de Moor 2008; van Bavel 2010a: 60–6). To us moderns, this seems normal, but the fact is that this kind of legitimate communal self-organisation, bound by law with articulated rights and prerogatives, was a wholly new thing not witnessed elsewhere. This new legal arrangement proved to be a boon to the rise of early modern capitalism, to the whole commercial revolution of the thirteenth and fourteenth centuries, as well as the 'little divergence' of northern Europe centred on Amsterdam, Utrecht and London (van Zanden 2009: 197), replete with a variety of new collective trading entities. These would include extra-familial firms (otherwise known as legally recognised companies), as well as emerging joint-stock companies (Scott 1912: vol. 1). Formally recognised banks, whose records constituted legal documents available to public scrutiny, became part of this early 'take-off' (Lopes 1977; de Roover 1953: 80–5; de Roover 1963; Usher 1934). Clearly, the legal revolution of this time had far-reaching consequences for political, economic and intellectual development.

Indeed, recent scholarship has added considerable weight to the assertion that Europe's legal revolution in all its dimensions contributed measurably to the economic ascendance of Europe in the early modern period in comparison to other parts of the world (Maddison 2010). Whether one discerns a causal link between the new legal science or the rise of the universities and the teaching of the new legal system, the evidence suggests that the availability of the new legal conceptions, lawyers and courts significantly facilitated economic growth in Germany and other parts of Western Europe (Cantoni and Yuchtman 2012; Shäfer and Wulf 2013).

Universities and the scientific agenda

When we turn to the rise of European universities, I believe their role as incubators of modern science and the scientific revolution is now well established, if not fully appreciated. Likewise, it is now understood that neither Islamic *madrasas* nor the Chinese academies had anything like the structure, legal autonomy or curriculum of medieval and early modern universities (Huff 2017: Ch. 6).

Given that context, I need only highlight a couple of elements. It should be apparent within the context of the foregoing legal history that the European universities were the salient example of 'whole bodies' or corporate entities embracing the new status of legally autonomous entities capable of creating their own rules and regulations while enjoying the bundle of rights granted to all corporate entities enumerated earlier. As Hasting Rashdall pointed out (Rashdall 1936: 4–5), it was only by an accident of history that schools of higher education retained the title of 'universities', which was the generic term for collective wholes (*universitas*, a whole body) recognised during the legal revolution of the twelfth and thirteenth centuries.

Second, the long-standing Arts curriculum (composed of the *trivium* and *quadrivium*) that had been a staple of the cathedral schools was transformed into the Three Philosophies: Moral Philosophy (or Ethics), Metaphysics, and Natural Philosophy (Grant 1996). This adaptation was an equally transformative outcome that reorganised the old Arts curriculum of the cathedral schools, giving them a progressive and, indeed, scientific new orientation. It did this by introducing into the curriculum the so-called 'New Aristotle' and especially his *natural* books. What the Europeans did was to institutionalise a whole new curriculum of naturalistic studies. These inquiries raised all sorts of questions about the natural world. The same method of compiling questions and working out answers that had been used in the study of law and theology was now employed with equal vigour in the study of the natural world.

For example, in naturalistic studies, scholars asked 'whether the world is round . . . whether the earth moves . . . whether it is possible that other worlds exist, . . . whether the existence of a vacuum is possible' and so on (Grant 1974: 199–209). What the founders of the new universities did was to place at the centre of this new curriculum the natural books of Aristotle, which included his *Physics*, [his book] *On the Heavens*, *On Generation and Corruption*, *On the Soul*, *Meteorology* and

The Small Works on Natural Things, as well as biological works such as *The History of Animals*, *The Parts of Animals* and *The Generation of Animals*. It is with these books, Edward Grant has observed, that we find 'the treatises that formed the comprehensive foundation for the medieval conception of the physical world and its operation' (Grant 1984: 78). This was indeed a core experience that was essentially scientific. Put differently, the Europeans institutionalised the study of the natural world by making it the central core of the university curriculum (Weisheipl 1984).

This curriculum was unique in the educational history of the world because the Muslim world prohibited the introduction of Aristotle's natural books into the centre of its teachings in the *madrasas*, while the Chinese did not have a philosophical tradition equivalent to Aristotle's natural books; nor did it mandate the study of naturalistic questions for the state-sponsored civil service examinations that served to select scholars to become government officials (Huff 2011: Ch. 4; Elman 1994).

In short, the medieval and early modern educational reforms led directly to the rise of modern science. If one looks carefully at the record, one will see that there is a direct continuity between many of the questions raised by the twelfth- and thirteenth-century naturalists and the experimental pursuits that were carried out in the seventeenth century during the scientific revolution (Clagett 1959; Moody 1957). These included experiments with magnetism and the discovery of electricity, the study of pneumatics, air pumps and the vacuum, and, of course, all the post mortem examinations of human bodies that had been going on in universities across Europe since the thirteenth century (and earlier), and were also encouraged even by Church officials (Huff 2017: 189–208).

From the twelfth century onwards, the teachings of the universities served to inculcate a spirit of scientific inquiry – that is, they instilled a fundamental intellectual curiosity that was to persist all the way to the present, while, conversely, that same spirit of innovative inquiry did not take hold outside of Europe. In the case of European universities, one might even suggest that the effect of studying natural philosophy there, in the period leading up to 1600, was so strong that many of the pioneers of the seventeenth-century revolution were highly educated laymen, not scholars attached to the universities. This is not to suggest that the universities of Europe had become less important, but rather that the ethos of science, of disinterested naturalistic inquiry, had jumped the bounds of strict university identification.

The long view

I submit that the deep structures enumerated above, etched in a unique legal tradition, constitute what I have called the hidden structure of modernity. These are, indeed, the fundamental touchstones of what it means to be a modern, democratic, constitutional order grounded in historic commitments to due process of law. This architecture also contains the essential legal mechanisms that make modern economies stable and efficient, though such devices always need revision and fine-tuning. This outcome was the result of following a particular developmental path for hundreds of years.

When the English colonialists ventured off to the New World, they did so organisationally as *companies*, mainly joint-stock companies. A narrow and blinkered view of this fact dwells only on the commercial side of the movement, entirely overlooking the earlier developments that established legally autonomous entities with their broad range of legal rights and prerogatives, available only in the unique Western legal tradition. Now, happily, many scholars have pointed out that just this set of legal and cultural resources resulted in the transition from a 'corporation to a commonwealth' in the USA, from what were sometimes failing economic enterprises into constitutionally structured democratic enclaves with *elected* leaders and elected *assemblies* of citizens who instituted representative government (Innes 1995, 2001). They brought not only all the 'rights, privileges and immunities of Englishmen', with special reference to the Magna Carta (Howard 1968: 14–34), but all the legal conceptions and guarantees of business and commercial activities that were embedded in the Common and Civil Law traditions of England and the continent. This occurred especially in the Massachusetts Bay settlement but also in Jamestown, among others.

In effect, the charters of the joint-stock company (as per the Canon and Civil Law traditions) provided for a constitutional framework within which 'We the people' could establish democratic institutions. These came

> complete with a representative assembly, an elected chief executive, and guarantees of individual rights. The assembly mandated by the charter had the power to enact 'orders, laws, statutes, and ordinances' necessary for the colony's governance. The company had a 'Governor,' a chief executive who was elected by the residents of the colony and served as commander-in-chief. (Winkler 2018: 19–20)

As in Jamestown, a key and historic innovation was 'the representative assembly' (Kuperman 2009: 287), though such an idea had clear roots in England and on the continent, found in self-governing cities and towns, professional associations, charitable organisations and so on.

When the dream of a European Union began to emerge after World War II, one of the first prerequisites, suggested by Winston Churchill, was a 'European Parliament', a clear reflection of the underlying values and commitments that Churchill and other Europeans anticipated as the first foundational step for a broader, more structured union of European countries that had been torn apart by the war. When and just how the EU can become the 'United States of Europe' (Reid 2004) is an open question. That there will be a significant but thriving 'unity' of European states, notwithstanding the perils of the present moment, seems highly likely.

References

Bartlett, R. (1993), *The Making of Europe: Conquest, Colonialization and Cultural Change, 950–1350*, Princeton: Princeton University Press.

Bavel, B. J. P. van (2010a), 'The Medieval Origins of Capitalism in the Netherlands', *BMCN – Low Countries Historical Review* 125(2–3): 45–79.

Bavel, B. J. P. van (2010b), *Manors and Markets: Economy and Society in the Low Countries, 500–1600*, Oxford: Oxford University Press.

Becker, S., and L. Woessmann (2009), 'Was Weber Wrong? A Human Capital Theory of Protestant Economic History', *Quarterly Journal of Economics* 124(2): 531–96.

Berman, H. J. (1983), *Law and Revolution: The Formation of the Western Legal Tradition*, Cambridge, MA: Harvard University Press.

Berman, H. J. (2003), *Law and Revolution, II. The Impact of the Protestant Reformations on the Western Legal Tradition*, Cambridge, MA: Harvard University Press.

Bisson, T. (2009), *The Crisis of the Twelfth Century: Power, Lordship, and the Origins of European Government*, Princeton: Princeton University Press.

Boli, J., and G. M. Thomas (eds) (1999), *Constructing World Culture: International Non-Governmental Organizations Since 1875*, Stanford: Stanford University Press.

Boli, J. (2001), 'Globalization and World Culture', in N. J. Smelser (ed.), *International Encyclopedia of the Social and Behavioral Sciences*, New York: Elsevier, pp. 6261–6.

Brundage, J. (2008a), *The Medieval Origins of the Legal Profession: Canonists, Civilians, and Courts*, Chicago: University of Chicago Press.

Brundage, J. (2008b), 'The Teaching and Study of Canon Law in the Law Schools', in K. Pennington and W. Hartmann (eds), *History of Medieval Canon Law in the Classical Period, 1140–1234*, Washington, D. C.: Catholic University Press of America, pp. 98–120.

Cantoni, D., and N. Yuchtman (2012), 'Medieval Universities, Legal Institutions and the Commercial Revolution', *NBER Working Paper 17979*, April. Available at: <http://nber.org/papers/w17979> (last accessed 26 June 2019).

Castells, M., O. Bouin, J. Caraça, G. Cardoso, J. Thompson and M. Wieviorka (2017), *Europe's Crises*, Cambridge: Polity Press.

Clagett, M. (1959), *The Science of Mechanics in the Middle Ages*, Madison: Wisconsin University Press.

Clark, C. (2012), *The Sleepwalkers: How Europe Went to War in 1914*, New York: Harpers.

Conrad, S. (2012), 'Enlightenment in Global History: A Historical Critique', *The American Historical Review* 117(4): 999–1027.

Drori, G. S., J. W. Meyer, W. F. O. Ramirez and E. Schofer (2003), *Science in the Modern World Polity: Institutionalization and Globalization*, Stanford: Stanford University Press.

Durkheim, E., and M. Mauss (1971), 'Note on the Notion of Civilization', tr. Benjamin Nelson, *Social Research* 38(4): 809–13.

Elman, B. (1994), *A Cultural History of Civil Service Examinations in Late Imperial China*, Berkeley: University of California Press.

Goldstone, Jack (2002), 'Efflorescence and Economic Growth in World History: Rethinking the "Rise of the West" and the Industrial Revolution', *Journal of World History* 12(2): 323–89.

Gorski, P. (2001), 'Calvinism and Revolution: The Walzer Thesis Reconsidered', in R. Madsen, W. M. Sullivan, A. Swidler and S. M. Tipton (eds), *Meaning and Modernity: Religion, Polity and Self*, Berkeley: University of California Press, pp. 78–104.

Gorski, P. (2003), *The Disciplinary Revolution: Calvinism and the Rise of the State in Early Modern Europe*, Chicago: University of Chicago Press.

Grant, E. (1974), *A Source Book in Medieval Science*, Cambridge, MA: Harvard University Press.

Grant, E. (1984), 'Science and the Medieval Universities', in J. M. Kittelson and P. J. Transue (eds), *Rebirth, Reform, and Resilience: Universities in Transition, 1300–1700*, Columbus: University of Ohio Press.

Grant, E. (1996), *The Foundations of Modern Science in the Middle Ages*, New York: Cambridge University Press.

Grant, E. (2001), *God and Reason in the Middle Ages*, New York: Cambridge University Press.

Hartmann, W., and K. Pennington (eds) (2016), *The History of Courts and Procedure in Medieval Canon Law*, Washington, D. C.: The Catholic University of America.

Hoeflich, M., and J. M. Grabher (2008), 'The Establishment of Normative Legal Texts: The Beginning of the *Ius Commune*', in W. Hartmann and K. Pennington (eds), *The History of Medieval Canon Law in the Classical Period, 1140–1234*, Washington, D. C.: The Catholic University of America Press, pp. 1–21.

Howard, A. E. Dick (1968), 'Road from Runnymede: Magna Carta and Constitutionalism in America', *American Journal of Comparative Law* 64: 14–34.

Huff, T. (2000), 'Science and Metaphysics in the Three Religions of the Book', *Intellectual Discourse* (A Journal of the Kulliyah [Faculty] of Islamic Revealed Knowledge and Human Science, International Islamic University Malaysia) 8(2): 173–98.

Huff, T. (2011), *Intellectual Curiosity and the Scientific Revolution: A Global Perspective*, New York: Cambridge University Press.

Huff, T. (2017), *The Rise of Early Modern Science: Islam, China and the West*, 3rd edn, New York: Cambridge University Press.

Hyde, J. K. (1972), 'Commune, University, and Society in Early Medieval Bologna', in J. W. Baldwin and R. Goldthwaithe (eds), *Universities in Politics: Case Studies from the Late Middle Ages and Early Modern Period*, Baltimore: Johns Hopkins University Press, pp. 17–46.

Innes, S. (1995), *Creating the Commonwealth: The Economic Culture of the Puritans*, New York: W. W. Norton.

Innes, S. (2001), 'From Corporation to Commonwealth', in J. Beatty (ed.), *Colossus*, New York: Broadway, pp. 18–22.

Kuperman, K. (2009), *The Jamestown Project*, Cambridge, MA: Harvard University Press.

Kuran, T. (2012), *The Long Divergence: How Islamic Law Held Back the Middle East*, Princeton: Princeton University Press.

Kuttner, S. (1964), 'The Date of the Constitution "Saepe": The Vatican Manuscripts and the Roman Edition of the Clementines', in *Melanges Eugène Tisserant*, Studi e Testi 234, vol. IV, Vatican City: Biblioteca Apostolica Vaticana, pp. 427–52.

Langbein, J. H. (2003), *The Origins of Adversary Criminal Trials*, Oxford: Oxford University Press.

Lopes, R. (1977), *The Commercial Revolution, 950–1350*, New York: Cambridge University Press.

Maddison, A. (2010), *Historical Statistics of the World Economy, 1–2008 AD*. Available at: <http://ggdc.net/maddison/Maddison.htm> (last accessed 26 June 2019).

Martines, L. (2003), *April Blood: Florence and the Plot Against the Medici*, Oxford: Oxford University Press.

Mitterauer, M. (2010), *Why Europe? The Medieval Origins of its Special Path*, Chicago: University of Chicago Press.

Moody, E. (1957), 'Galileo and Avempace: Dynamics of the Leaning Tower Experiments', in P. Wiener and A. Noland (eds), *Roots of Scientific Thought: A Cultural Perspective*, New York: Basic Books, pp. 176–206.

Moor, T. de (2008), 'The Silent Revolution: A New Perspective on the Emergence of Commons, Guilds, and Other Forms of Corporate Collective Action in Western Europe', *International Review of Social History* 53: 179–212.

Moore, R. I. (2000), *The First European Revolution, c. 950–121*, Oxford: Blackwell.

Nelson, B. (1973), 'Civilizational Complexes and Intercivilizational Encounters', *Sociological Analysis* 34(2): 79–105.

Nelson, B. (1981), *On the Roads to Modernity: Conscience, Science and Civilizations. Selected Writings of Benjamin Nelson*, ed. T. Huff, reprinted with a new Introduction 2012, Lanham, MD: Lexington Books.

Ozment, S. (1993), *Protestants: The Birth of a Revolution*, New York: Doubleday.

Pennington, K. (1993), *The Prince and the Law, 1200–1600: Sovereignty and Rights in the Western Legal Tradition*, Berkeley: University of California Press.

Pennington, K. (1998), 'Due Process, Community, and the Prince in the Evolution of the *ordo iudiciarius*', *Rivista internazionale di diritto commune*, 9: 9–47.

Pomeranz, K. (2000), *The Great Divergence*, Princeton: Princeton University Press.

Post, G. (1964), *Studies in Medieval Legal Thought: Public Law and the State, 1100–1322*, Princeton: Princeton University Press.

Rashdall, H. (1936), *The Universities of Europe in the Middle Ages*, new edn in 3 vols, ed. F. M. Powicke and A. B. Emden, Oxford: Clarendon Press.

Reid, T. R. (2004), *The United States of Europe*. New York: Penguin.

Robertson, R. T. (1986), *The Making of the Modern World*, London: Zed Books.

Roover, R. de (1953), 'The Commercial Revolution of the Thirteenth Century', in F. Lane and J. C. Riemersma (eds), *Enterprise and Secular Change: Readings in Economic History*, Homewood, IL: American Economic Association, pp. 80–5.

Roover, R. de. (1963), 'The Organization of Trade', in M. M. Postan, E. Rich and E. Miller (eds), *Cambridge Economic History of Europe*, vol. 3, New York: Cambridge University Press, pp. 42–118.

Schiavone, A. (2012), *The Invention of Law in the West*, Cambridge, MA: Harvard University Press.

Schofer, E., and E. H. McEneaney (2003), 'Methodological Tools for the Study of Globalization', in *Science in the Modern World Polity*, Stanford: Stanford University Press, pp. 43–74.

Scott, W. R. (1912), *Constitution and Finance of the English, Scottish and Irish Joint-Stock Companies to 1720*, vol. 1, Cambridge: Cambridge University Press.

Shäfer, H.-B., and A. J. Wulf (2013), 'Jurists, Clerics and Merchants: The Rise of Learned Law in Medieval Europe and Its Impact on Economic Growth', 1 April. Available at: <https://ssrn.com/abstract=2242110> (last accessed 5 July 2019).

Skinner, Q. (1979), *The Foundations of Modern Political Thought*, New York: Cambridge University Press.

Stiglitz, J. (2016), *The Euro: How A Common Currency Threatens the Future of Europe*, New York: Norton.

Udovitch, A. (1970), *Partnership and Profit in Medieval Islam*, Princeton: Princeton University Press.

Usher, A. (1934), 'The Origins of Banking: The Primitive Bank of Deposit, 1200–1600', *The Economic History Review* 4(4): 399–428.

van Zanden, J. L., E. Buringh and M. Bosker (2012), 'The Rise and Decline of European Parliaments, 1188–1789', *The Economic History Review* 65(3): 835–61.

Vries, P. (2013), *Escaping Poverty: The Origins of Modern Economic Growth*, Vienna: University of Vienna Press.

Vries, P. (2015), 'Replies to my Commentators', *Tijdschrift voor Sociale en Economische Geschiedenis* 12(2): 105–20.

Weber, M. (1958), *The Protestant Ethic and the Spirit of Capitalism*, tr. Talcott Parsons, New York: Charles Scribner's Sons.

Weisheipl, J. A. (1984), 'Science in the Thirteenth Century', in J. I. Cato (ed.), *History of the University of Oxford*, Oxford: Clarendon Press, pp. 435–69.

Winkler, A. (2018), *We the Corporations: How American Businesses Won their Civil Rights*, New York: Liveright.

3

To Hell and Beyond: The European Civilisational Crisis of the Twentieth Century

Johann P. Arnason

THE FIRST HALF of the twentieth century is often referred to as the time of a 'European civil war'. This does not necessarily imply that the war ending in 1945 was an inevitable sequel to the one that began in 1914. Recent scholarship has reinforced interpretations of the interwar decades as a phase of open possibilities and contingent outcomes. But if World War II is taken to have reopened a conflict that the 'overstretched peace' (Leonhard 2018) constructed in 1918–23 failed to settle, the dynamic of disintegration outweighs the untested alternatives.[1]

That said, it remains to clarify what kind of continuity can be attributed to the breakdown that unfolded in two stages with a long interval. The whole process is obviously a key part of the background to later developments, including – not least – European integration. The metaphor of a civil war, interrupted by a truce and followed by a more lasting settlement, is in many ways misleading. It obscures the extra-European dimensions already evident in 1914. This was not simply a matter of power struggles, unleashed and decided in Europe, spreading beyond its borders. Closer analysis must take note of changes to war aims and dynamics, resulting from global extension, and of their retroactive impact on the European field. The initial constellation linked a crisis on the European periphery (due to the rivalry of Austria–Hungary and Russia in the Balkans, exacerbated by the rising and ambitious Serbian state) to ongoing tensions between imperial states with global possessions and interests. Concerns about German *Weltpolitik* were of some importance for the British decision to draw closer to France and Russia; but conversely, there were – as Paul W. Schroeder (2004) has emphasised – compelling reasons for Britain to reach a compromise, gradually transformed into an alliance, with its main rivals in the global arena, already allied with each other and too strong to be jointly defeated.

As recent historical work has stressed more than used to be done, the outbreak of war resulted from a crisis where ill-advised initiatives and decisions on all sides compounded each other, and war aims were at first very unclearly defined. They had to be determined in the midst of conflict, and to a significant extent away from public notice, thus causing aggravated problems when they had to be pursued more openly. The upgraded war aims not only escalated the struggle between the two warring blocs; they also revealed dissonances among the Allies and generated discord where incompatible promises had been made to interested sides (the intertwining of Anglo-French rivalry and Jewish–Arab conflicts in the Middle East is a familiar example).

Several new dimensions emerging during the war should be noted. The East Asian offshoot of the conflict, although neither very visible nor strategically significant at the time, paved the way for future developments. Both Japan and China joined the war on the side of the Allies, in the hope of profiting from a likely victory. The postwar settlement favoured Japan at the expense of China, thus reinforcing a dominant position that had been achieved around the turn of the century. This provoked a massive protest movement that became a spearhead of Chinese cultural modernisation, a crucible of rival nationalist and Communist projects, and a protagonist of more adversarial relations with Japan. Japan's postwar ascendancy in the region culminated in a war of conquest against China, which, in turn, became the main reason for a collision with the USA. The latter conflict was a crucial part of World War II and therefore a major determinant of international relations in its aftermath. At the same time, the defeat of Japan paved the way for a revolutionary transformation of China; this process went through successive reorientations and is still reshaping China's relations with the rest of the world, not least with Europe. The conflict that began in 1914 was thus reflected in changes to the global environment of European integration, and the long-term consequences are a major matter of debate.

Another, more rapidly visible complication of that kind arose from the abortive end of the war on the eastern front. The German victory over Russia opened up possibilities of imperial expansion, unprecedented in the European setting; the eastward offensive of German armies in 1917–18 was a war of conquest, not remotely comparable to a civil war and all the less so because it took place in a virtual vacuum. Bolshevik power was still a pretence rather than a functioning regime. From the German point of view, the sudden breakthrough reinforced hopes of all-round victory; civil and military power-holders disagreed

on the options of colonisation or indirect rule, but they also enter-
tained visions of expansion much further to the east. Both conquests
and expectations vanished in the autumn of 1918, but their afterlife was
arguably more important than the original episode. The lost empire on
the eastern frontier became the most direct experiential anchor for the
phantasms of conquest that were both central to Hitler's ideology and
essential to his alliance with the German army. Empire-building at the
expense of Russia and East Central Europe was a key war aim of the
Nazi regime, and its pursuit proved the most self-destructive part of
a *va banque* strategy. The final defeat of the bid for an eastern empire
set the scene for post-1945 European history. This is a crucial but often
underestimated aspect of the continuity between the two world wars.

The decisive factor in the German collapse on the western front was
an extra-European one. Notwithstanding the superior resources and
more effective command structure of the Allies, it seems likely that,
without American intervention, the German position after victory in
the east would have been strong enough to ensure a more mitigated
setback, if not a stalemate. A closer look at the American intervention
and the postwar settlement reveals a complex picture. The first step was
direct participation in the war, hastened by German provocations and
not preceded by a debate on war aims. The first indication of a global
vision came with Wilson's 1918 declarations. They responded to the
challenge posed by the rise of Bolshevik power in Russia, and at first
adopted a rather conciliatory attitude to this new force. Bolshevik policies and Allied strategies soon put paid to the latter effort. Although
Wilson's initiative was triggered by the October Revolution, it was, in
the short run, much more globally influential than the Russian events
(Manela 2009); but, by the same token, the subsequent disappointment
came more quickly and with broader impact, and that in turn created
new opportunities for Bolshevism as a global force. As for direct effects
on the postwar settlement, the American retreat from Wilson's project
came in two steps. The laborious compromise with European victors
during the Versailles conference was followed by the decision to with-
draw from involvement in the international consolidation of the peace.
However, recent scholarship has corrected earlier views of American
'isolationism' after 1920. The transatlantic great power retained a massive presence in world affairs, all the more so when its multiple non-
political influences are taken into account. An epoch-making and
irreversible step towards the 'globalizing of America' (Iriye 1993) had
been taken, but in a markedly indecisive way, leaving open questions

about future courses of action, and thus leading to uncertainty about the strategies to adopt in response. This ambiguous entry into a new chapter in Atlantic history was to prove important for developments during the following decades.

To sum up, the global sources, extensions and repercussions of World War I add up to a strong case against the notion of a European civil war; the input from the Western hemisphere was eminently significant. Another line of argument concerns events within Europe. The period in question was characterised by a high frequency of civil wars in the proper sense, and their relationship to the interrupted global conflicts varied widely. The overstretched metaphor of a continental civil war obscures this complex picture. A closer analysis of the interconnections might start with the revolutionary venture that aimed at turning World War I, perceived as a clash of rival imperialisms, into a civil war. This was the attempted breakthrough of Bolshevism as an international force; it did not come anywhere near its ultimate goal, and success within a large political arena – imperial Russia – was achieved in circumstances that changed both the project and the protagonists in unprecedented ways, conducive to a revival rather than an overcoming of the global conflict. Apart from this decisive but paradoxical case, another concatenation of defeat in war and the outbreak of civil wars unfolded in the domains of the Central European powers; it was neither controlled by nor fully aligned with the Russian strategists of revolution, its key episodes were separated in time and space, and the outcome was very different from the Russian upheaval. A half-collapse of the established order led to the simultaneous mobilisation of revolutionary and counter-revolutionary forces; at the same time, key parts of the old power elites rode out the storm and reached a temporary modus vivendi with reformist forces facing a radical threat. The end result was the victory of an extreme counter-revolutionary current, in control of the German state from 1933 onwards and rapidly dominant in the whole region before it self-destructed in a continental war of conquest.

These two major cases are prime examples of the intertwined dynamics of imperial war, civil war and revolution in twentieth-century Europe. A broader survey would have to deal with a range of more singular constellations. One of them often looms large in historiographical and ideological accounts of the twentieth century. The Spanish civil war brought a long-term dynamic of deepening enmity between rival sociopolitical blocs to a climax, but its particular course and perceived significance also reflected both the growing radicalisation and the shifting fronts of pan-European antagonisms that became central to the second global war. Within Europe, the latter did not spark any transformative social conflicts comparable to those of the years 1917–23, but local resistance movements enmeshed in civil wars developed in the margin and the aftermath of the main contest (especially on the southeastern periphery), and the outcome depended on stronger powers. The Greek civil war stands out as a particular case; the Communist bid for power was launched without Soviet support, but Western assumptions of such involvement played a disproportionate role in converting this local conflict into one of the opening moves of the Cold War.

In short, Europe's time of troubles was marked by complicated intertwinings of local, national, regional and multipower conflicts (the last-named went rapidly global, but the first of them grew out of regional upheaval in the Balkans, while the second was precipitated by the reassertion of German regional power in Central Europe, with consequences uncontainable by rivals and uncontrollable by those who spearheaded the move). The variety of relationships between these different levels is still an underdeveloped theme of comparative history, and shorthand descriptions applied across the board are unhelpful. If we want to come up with more precise conceptual pointers, it seems appropriate to begin with the level that shaped the context of the others and set the scene for later developments. The following remarks will outline a case for the concept of civilisational crisis. It is not uncommon to use the term 'civilisation' with reference to the events and processes discussed here. Both world wars have been described as civilisational breakdowns or ruptures, but mostly without any clarification of the adjective. Here, the next step will be to examine the interlinked meanings of both categories, civilisation and crisis.

In the context of twentieth-century catastrophes, it is intuitively plausible to describe the afflicted civilisation as European. Closer consideration raises doubts about this assumption of continuity. As suggested in the Introduction to this volume, there are good reasons to trace the history of Europe as a historical complex back to the transformation of the Roman world, but that does not justify the construction of an enduring civilisational pattern. If we follow the line that has proved most fruitful in comparative civilisational studies – that is, the analysis of interconnections between cultural articulations of the world and institutions of social power (most seminally developed in the work of S. N. Eisenstadt) – the contrast between medieval and modern patterns is too massive to be bridged by a supposedly intact civilisational model. The world of Western Christendom was dominated by the Catholic Church as a central and authoritative institution, weaker but recurrently active aspirations to imperial rulership, and a broad spectrum of political formations with a more limited reach (from dynastic kingdoms to city republics), variously dependent on and deviant from the interplay of papacy and empire. This medieval constellation was radically different from the modern one that took shape from the sixteenth and seventeenth centuries onwards. An irreversible split of Western Christendom into two violently opposed religiopolitical cultures, slow to find a modus vivendi and conducive to major geopolitical as well as social differences, was accompanied by new developments in state formation, the first steps towards a radical change in the relationship between religion and politics, and transformative trends in various fields of human activity, from scientific thought to the economy. It should be noted that this emphasis on early modernity as a time of rupture is contested by another narrative centred on the 'long Middle Ages', from the third to the late eighteenth century, most clearly formulated by Jacques Le Goff. In that case, the transition to modernity is equated with the industrial and democratic revolutions. The debate is not easily settled, but here it suffices to observe that the latter claim also undermines the claim to civilisational continuity. Le Goff explicitly defined the long Middle Ages in terms of the beginning and the end of a civilisation (Le Goff 1991).

Doubts about the idea of a continuous European civilisation are reinforced by the fact that such visions of ancestry have not proved very usable for identity-building purposes. Efforts to legitimise European integration in terms of a heritage have occasionally appealed to classical antiquity, but given the declining influence of classical studies, that could never go far. The invocation of Greek democracy to justify the accession of Greece to the EU was a rhetorical ornament of action in support of a fragile parliamentary regime in a sensitive region. It gave a certain boost to popular notions of classical Athens as a direct ancestor of modern democracy, but this grossly oversimplified view – an offshoot of nineteenth-century liberalism in search of a pedigree – was now too weakened by scholarly criticism to regain much ground. Following Marcel Gauchet (2007: 21–2), modern democracy is best described as a mixed regime (constituted by the rule of law underpinned by basic rights, a sovereign political community, and a regime of historicity that focuses expectations on collective action shaping the future). Greek democracy was also a mixture, but a different one; it is legitimate to compare the two cases, but ancient democracy was neither a model nor an embryo of the regime that borrowed its name.[2]

The question of Christian sources as a defining aspect of European identity has been a matter of somewhat more active debate. However, the outcome seems unequivocal: the idea of Europe as a Christian civilisation does not carry the weight or conviction that would make it a viable cultural framework for integration. The appeal that it now seems to have in specific and limited contexts (as in Poland and Hungary) depends on political conjunctures with uncertain prospects.

If historical and contemporary experiences speak against the construct of Europe as a continuous civilisation, it remains to explore another variation on the civilisational theme. The interpretation of modernity as a new type of civilisation was, to the best of my knowledge, first suggested by the Czech philosopher Jan Patočka, in an unfinished text written in the 1950s but not made accessible until much later (Patočka 1996) and unknown to those who brought this idea into sociological debates. The most decisive move was made by S. N. Eisenstadt, who set out to theorise both the novelty and the diversity of modern civilisation in terms of human autonomy, although the latter concept was not as explicitly developed as the project would, in principle, entail. If the conception of modernity as a distinctive civilisation of autonomy is to be linked to the general perspective mentioned above (the intertwining of world articulation with institutional patterns and processes), a broad understanding of autonomy is required, and it must go beyond the philosophical arguments that tend to equate the foundations of modernity with more or less emphatically Kantian principles. Autonomy as a civilisational horizon is not reducible to higher degrees of rationality or aspirations to self-determination; it also implies new and inherently expanding ways of accumulating wealth and power. In the economic sphere, the field of alternatives includes entrepreneurial innovation in the never-ending quest for wealth, as well as the revolutionary project of a 'free association of producers'. On the political level, the turn to autonomy involved a theoretical and practical disconnection of state power and its reasons from religious frameworks, but also – in the longer run – the affirmation of democratic sovereignty. In cultural terms, the orientations grounded in autonomy range from articulated abilities to intervene in the world and question existing social orders, to the highly variegated models of self-realisation.

Given these multiple contexts, overall ideological elaborations of autonomy have inevitably been conflict-prone. In particular, the dispute between individualistic and collectivistic versions – emphasised by

Eisenstadt – grew into one of the central antinomies of modernity. Both the plurality of domains and the polarity of encompassing interpretations can be seen as preconditions of a civilisational crisis and a further reason to reject the metaphor of a civil war. The most fundamental flaw in Huntington's unfortunate adaptation of civilisational theory was the assumption that civilisations are the 'ultimate tribes', hence defined by a collective identity analogous to that of nations, but broader and stronger. In such a context, the comparison to civil wars within nation-states would make sense. But the above remarks on modernity suggest that a civilisational problematic (with conflicting interpretations), rather than civilisational identity, was the core factor; and although this is not the place for broader comparisons, it may be noted that similar conclusions seem to apply to other cases.

More specific considerations will clarify the trends and problems that made Europe the epicentre of the crisis. Current debates on the question of modernity as a new civilisation suggest multiple regional origins; historians have highlighted changes with modernising implications in East Asian societies and the empires that dominated much of the Islamic world in the sixteenth and seventeenth centuries. The idea of modernity as an exclusively European invention, subsequently diffused to the rest of the world, is untenable. But transformations in the European arena were more radical than elsewhere, more conducive to the formation of a whole civilisational pattern, and accompanied by conflicts on a scale unknown elsewhere. There is no extra-European parallel to the split of Western Christendom, the religious wars that followed in its wake, or the restructuring of the political order undertaken – within states as well as between them – to contain the conflicts. This distinctively European dynamism led to global expansion in successive stages and with varying impact on other parts of the world; the long-term pattern was a mixture of European domination, adaptation of models borrowed from Europe to indigenous contexts, and the use of European techniques, institutions and ideas to boost resistance to European rule. The other side of European expansion was entanglement in a global constellation and its ultimately uncontrollable dynamics. The globalising processes that began in the early modern era set a course that culminated in global repercussions of the twentieth-century crisis.

Further civilisational aspects, crucial to the disaster dynamics of 1914 and beyond, should be added to the picture. Figures of autonomy, as distinct from the institutional spheres and ideological visions mentioned above, have played a more prominent historical role and taken clearer shape in the European world than elsewhere. Nation and class are two key figures of that kind. Historical sociologists – notably, Mann (2012) – have identified nations and classes as the most salient collective actors of modern times. Both types are still alive and well; the long-drawn-out and erratic process of adjusting their modes of action and organisation to modern democracy is not about to end. But the imaginaries that accompanied and co-determined the trajectories of nations and classes are also integral to the story. The most ambitious images of nation and class have cast them as privileged claimants to self-determination, the former with an emphasis on continuity between a legitimising past and a more advanced future, the latter in the name of a more radical and universalistic break with the past but still with promises of continuing progress. The invocation of self-determination established a link to democratic transformations, but the projection of national and class identities beyond historical experience and horizons could also turn against more fundamental democratic presuppositions. It has been convincingly argued that racial ideology, especially in its extreme National Socialist form, was a significant step beyond nationalism; but its appeal was clearly based on an apparent upgrading and closure of national identity. As for the class imaginary and its offshoots, the turn to absolutist claims occurred in a very different context. Gone are the days when interpreters of the twentieth century could identify the rise of the Leninist party, defined by its quest for a monopoly of power in the name of superior knowledge, as the most decisive event; however, it remains true that this model proved remarkably attractive and useful to a variety of forces in search of power, often in circumstances altogether unlike the situation of emerging Bolshevism. Even so, the idea of a universal class – and of an exclusive authority to define the objective interests of that class – was a legitimising background of lasting importance.

Although the idea of the nation as a solely European invention is still defended by some eminent scholars (notably Hroch 2015), it is open to weighty objections (Japan is the most striking counter-example); in any case, processes of nation formation were a particularly sustained, conflict-prone and diversified aspect of European history. Class formation and class conflict are no longer seen as a universal key to the European experience of revolutions, but their importance for the paths of modern history is not in doubt. One of the most seminal liberal interpretations of twentieth-century trends (Halévy 1967) portrayed the events of 1914 as a triumph of national forces, antagonisms and imaginations over class-determined ones. On this view, the aftermath of the war saw a resurgence of conflicts based on or defined in relation to class divisions. In the long run, though, the national factor prevailed through increasingly statist policies, linking up with the advances of state intervention and state-directed mobilisation during the war. As a result, the statist current of the socialist tradition won a decisive victory over the liberal one, and also over the goals and ideas linked to social movements.

This line of argument highlights some aspects of the 'inaugural catastrophe' and its consequences, but a more complex perspective is needed. European versions of modernity were too diverse and their paths too divergent to be adequately grasped through the bipolar scheme of class and nation. The first point to add is one that recent reinterpretations of World War I have foregrounded: it was very much an inter-imperial conflict. Recognition of that fact is already an important step beyond earlier habits of placing the whole blame on nation-states and nationalism, but the synthesising grasp of its implications still leaves something to be desired. An obvious starting point is the insight that all the great powers that went to war in 1914 had imperial interests with specific strategic preferences and potential conflict zones, and thus contributed to the evolving crisis culminating in 1914. On this issue, as well as some of those discussed below, Christopher Clark's magisterial work on the outbreak of World War I (Clark 2013) has brought a decisive clarification. It is still possible to argue that German responses to events in the summer of 1914 were particularly risky, and to relate that observation to structures of power and decision-making in the Wilhelmine regime, but the idea of a uniquely aggressive bid for world hegemony is untenable.

Some further aspects of the multi-imperial constellation should be noted. On the one hand, it meant that the imperial powers interacted in a global arena where events on the periphery or the rise of outsiders (exemplified by Japan's victory over Russia) could affect the European epicentre and have a significant effect on relations between the major players. In the global field, perceptions and expectations could enter into the alignment of forces. One noteworthy case was the growing prominence of China as a future stake of great-power rivalry (Otte 2007), and the de facto settlement of that issue by two Japanese victories, over China and Russia. As a result, Russian imperial ambitions in the east were scaled down and redirected towards the Balkans; Britain settled for alliance with Japan; and both shifts affected the line-up of power blocs in Europe. On the other hand, interstate competition on the European periphery – more specifically, in Southeastern Europe – was marked by the neighbourhood of empires in contest; none of the Balkan states can be described as an imperial one, but their mutually damaging struggle for status and territory involved efforts to gain patronage and a less unequal footing within the European order. It was the interaction of those two asymmetric patterns of rivalry that triggered war in 1914. This entanglement combined with the collapse of the Ottoman empire, more protracted than the other imperial endings that followed: it began before the war, continued after defeat and, in conjunction with a series of abortive and uncoordinated Western incursions, left behind a geopolitical problem complex that has yet to be solved.

The constellation that descended into all-out conflict was characterised not only by the presence of multiple empires, but also by multiple types of imperial structure and rule. Some of them were contiguous, others trans-maritime; some retained a monarchic centre with real power but ambiguous effects, others had established a more coherent parliamentary regime. The formation of rival blocs in the last two decades before 1914 was determined neither by ideological orientations, nor by any straightforward geopolitical logic. The alliance most consistently strengthened was the Franco-Russian one, despite the stark contrast between republican and autocratic regimes; the British empire had more direct and potential conflicts of interest with the French and Russian ones than with Germany. Arguments about a German challenge to the whole international regime of unequal imperial power have been subjected to effective criticism. The line-up that prevailed on the eve of the war can be explained only in historical terms, as a result of combined global, European and national processes. If we look for the historical origins of the multi-imperial pattern as such, the story can be traced back to the transformation of the Roman world. Multiple heirs divided the legacy of the Roman empire, and attempts to impose unity were, in the long run, unsuccessful. The variety of imperial formations became more pronounced in the course of later European expansion.

These long-term perspectives concern Europe as a historical complex. A closer analysis of distinctively modern patterns can begin with the above-mentioned figures of autonomy. Both nations and classes were involved in changes linked to the apogee of imperialism before 1914 and the postwar disruptions, and neither category is reducible to anti-imperial aspects. The 'nationalizing of empires' (Berger and Miller 2014), strengthening the links between national identity and imperial rule, was a prominent trend of the period in question, although one that had uneven results. The most problematic case was the Habsburg empire, where the two component states diverged: uncompromising nationalisation in the Hungarian kingdom contrasted with the unavoidable acceptance of multinationality on the Austrian side, which in turn opened the way for pan-German currents as a substitute for self-contained nationalisation. As for the general postwar pressure to redefine relations between empires and nations, four main patterns may be distinguished. The victorious Western powers retained the identification with empire (in the British case, with a clear but adaptable distinction between dominions and possessions) and did not abstain from further expansion. Germany and Italy found themselves in a comparable situation, for different reasons but with analogous outcomes. The former was defeated and meant to be marginalised in a new world order, with both the losses and the stigma gradually revealed in the aftermath of the war and therefore open to ongoing mythologisation; the latter was denied both the expected gains from victory and a corresponding role in the peace settlement. In both cases, the result was a renewed bid for imperial power, backed up by a nationalism radicalised far beyond its traditional versions. The Habsburg empire collapsed entirely and was succeeded by states retaining the character of imperial fragments, either as incomplete nation-states (Austria, Hungary), or as multinational ones with unsustainable claims to constitute nation-states (Czechoslovakia, Poland, Yugoslavia). Finally, the Russian empire was reconstructed in a new form, with redefined relations between the centre and its subordinate national units, but the fragility of that arrangement was starkly highlighted by the massacre of national elites in the mid-1930s.

The destinies of class-based movements and ideologies differed from those of nations and nation-states, but they can also be analysed in relation to the imperial background. Advances of the workers' movement, both trade unions and political parties, were a core feature of the decades before World War I, so much so that later historians have even seen them as indications of a possible alternative to the path taken in 1914. On the other hand, the emerging split of reformist and radical wings within this apparent challenger of the established order was to prove to be fraught with consequences. It has been interpreted as a prelude to more serious conflicts of the interwar period or – more sweepingly – as one of the sources of the Cold War (Westad 2018). The view that now seems most plausible is that a broad spectrum of possibilities was channelled into a particular path by the constellation that crystallised in and through World War I. Reformist (not, eo ipso, openly revisionist) currents had been moving towards closer integration into the existing social and political framework; Social Democratic support for the war took the implications of this shift to more extreme lengths, making them more binding than before, and in the core victorious powers this led to long-term alignment with imperial outlooks and policies. Prewar radical socialism appeared in many guises and contexts; a shared effort to reactivate visions of revolution and mass mobilisation did not prevent major divergences, and the Russian imprint on the Leninist offshoot – the notion of a revolutionary vanguard – made it crucially different from all other versions. But it was this version of radicalism that found a historical outlet, provided by an inter-imperial conflict that it mistook for a terminal crisis of capitalism. The paradox of a successful revolution fuelled by a massive misunderstanding was compounded by a post-revolutionary mutation: class-based universalism became the universal ideology of a rebuilt imperial state, compatible with appeals to all sorts of allies and open to nationalist variations when it came to its application in other contexts.

This last observation brings us to the final point about imperial dynamics and legacies. The totalitarian regimes that rose and fell during the twentieth century are best understood as avatars of empire. To clarify this claim, it is important to note that we are dealing with the totalising logic of regimes, not with the achievement of total control over individuals or societies. The basic principle of this logic was a unification of political, economic and ideological power. In the Soviet model, unity was ensured by a distinctive type of double statehood, with party institutions superimposed on those of the administrative state; and for the higher level of that institutional edifice to function, the party had to combine power with authority over law and knowledge (this last aspect was particularly emphasised in the writings of Claude Lefort). By contrast, the much less institutionalised and more self-destructive regime of Nazi Germany rested on the alliance of a charismatic leader and movement with key parts of the established elites, but the drive for total power was built into its project.

Three fundamental aspects reveal the affinity between imperial and totalitarian regimes. Although it remains difficult to agree on a general definition of empires, some kind of supreme rulership – transcending more common types of kingship – is widely seen as a defining feature. The relatively short-lived modern European attempts to nationalise empires reflect a tension between this inherited model and the democratic imaginary, but the proposed alternative had to rely on the supposedly exemplary institutions and cultural missions of the imperial states. A transfiguration of the centre was thus to be achieved by other means. Totalitarian movements and regimes turned to a new way of personalising power: the institutionalised image of a supreme leader, empowered for decision-making across the board. This figure was not so much an outright negation of democratic transformations as an attempt to invert their logic. An extreme form of authoritarian rule was to be stylised as the most adequate expression of popular will and interest.

A second reason to stress imperial antecedents is the aspiration to power beyond the borders of ethnic, cultural or national communities, almost unanimously attributed to empires. The totalitarian regimes had vast trans-national ambitions, although their visions of mastery on that scale varied widely. Nowhere was the invocation of a past imperial tradition as explicit as in the Italian Fascist claim to *romanità*.

Finally, imperial domination tends to be associated with more or less emphatically universalistic ideological frameworks. This applies to the totalitarian episodes. The case of Marxism–Leninism is uncontroversial. National Socialism has often been described as a paradigm case of radical particularism, but the invertedly universalistic implications of racial doctrines have not gone unnoticed and Nazi ideology may be characterised in the paradoxical terms of an exclusivistic universalism.

The years between the wars were no mere interlude in a predetermined countdown to renewed war, but they were a short period, heavily conditioned by beginnings and marked throughout by fateful turns. Following recent reappraisals (especially Gerwarth 2017), the interwar phase can be dated from 1923, when the last of the peace settlements was imposed and local offshoots of the global conflict came to an end. The most appropriate terminal date is 1938, which saw Hitler's first conquests, although they were not perceived as such by those whom he set out to challenge. Key determinants of this decade and a half are easily identifiable. An intrinsically unsustainable project of world order – centring on the Versailles settlement – was further undermined by the inability or unwillingness of its protagonists to defend it. Uncontainable adversaries became the main bearers of totalitarian counter-projects. International disputes and upsets took place in a context of structural crises; if the whole record so far suggests that the relationship between modern capitalism and modern democracy is best understood as a troubled co-habitation, rather than a perfectible harmony or a fundamental conflict, the interwar chapter of the story was particularly fraught with disruptions on both sides.

Within the limits of this chapter, it is not possible to trace later developments in the same detail as the primal disaster of 1914 and its direct implications. Suffice it to note that, after another round of global conflict, more destructive and more conclusive than the first, the century-long crisis was channelled into the unprecedented constellation known as the Cold War. A closer look at that phenomenon will suggest a final objection to the metaphor of a European civil war. One of the main problems with the latter was its easy convergence with triumphalist accounts of the short twentieth century's end. An excessive focus on the European arena of the Cold War combined with the subsumption of Fascism and Communism under a unified theory of totalitarianism (this particular use of that concept should not be mistaken for the only possible one). In this way, the Cold War could be construed as a continuation of the European civil war that had supposedly reached a turning point but not a conclusive ending in 1945. The defeat of Communism was then equated with an 'end of history', a final triumph of the modern paradigm first exemplified by 'the West', and built on an unbreakable unity of liberal democracy and market economy.

This expanded narrative did not necessarily invoke the metaphor of a European civil war but fundamental affinities with that preconception are obvious. The shared longer-term vision also implies a certain perspective on European integration and its part in the developments that led to the world political sea change of 1989–91. Tony Judt, writing in the mid-1990s, described the reconstructed and slowly integrating western part of Europe between 1945 and 1989 as 'cosseted and amnesiac' (Judt 2011); it evolved within the protective framework of stable borders between zones of influence controlled by the two superpowers, and its break with a violent past was accompanied by far-reaching suppression of memories. The first impression of the new horizon after 1989 was that these limitations could be overcome in a more activist spirit. Post-Communist Eastern Europe appeared as a new domain to be added to the union in progress and promising to boost its strength and appeal on world scale; the farewell to a divided present was to enable a more shared and sovereign approach to memories of the past. It is of some importance that East European attitudes after 1989 matched these expectations. Whether the transfers of power in the erstwhile Soviet satellites can be understood as revolutions is a much-debated question that will not be addressed here, but the widespread notion that there was no

utopian element is easy to refute. In fact, the political and social transformations were accompanied by a cluster of imaginary themes best
described as a triune utopia. There was a marked difference between
visions of an active civil society, conducive to a new kind of politics, and
plans for rapid privatisation as a shortcut to a society of responsible and
market-literate proprietors; the two projects temporarily converged in
the mirage of a really existing West imagined as a successful synthe-
sis of their aspirations. The 'return to Europe' functioned as a unifying
slogan. Three decades later, the record of internal change and participation in the EU can at best be described as a very mixed result.

From the Western European angle, new problems and challenges
emerged almost simultaneously with the perspective of further progress.
Three developments changed the prospects of European integration, all
with gradually unfolding consequences. The unification of Germany
affected interstate relations, power balances and economic policies,
within and beyond the union. Enlargement eastwards confronted the EU
with historical legacies and emerging problems, unlike those inherited
or experienced by its established members. Last but not least, the new
eastern borders of the union necessitated a new approach to relations
with Russia. And if it took time for that situation to mature, responses
were also shaped by enduring triumphalist illusions. The Ukrainian
crisis is the most revealing example of such missteps.

Reflections on the problematic record of European integration after
the Cold War call for a closer look at the latter. Apart from the shift
to a stronger focus on its global reach and varying impact on different world regions, there are several significant aspects to be noted. It
is a familiar thesis that the period from the late 1940s to around 1990
was an unprecedented mixture of war and peace. Up to a point, we can
speak of a global conflict ending with the victory of one side but kept
from escalating to extremes; the successful containment of violence
was most obviously due to the threat of mutual destruction but probably facilitated by memories of an alliance against common enemies.
That said, a major qualification is in order: the balance between war
and peace was intrinsically unstable, permanently at risk because of the
armaments race, and it did not exclude local wars of a more or less
proxy character but also capable of developing their own dynamics and
unforeseen repercussions. The most momentous conflict of that kind
was the Vietnam war, whose international impact was more ambiguous
than it seemed at the time. It weakened the authority and the morale
of the dominant Western power, but also hampered the ability of an

emerging New Left to break with Communism. A Leninist party-state fighting to reclaim what it saw as its historical inheritance was mistaken for a popular liberation movement.

This link between global division and local conflicts was not the only destabilising factor. If the threat of mutual destruction was instrumental in averting a third world war, that should not obscure other implications: on both sides, the availability of nuclear weapons became an incentive to look for ways of making them operational. It was not pre-ordained that such temptations (and corresponding suspicions) would be kept in check, and there is no reason to believe that they have disappeared with the transition to a new 'world order'. The fragility of that order is another reminder of the need to reconsider understandings and outcomes of the Cold War. Western perceptions of events at the end of last century as a 'collapse of Communism' translated into a triumphalism that now seems decidedly misplaced. On the American side, this gave rise to the mirage of unipolarism, still strongly present in foreign policy. European versions ranged from a vision of a union rising to the rank of a great power, in its own right and in a new environment, to the claim that a European model would represent a more attractive way of life than either the more powerful ally or the defeated adversary. The former expectation has proved empty; there is more to the latter, but it has also – in conjunction with other factors – generated a migration crisis to which the EU has yet to find a common answer.

Thirty years later, the defining events of the last fin de siècle appear as an exit from Communism through multiple mutations, in some cases involving a collapse of power structures, though not on a scale comparable to the one that had paved the way for their constitution. The result was a more multipolar world, with a less firmly settled distribution of power, but also with more confused interpretive mappings and mutual definitions. Among the unique features of the Cold War, not the least important was the close fusion of ideological and geopolitical aspects; it was this combination that gave a civilisational dimension to the conflict. To Western eyes, it seemed at first that both sources of division were being overcome after 1989, but the geopolitical force-field did not take long to resurface. The return of ideology has been a more diffuse process. Both Russian and Chinese reorientations resulted in eclectic patterns, drawing on selective use of traditions and Western borrowings, as well as some aspects of the Communist past. On the Western side, there are more signs of a wholesale reversion to the Cold War imaginary, most markedly when the new frontline is defined in terms of the defence of liberal democracy against a Eurasian model of autocracy.

A retrospectively balanced interpretation of the Cold War will also have to place more emphasis on the fact that it was a conflict of coalitions, made up of different sociopolitical forces as well as states with divergent interests, and open to shifting relationships on both counts. A reformist Left component was important for the original Western bloc, but such trends were sidelined at a later stage and not given much credit for the apparent triumph at the end of the century. As for the multistate level, it is a commonplace that there was no complete harmony between the policies of the USA and its European allies, and a matter of debate among historians as to how far these dissonances affected the course of events. On the Communist side, there was, for obvious reasons, next to no space for sociopolitical divergences, but the original geopolitical bloc – a defining adversary for the West – proved so brittle that a split between its main pillars, the Soviet Union and China, developed into a conflict aptly described by historians as a second Cold War, of lesser duration and more limited impact, but certainly a major contributor to the crisis of the Communist alternative.

The implications of these correctives to the mainstream vision merit a more detailed discussion than can be undertaken here. Indisputably but paradoxically, perceptions of the Soviet collapse as the failure of a rival model reinforced the decline of internal counterweights that had helped to build the case for a superior Western version of modernity, and this paved the way for the neo-liberal hubris that culminated in the great recession. The spectres that surfaced in the wake of that experience, thoughtlessly lumped together under the umbrella of 'populism', suggest a backlash in progress.

Finally, the trajectory of the Cold War and its outcome must be reconsidered from a more complex perspective than the triumphalist narrative allowed for. If the rivalry between superpowers with global aspirations unfolded across different spheres of social life – economic, political and cultural – explanations of the outcome must deal with the combined effects of these plural dynamics. In the aftermath of 1989, the most favoured explanation rested on the claim that Western ways of practising capitalism and democracy had been perfected to a point that made them immune to ideological challenges. The factor most instrumental in bringing this truth home was the inability of the Soviet regime to sustain military competition with an adversary that could draw on vastly superior economic resources. A more diffuse point often added to this argument was the 'soft power' of Western cultural models, not least so-called popular culture. More recent developments have cast doubt on the triumph of democracy and revealed the fragility of global capitalism; at the same time, the limited and ambiguous impact of 'soft power' became clearer. What remains widely accepted is the notion of an arms race won by a richer and more resourceful power, but this view overlooks the lessons to be drawn from the very different experiences of the two major Communist powers. In the Soviet case, a reform project, certainly not the only possible response to decline in relative power, had unleashed internal dynamics of dissent and division, and at the same time failed to achieve an expected breakthrough in international relations. The joint effect of these processes was an imperial collapse. The Chinese strategy of reconsolidating the party-state went hand in hand with effective economic and – more cautiously – military competition on the interstate level. There is, in other words, no simple common pattern that would account for the exits from Communism.

Perspectives on integration

To conclude, the implications of this approach to twentieth-century history for the understanding of European integration should be briefly outlined. As noted above, the metaphor of a European civil war has a basic affinity with simplifying and optimising narratives about the post-war decades, not least in relation to the unification of Europe. In that vein, the steps taken from the late 1940s onwards can be described as an ongoing effort to close the book on civil war and overcome its legacy; the downfall of dependent Communist regimes in Eastern Europe appears as a sequel to the victory over a more aggressive totalitarian enemy in 1945, and the subsequent eastern enlargement of the EU as the completion of a European order no longer threatened by disasters of the kind exemplified by civil war.

The ideas adumbrated here suggest a less benign vision, but to clarify the thrust of this alternative some theoretical premises must be brought into the open. As mentioned in the Introduction to this volume, the strong and temporarily influential theories of European integration were clearly inspired by the strong concepts of society that had already been subjected to telling criticism but had not ceased to influence social and political thought in less explicit ways. This applies to the functionalists who saw integration as a cumulative result of self-reinforcing needs for cooperation, and to the advocates of a European project supposedly rooted in cultural values with normative force; the latter could appeal to the notion of a cultural programme, accepted by the more sophisticated version of functionalist sociology. But if these models are discarded, alternatives can still be disputed. An influential, though ultimately self-limiting, school of thought retreats from orthodox functionalist views, but transfers the same kind of comprehensively utilitarian rationality to individual actors and subsumes more complex cases under that model. In analyses of European integration, this approach has emphasised the rational choices of negotiating actors, thus reducing a historical process to the interplay of state strategies. On this issue, Perry Anderson's critique (directed against Moravcsik 1998) seems definitive: what this construction is

> *ab initio* unable to explain is why the standard objectives of intercapitalist state cooperation . . . could not have been achieved after the war in Western Europe by free-trade agreements of a conventional kind, without creation of any complex of supranational institutions, or derogation of national sovereignty.

It ignores 'the critical fact that the institutional origins of the European Community were deliberately framed in open-ended terms . . . , declared to be stepping-stones in view of an ultimate objective whose exact shape was left unspecified' (Anderson 2009: 86). To put it another way, a civilisational surplus has been central to the whole process of European integration.

The factors that brought this transcending theme to the fore are easily identified. The experience of two disastrous wars provoked strong demands for an end to interstate violence and efforts to found an order of peace. It is true that the postwar geopolitical constellation entailed a stable division of Europe and excluded armed conflict within the Western bloc; but the intention to transform this favourable conjuncture into a lasting regime was, from the outset, one of the driving forces. The key precondition for such an innovation, a consolidation of peaceful relations between France and Germany, could not be realised without broader changes. At the same time, the reconstruction and pacification of Western Europe was seen as inseparable from a restoration of democracy, but memories of the interwar years inspired moves to protect democratic rule against breakdowns and threats from within. This translated into more elitist conceptions of the institutions to be restored and that bias was even more pronounced when it came to the new frameworks of European integration. Not only was the pursuit of European unity an elite strategy from the outset, without any broader popular mobilisation; there was, as Marc Joly (2007) argues, a distinctive vision of a European power (*pouvoir Europe*), never envisaged as a negation of democracy, but consistently aligned with the idea of constitutional protection against the temptations and vulnerabilities of democracy.[3]

But if we can thus speak of a definite twist to the floating signifier of integration (described above as a civilisational surplus), it was and remains an elusive and controversial goal, a horizon rather than a project. It is open to conflicting interpretations with different emphases on agencies, procedures and preferred outcomes (by the same token, adversaries of integration have been able to construct vastly divergent images of the enemy to be resisted, from a Soviet-style superstate to a neo-liberal arena). These multiple meanings, attributed to a shared but underdetermined field of action and imagination, raise the question of contextual backgrounds. As indicated above, the strong theoretical models that reduce social–historical contexts to systemic logics or interacting decisions, have been challenged on general grounds, and they seem particularly unsuited to analyse situations as ambiguous and open-ended as those of postwar Europe. Rather, the kind of social theory needed here is one that begins with major concessions to comparative history. A radical conceptual alternative in that style was proposed by Norbert Elias (most succinctly in Elias 1984), whose image of society centred on the twin concepts of figuration and process. Figurations are constellations of interdependent actors, always already entangled in constraining and enabling interrelations, of which they have only partial and divergent understanding, and which their actions modify in multiple but only partly intentional ways. This perspective goes beyond the more conventional focus on intentional action and unintended consequences.

There is no problem with adding collective actors of various kinds and strengths to the field of figurations. Further implications emerge when the interconnections in question are understood as formations of power. The dynamics of figurations reveal the relational character of power, misconceived by theories that reduce it to an instrument or possession of actors. This point of view enables the inclusion of institutions (not duly emphasised by Elias), seen as culturally defined patterns of power. Through the cultural aspect, a connection can be made with the classic Weberian argument about ideas channelling interests (and thus also the pursuit and exercise of power); institutions represent stabilised complexes of orienting meanings. On the other hand, figurations can involve conflictual relations and escalation into violence; interdependences can, as Elias noted with an obvious allusion to twentieth-century disasters, lead to mutual killing. On that level, the role of ideas reappears in another way: through the ideological conflicts that can intertwine with various degrees of violent struggle.

The concept of figuration seems to be the prototype of other recently proposed alternatives to the systemic image of society, such as the notion of networks of power. Such conceptions are also closely linked to the emphasis on process, already central to Elias's work and shared by those who have more or less explicitly followed his lead. The idea of processual analysis stresses a dynamic that transcends specific causal links but can do so in different ways. Cumulative processes with an enduring and unequivocal direction have attracted more attention than other types, but schismogenic processes, conducive to divergences and ruptures, are also an important theme for historical sociology. In yet other cases, a processual dynamic may result in breakdowns, or in mutations that open up a spectrum of possibilities and pave the way for the intervention of contingent factors. A particular example worth mentioning is the kind of process that accumulates and exacerbates problems, while at the same time undermining the ability of concerned actors to solve them. Christian Meier's work on the long-drawn-out crisis of the Roman republic (Meier 1980) is a classic case study in that vein, and the same historical episode has more recently been compared to the present troubles of the EU (Engels 2013).

Elias dealt most extensively with processes of state formation; he analysed the emergence of gradually strengthening centres from diffuse constellations of power, and the twin monopolies of taxation and violence appeared as inbuilt goals of such developments. That model is obviously inapplicable to the EU. One of the most salient landmarks in its history is the failure of an attempt to set up a common defence force; as is well known, it has no power of taxation, and member states have effectively resisted efforts to increase its control over financial resources. A case can, however, be made for a more flexible connection. As with other classics, the merit of Elias's work has more to do with the formulation of problems and perspectives than with detailed arguments. His general approach to state formation as a long-term process allows for closer consideration of factors that did not enter into concrete analyses. From legal frameworks to cognitive resources, from religious traditions and evolving political cultures to imaginary horizons and ideological projects of change, the cultural context of state-forming processes affects their course in complex ways; such inputs may reinforce or resist the trends at work, or even compensate for their limits.

If the model actually applied in Elias's account of European state formation is seen as a first step towards a more pluralist framework, we can more easily envisage cases where divergent processes may be going on: one level of state formation is then accompanied and perhaps counteracted by another. An obvious historical example is the Holy Roman Empire. It undeniably developed some features of statehood, but in the longer run, the stronger elementary structures of units emerging within its frontiers proved more significant. In view of attempts to compare the EU to the empire, this experience is worth noting. But if the expanded problematic of state formation is to be linked to questions of European integration, the most promising starting point is Alan Milward's work on the 'European rescue of the nation-state' (Milward 2000). There is, to the best of my knowledge, nothing to suggest that Milward drew on Elias's work, but some basic parallels stand out. Both authors link changes of state structures to interstate relations, as well as to changing alignments with social forces. Milward's main emphasis was on the innovative reconstruction of states that had to rebuild institutions after wartime destruction, face an expanded field of governmental tasks, and construct a new basis of legitimacy through more complex reciprocal relationships with their respective societies. He rejected the widely accepted claim that European integration was an antithesis to the nation-state and argued that strategies of interstate cooperation and coordination developed in close connection with domestic policies. Yet he also noted that the nation-states in question continued to declare their intention of voluntarily achieving political unification, and described this as an ideological position. His comments can be read as a negative version of the self-interpretive overload described by Anderson. A closer examination of the context will help to reconcile the two views.

Milward analysed policy areas in detail, and distinguished between those calling for interstate cooperation and others more internal to each state. As he showed, the Common Agricultural Policy was more important for the pioneering integrative moves than later interpretations have often assumed, and left a significant historical legacy. By contrast, he regarded the politics of the welfare state as less directly related to integration. But there is another side to the latter example. Three key states – France, Italy and West Germany – were particularly exposed to

the frontlines of the Cold War (France and Italy had strong Communist parties, Germany was divided), and welfarist policies were part of
the effort to defuse that problem, even if they developed along specific
lines. Similar goals in domestic affairs reinforced the primary dynamic
of integration through exchange and pooling of resources.

The parallel moves towards welfare states, to some extent pioneered
by the reformist turn in Britain at the end of the war, were thus not
unrelated to a global context that had other implications as well. Two
main components of that context should be distinguished: geopolitical constellations and patterns of capitalist development. To grasp their
interrelations, it is essential to avoid systemic images of both sides. This
is, in view of the massive but ambiguous changes, easier on the geopolitical side, although systemic notions of a 'liberal world order' are not
quite extinct. The trends that have discredited it can be traced back to
early postwar times. On the Western side, the asymmetric European
alliance with the USA (described as 'empire by invitation' by favourable observers) was never a model of stable harmony. Notwithstanding the attempts to portray American influences on Europe as moves
towards modernisation, tensions between different sociocultural models remained strong enough to translate intermittently into visions of
unifying Europe as an alternative to the dominant transatlantic partner.
Divergent power strategies continued to affect foreign policies, not least
in the Middle East; this arena par excellence of Western adventures,
rivalries and miscalculations is part and parcel of the legacy of World
War I. However, the end-of-century sea change showed that such dissonances did not add up to significantly different perceptions of the
new global constellation. The policy-makers of the EU adopted the triumphalist perspective aligned with American unipolarism, and eastward enlargement, as well as the expected raising of global profile, was
conceived as a way of building a new order on that basis. Long-term
consequences of this attitude came to the fore in the Ukrainian crisis
and in the unsolved problem of developing a response to the sharpening antagonism between China and the USA.

Changes on the eastern side of the postwar frontline were more
momentous than in the west. Here we need only note the ones most
salient in the geopolitical context. In that regard, it now seems appropriate to highlight a double series of mutations. In the Russian case,
the disintegration of the Soviet model is – geopolitically speaking –
subsumed within a process whose landmarks are the successive reorientations of Russian great-power politics. The changes after 1953,

erratic at first, were stabilised and modified under the Brezhnev regime from 1964; Gorbachev's foreign policy, short-lived but highly consequential, marked a new departure. Russia under Putin still aspires to the role of a major power, but has inherited a massive disproportion between military strength and other forms of power, and a coherent strategy has yet to emerge. As for China, the revolution that seemed at first to have given rise to a Eurasian Communist bloc was soon followed by a Sino-Soviet split that had a major impact on the Cold War power balance. In the longer run, this geopolitical upheaval, together with the accompanying ideological adventurism, turned out to be a roundabout prelude to the unprecedented path taken by China since the end of the 1970s. At this stage, the ongoing adaptation of a Leninist party-state to an eclectic pattern of capitalist development is probably better described as a balancing act than as a model, but there can be no doubt about the significance of this venture for global affairs and future perspectives.

All the above considered, the late twentieth-century transition looks more like an entry into uncharted territory than a great leap from a tried and tested model to a new world order. There is, to put it mildly, very little to suggest that the EU has adapted its policies to changing perceptions of this historical juncture. It remains to comment briefly on its responses and relations to the other main determinant of globalising processes: the capitalist economy. It is not proving easy to overcome systemic conceptions of capitalism, shared by admirers and adversaries of this economic regime, and invoked to justify correspondingly opposed verdicts on the EU: one side proposes to align it with the logic of a spontaneously self-improving capitalism, while the other condemns a supposedly unconditional surrender to the neo-liberal radicalisation of capitalist practices. Recent debates have seen some noteworthy attempts to question the common presuppositions of these sweeping judgements (for example, Wallerstein et al. 2013, Delanty 2014). The dynamics of production, trade and finance diverge too significantly for a streamlined model of capitalist principles to be applicable. Similarly, the changing weight and ways of state intervention refute both the simple equation of capitalism with a market economy and the notion of a polarised contest between liberal and statist capitalism (during the past decade, the latter view has, to some extent, superseded the fin-de-siècle vision of one authentic and triumphant model left standing). The unfolding and the aftermath of the great recession that began in 2007 have memorably clarified these issues.

Adam Tooze's remarkable analysis of the financial crisis and responses to it (Tooze 2018a) throws much light on the interaction of multiple factors. For our present purposes, four lessons in his account should be underlined. In the first place, initial European perceptions and portrayals of the crisis as an American one were quickly dissipated; European banks turned out to be deeply implicated and highly vulnerable. Anti-crisis measures on the part of member states and institutions of the EU were less prompt and less coordinated than in the USA, hampered by tensions and divergences between the main actors, and more dependent on the ideological prescription of austerity. The whole process of crisis management highlighted the power balance between the key players, and more specifically the role of the European Council in conjunction with the European Central Bank; it was within this framework that the distinctively oblique and self-limiting exercise of German power took place. Finally, Tooze emphasises the intertwining of economics and geopolitics, and that means, above all else, the importance of the Chinese connection. Not only is the awareness of China's rise and rise an integral part of policy-making by Western powers; also, more tangibly, the economic strategy implemented by the Chinese government during the crisis (a major case of Keynesianism sui generis, as Tooze (2018b) has argued elsewhere) was crucial to the global course of events.

To sum up, the above points may serve to clarify the present relationship of European integration to core capitalist trends. If the last few decades have left next to no grounds for expecting the EU to invent macro-economic and international correctives to neo-liberalism, it is equally unconvincing to dismiss it as from the outset as nothing but an engine of capitalist expansion. The relevant questions concern the interaction with – or exposure to – the new turns of capitalist development, unfolding from the 1980s onwards. The dominant narrative has portrayed the whole process as a triumph of markets over states but a more complex picture is now very visible. A massive advance of financialisation stands out as the most decisive shift; the point that financial markets do not function according to models derived from product markets has been developed by various schools of thought, but in the public sphere it is still obscured by ideological preconceptions. Financialisation has drawn support from new technologies and this combination has resulted in new waves of globalising processes, but they do not add up to a harmonising finale of the globalising dynamic that has a long history and an uncertain future. On the geo-economic and geopolitical levels, the new constellation gave rise to multiple centres of capitalist development, at first labelled 'emerging markets' but increasingly seen as divergent models, not least because of varying interconnections with state structures. Finally, the geopolitical triangle of China, Russia and the USA, with inbuilt possibilities of changing alliances or compromises, constitutes a fragile and upset-prone framework for world affairs, capable – as current events are showing – of significant interference with economic networks.

The incomplete and contested European polity – an unidentified political object, as it was famously called by one of its foremost protagonists, Jacques Delors – facing this environment has its own internal sources of uncertainty. As noted above, the question of European integration can usefully be approached in terms of state formation dynamics, and the appropriate starting point is a connection between Alan Milward's work on the reconstruction of the nation-state and Norbert Elias's processual conception of statehood. The latter approach can allow for extensions and offshoots that go beyond the primary and decisive foci of state-forming processes; in that perspective, Milward's emphasis on the reconstruction of European nation-states as the bedrock of postwar European revival is easily compatible with the fact that this in turn involved transnational innovations. From the outset, the reconstructive process required and enabled institutional bridges across borders, the added civilisational ambitions magnified such measures into institutional projects, and they gave rise to significant elements of statehood at a new level.

The configuration that grew out of these developments is too complex to fit either Anderson's description of the EU as an 'unscrambled and disjoined' version of historical state-forming processes, or Collier's verdict on the EU as a failed state (Anderson 2009: 518; Collier 2017). The vision of an emerging superstate has periodically gained some traction but now seems very unlikely to revive. Three fundamental failures mark the trajectory of moves to supranational state-building and reveal their inbuilt flaws: the rejection of the European Defence Force in 1954, the defeat of the proposed European Constitution in 2005 (partly offset by the Lisbon Treaty, but the latter cannot claim the same level of statehood as the original project), and the failure of the euro to overcome economic disparities, let alone promote the ever closer political union envisaged by its advocates. What survived on the supranational level is perhaps best described as a prefragmented and dysfunctionally developed (not designed) constellation of powers. The interplay of the institutions in question was at its most revealing during the financial crisis and its eurozone sequel. Following Tooze's close analysis of those events, the intermediate level between member states and the Union – the European Council, made up of heads of state or government – stands out as a crucial but neither internally unified nor externally uncontested factor. Its interaction with the European Commission and the European Central Bank determined the scope and the limits of interventions to counter the crisis.

The phenomenon of state formation reaching beyond its primary context, with partial and structurally self-limiting results, is perhaps the most significant analogy between the EU and the Holy Roman Empire. In the latter case, effective long-term state formation took place in ostensibly subordinate domains, finally replacing the imperial framework with a cluster of contending states; but the empire had, on various occasions and in changing situations, advanced its claims to superior statehood. Parallels between the EU and the Holy Roman Empire were discussed by Jan Zielonka (2007). That book remains one of the most interesting interpretations of European integration, but its advocacy of a 'neo-medieval' model reflects an optimism later abandoned by the author. Moreover, his analysis of the Holy Roman Empire did not deal with its decisive early modern setback: its failure to prevent the Thirty Years' War.

Notes

1. Readers will note that the title of this chapter is inspired by Ian Kershaw's history of Europe in the first half of the twentieth century (Kershaw 2016). The variation is not meant to detract from the merits of this valuable book but I do want to stress, more than Kershaw does, the novelty of the postwar condition, rather than any kind of return to normalcy.
2. Joly (2007) convincingly criticises the mythologisation of Jean Monnet as the 'father of Europe'. However, he also shows that Monnet was anything but a negligible figure, and that his political initiatives were guided by a certain idea of a civilising process, centred on institutions as ways of stabilising efforts to improve the human condition.
3. The oversimplified and overblown invocations of Greek democracy generated a backlash, equally oversimplifying excursions into world history, based on very loosely defined notions of democracy and finding examples in vastly different cultural settings. Keane (2010: Ch. 2) is a representative example.

References

Anderson, P. (2009), *The New Old World*, London: Verso.
Berger, S., and A. Miller (2014), *Nationalizing Empires*, Budapest: Central European University Press.
Clark, C. (2013), *The Sleepwalkers: How Europe Went to War 1914*, London: Penguin.

Collier, P. (2017),'Europe and Refugees: Tragedy Bordering on Farce', in Castells, M., O. Bouin, J. Caraça, G. Cardoso, J. Thompson and M. Wieviorka (eds), *Europe's Crises*, Cambridge: Polity Press, pp. 224–39.

Delanty, G. (2014),'Europe's Nemesis: European Integration and Contradictions of Capitalism and Democracy', in S. Champeau, C. Closa, D. Innerarity and L. M. Poiares Pessoa Maduro (eds), *The Future of Europe: Democracy, Legitimacy and Justice after the Euro Crisis*, London: Rowman and Littlefield, pp. 135–56.

Elias, N. (1984), *What is Sociology?*, New York: Columbia University Press.

Engels, D. (2013), *Le Déclin: La crise de l'Union européenne et la chute de la république romaine*, Brussels: L'Artilleur.

Gauchet, M. (2007), *La Révolution moderne* (vol. 1, *L'Avènement de la démocratie*), Paris: Gallimard.

Gerwarth, R. (2017), *The Vanquished: Why the First World War Failed to End, 1917–1923*, London: Penguin.

Halévy, E. (1967), *The Era of Tyrannies: Essays on Socialism and War*, London: Allen Lane.

Hroch, M. (2015), *European Nations: Explaining Their Formation*, London: Verso.

Iriye, A. (1993), *The Globalizing of America, 1913–1945* (*Cambridge History of American Foreign Relations*, vol. 3), Cambridge: Cambridge University Press.

Joly, M. (2007), *Le Mythe Jean Monnet*, Paris: CNRS.

Judt, T. (2011), *A Grand Illusion? An Essay on Europe*, New York: New York University Press.

Keane, J. (2010), *The Life and Death of Democracy*, New York: Simon and Schuster.

Kershaw, I. (2016), *To Hell and Back: Europe 1914–1949*, London: Penguin.

Le Goff, J. (1991), *Medieval Civilization*, Malden, MA: Wiley.

Leonhard, J. (2018), *Der überforderte Frieden: Versailles und die Welt 1918–1923*, Munich: C. H. Beck.

Manela, E. (2009) *The Wilsonian Moment: Self-determination and the International Origins of Anticolonial Nationalism*, Oxford: Oxford University Press.

Mann, M. (2012), *Sources of Social Power*, vol. 2: *The Rise of Classes and Nation-States, 1760–1914*, 2nd edn, Cambridge: Cambridge University Press.

Meier, C. (1980), *Res publica amissa: Eine Studie zu Verfassung und Geschichte der späten römischen Republik*, Frankfurt am Main: Suhrkamp.

Milward, A. (2000), *The European Rescue of the Nation-State*, 2nd edn, London: Routledge.

Moravcsik, A. (1998), *The Choice for Europe: Social Purpose and State Power from Messina to Maastricht*, London: Routledge.

Otte, T. G. (2007), *The China Question: Great Power Rivalry and British Isolation, 1894–1905*, Oxford: Oxford University Press.

Patočka, J. (1996),'Nadcivilizace a její vnitřní konflikt' (Super-civilization and its Inner Conflict), in Patočka, *Sebrané spisy* (Collected Works), vol. 1, Prague: OIKOUMENH.

Schroeder, P. W. (2004), *Systems, Stability and Statecraft: Essays on the International History of Modern Europe*, New York: Palgrave Macmillan.

Tooze, A. (2018a), *Crashed: How a Decade of Financial Crises Changed the World*, London: Allen Lane.

Tooze, A. (2018b), 'Tempestuous Seasons' [review of G. Mann, *In the Long Run We Are All Dead: Keynesianism, Political Economy and Revolution* (London: Verso, 2017)], *London Review of Books*, 9 September, 40: 17.

Wallerstein, I., R. Collins, M. Mann, G. Derluguian and C. Calhoun (2013), *Does Capitalism Have a Future?*, New York: Oxford University Press.

Westad, O. A. (2018), *The Cold War: A World History*, London: Penguin.

Zielonka, J. (2007), *Europe as Empire: The Nature of the Enlarged European Union*, Oxford: Oxford University Press.

4

The Fall of the Habsburg Monarchy and the Crisis of Modern Europe: A Historical–Sociological Comparison

Helmut Kuzmics

The problem

FOR ROUGHLY FOUR CENTURIES (1526–1918), the Habsburg Monarchy was a major power centre within the European system of states. Its final failure to survive warlike state competition created a security vacuum persisting in Europe until today. The Balkan wars of the 1990s, following the collapse of the Soviet Union, are only the latest reminder of this fact.

Trying to find the causes of the Habsburg Monarchy's downfall, historians and historical sociologists alike have developed highly divergent theories. It is conventionally agreed that Austria's period of successful military expansion was relatively short – it ended, all in all, with the victories of Prince Eugene of Savoy – and that, among the manifold wars waged later on, most led to defeat or unsatisfactory compromise. Most observers would also say that the Monarchy constituted a state sui generis, forming a conglomerate of kingdoms, princedoms and many ethnic groups speaking different languages, ruled and administered in a patrimonial way, and seen by her contemporaries at the beginning of the twentieth century as a living anachronism in a world of ambitious nation-states.

A hundred years later, the global situation of Europe is mirror-inverted. There exists a supranational structure comprising European nation-states that are intensely interwoven economically, even more intensely than some would like. The 'survival unit' of the nation-state seems to have given way to a new, higher-level survival unit, 'Europe' (Elias [1987] 2010: 137–208). Will it really be able to 'survive' or to enhance the chances of 'survival' for its citizens? As a unit to protect and to defend itself against a possible threat from outside, can the European Union be expected to cope with severe crises efficiently and, at the same time, democratically? Can we learn something by comparing today's multinational Europe with yesterday's multinational Austria–Hungary? The latter was a real empire, with a real army, with real central taxation in both halves of the Dual Monarchy and the hereditary charisma of an emperor. Europe today has none of that; in a certain sense, what can be compared is an entity of the past with a project of the future. But some educated guesses can be made by pointing to the challenges of Austria's past and the attempts to cope with the new problems faced by Europe.

The argument of this chapter unfolds in four steps. It will first sketch out some explanations for the downfall of the Habsburg Monarchy, and how they deal with the role of military efficiency in securing or impeding its success in state competition; then it discusses the prolonged history of hesitation and failure that characterises Austria's record in the great-power rivalry with Prussia and France, and during World War I, putting emphasis on the structural causes found in the inner dynamics of state formation with the transition from feudal–aristocratic to national centrifugal forces. The focus then shifts to Europe's history of integration after World War II and the place given in historical–sociological explanations to the 'survival' function of the EU in terms of its ability to act as a truly 'supranational' entity. Finally, it will address the paradox that the big crises demanding determined political action of the EU as a 'survival unit' (the Balkan wars of the 1990s, credit crunch of 2008, refugee crisis of 2016) affect national sentiments and interests that threaten to disintegrate the union. If we compare the situation with that of the Monarchy at the turn of the twentieth century, we see that the remedy of parliamentarisation might easily bring the opposite of a cure: the broad catch-all parties of the European parliament would take a particularistic turn, narrowly defined by national interests.

Explanations for the downfall of the Habsburg Monarchy with respect to its performance in wars

Before the demise of the Habsburg empire can be discussed, it seems necessary to consider its formation.

The territory that later became the Habsburg Monarchy of 1526 – with the Austrian lands, Bohemia and Hungary coming together as a consequence of a treaty securing mutual succession between two dynasties and the loss of life and land of the Hungarian King, Ludwig II (Lajos; Ludevik Jagiello), in the battle of Mohacs against the Turks – was inhabited right from the start by ethnic Germans, Hungarians and Slavs. Its medieval origins lie partly in the same feudal knock-out competition that can be observed elsewhere in Western Europe (Elias [1939] 2000; Bloch [1939/40] 1982), and are partly under the particular influence of the onrush of eastern nomadic peoples like the Avars, Magyars or later the Turks.

The power ratio of the armed aristocracy, resulting from their role as defenders against enemies from outside, remained high for a long time; central taxation met with strong resistance from estate-assemblies everywhere. The Habsburgs, as German emperors over a huge area, with obligations resulting from competition on a larger, European scale, repeatedly came close to financial ruin and blackmail by the various diets (Elias [1939] 2000, vol. II: 263). Internal state formation in Central Europe can be roughly described as falling into four phases (Kuzmics and Axtmann 2007: 69–113): first, manorial absolutism, based on feudal authority over unarmed peasants; second, courtly absolutism, as a product of the victory of prince and emperor over their aristocratic rivals, accompanied by, third, confessional absolutism, together with the Catholic Counter-Reformation (Heer 1981: 40–87) securing the administrative and disciplinary power of the Church; and fourth, reform absolutism, based on an alliance of the Crown with bureaucrats, the working middle class and the peasantry against the nobility.

For a long time, centralisation was slow and ineffective, all 'councils' and 'chancelleries' for the empire or the Habsburg countries becoming overextended and clumsy bodies. Since 1526 – when Bohemia and Hungary fell under Habsburg rule – the heterogeneity and openness of the system were unique, anticipating today's EU in a way that makes it suitable for comparison. This unification was partly accidental, partly caused by the Turkish threat, and partly the result of dynastic striving for power (Kann 1982: 37–8). The first really effective modern state was a response to the real danger of annihilation of the Habsburg Monarchy after 1740, when Prussia, France, Saxony and Bavaria simultaneously attacked Maria-Theresa. 'Enlightened Despotism' or, as Austrians call it, 'Enlightened Absolutism' meant a strengthening of administrative power (centralisation of administration and police, taxation of the aristocracy, reorganisation and enlargement of the army, secularisation, reformation of censorship and so on; Kann 1982: 150–225). These administrative reforms created, somewhat belatedly, a real state (Bohemia and Austria proper were united; Hungary, which had never been part of the Holy Roman Empire, was a different case). What we find is the strange simultaneity of state formation (or empire formation) and decline; at least, if we regard the largest territorial extension of Habsburg power as being achieved with the victory over the Turks and the acquisitions resulting from the peace accord after the War of the Spanish Succession, developments since then have meant territorial shrinking – loss of Sicily, Serbia, Silesia, Upper Italy and so on.

Industrial revolution came rather late. The Habsburg Monarchy bore a closer resemblance to Gellner's 'agro-literate societies' (Gellner 1983: 8–18), with a small literate class in combination with a landed aristocracy controlling a rather backward economy (but with respectable growth rates). This is the sociological meaning of the so-called *Hofratsnation* – a nation of 'court councillors', or high bureaucrats. The French Revolution, the Napoleonic wars and the nationalist–romantic reaction to French occupation promoted the idea of the so-called 'nation-state'. During the nineteenth century, such states were taking shape, with ever more extended armies (Van Creveld 1998) until they reached the stage of 'nations in arms'. Their triumph created big problems for the Austro-Hungarian empire (after the defeat by Prussia in 1866, the so-called *Ausgleich* had become reality and Hungary had become a state in its own right). National 'we-feelings' of the more than twelve ethnic groups that lived within the boundaries of the Monarchy seemed to conflict massively with the empire-patriotism and dynastic loyalty of army and bureaucracy (Kann 1982: 399–406). But the Monarchy had also moved toward constitution and democracy. Its feudal and absolutist heritage was certainly a hindrance, but so too was the struggle of the nationalities. Political parties formed quite closed *Lager* (political 'camps'), which fought against each other passionately.

Explanations for the final demise of the multinational Central European empire of the Habsburgs can be classified according to the role they attribute to military strength or weakness of the system compared with non-military and more general factors, among these economic backwardness or reduced loyalty towards empire and emperor. Since both of the latter can also lead to military weakness, causal analyses will necessarily overlap. A further complication is the fact that Austria–Hungary went down in the catastrophe of World War I and was seen by many of her opponents as guilty of starting it; the question of structural reasons for its collapse has also led to moral condemnations of the behaviour of the dynasty and the political elites of the Dual Monarchy. For the purposes of comparison with today's Europe, this perspective can be neglected. More relevant is the balance between exogenous forces (geopolitical competition with its challenges; cf. Kennedy 1990, Mearsheimer 2001, Lieven 2000) and endogenous ones (including the internal structural problems mentioned above); the former's culmination in short, potentially catastrophic crises adds the possibility of good or bad luck (Clark 2012) determining their outcome.

For those who stress the importance of geopolitical constraints, military strength is the decisive factor. For Kennedy and Mearsheimer, the army was important but the Monarchy was too weak economically to be a serious contender – at least in the nineteenth century. This overstretch view is also shared by a recent detailed historical analysis of the eighteenth century (Hochedlinger 2003). For Lieven, military success was also decisive, but he directs his attention to the centrifugal forces that led Hungary, for instance, to adopt a policy to sabotage all attempts to provide the financial means necessary to sustain a credible common Austro-Hungarian great-power army. Supporting this view, which focuses on the violence dimension of survival units, Elias ([1983] 2006), in his theory of power sources, distinguishes control of the means of physical violence from control of economic means and control of knowledge. Other authors have placed their emphasis elsewhere. For Anderson (1974), the focus is on the army only in so far as its efficiency suffers from economic backwardness, but much more weight is given to the internal power dynamics between different classes and ethnic groups. Mann (1993), who shares many insights with Anderson, nevertheless has a more positive view of Austria's economic performance (following Good 1984). It is rather the fiscal exploitation of economic strength that leaves something to be desired. Referring to war, Mann traces Austrian decay to the 'militaristic dynasticism' of the Habsburgs. The most dramatic reversal of opinion regarding the Habsburg empire, though, can be found in the work of two authors who have both shifted their attention away from the evolutionary 'telos' of the nation-state and towards the acceptance of something different: namely, the persistence of a composite, supranational entity defying the conventional assumption about its anachronism. The first is Ingrao (1994), whose interpretation of the development of Habsburg power starts in the year 1618 (the beginning of the Thirty Years' War) and ends in 1815, when the Vienna Congress, held after the Napoleonic wars, resulted in the relative peak of Austria's status as a great power. For him, it is a great achievement of the dynasty to have rebounded after every defeat (1618–20, 1683, 1704/5, 1740/1, 1790/1815). This perspective renders its final fall in 1918 even more puzzling. The second is Judson (2017), who also refutes the 'telos' of the nation-state and the methodological bias of the thoroughly nationalistic perspective adopted by opponents and nationalistic successors of the Habsburg Monarchy alike: contrary to the conventional view, dynasty and citizens had formed one of the most successful liberal, minority-friendly and pluralistic empires imaginable – one could say an early European Union. State formation was something effected not only from above, but also from below. Imperial patriotism did not collide with the nationalistic sentiment of Czechs, Croats or Slovenes, but more often was complementary and self-evident in the face of the astonishingly uniform material culture of railway stations, opera houses, court buildings and tobacco shops in all parts of the empire. In particular, he devotes a lot of space to the analysis of horizontal political movements, in associations, diets, assemblies and town councils, that were on the path to ever greater participation, boosted by electoral reforms and also by economic upturn in the more distant and forgotten provinces of Galicia and Bosnia-Herzegovina. Judson cannot deny the surge in nationalism; however, drawing on extensive recent empirical evidence collected by scholars of a younger generation, he argues that it has been exaggerated and was largely due to the mutually reinforcing rhetoric of the political elites whose fortunes were promoted by the very enlightened administration they were fighting against. But what of the catastrophe of World War I and the apparently easy dissolution in the year 1918? Here, like so many of his colleagues, he blames the officer caste, who tried to impose their disciplinary, authoritarian world-view, shaped by the backward-looking mentality of a beleaguered, privilege-sustaining group within a rapidly changing environment. To prevent their own downfall as a group, their members exaggerated the threat from outside and rushed thoughtlessly to preventive war. State repression during the war, economic hardship and huge human sacrifices on every front led to the final estrangement of the Habsburg peoples from the centuries-old empire.

We thus have at least two conflicting narratives about the causes of the dissolution of the Dual Monarchy. But is it not possible to combine both interpretations – to see the unfolding of the internal and the external forces in their entanglement – in order to gain a more realistic, less normative picture of the chances of survival of this multiethnic empire? And can we learn something important from this story for the understanding of Europe in the making?

Lost battles: the Habsburg army's history of hesitation and failure

Austria's great-power status was a result of its victory over the Ottoman empire at the turn of the eighteenth century. The slow decline of Austrian greatness lasted two centuries, though, and provided ample opportunities for successes on the battlefield. In the wars against Prussia (1740–63), France (1792–1815), France again (1859), Prussia again (1866) and the Entente powers (1914–18), the Austrian armies even enjoyed, time and again, the advantage of substantial numerical superiority over their opponents, at least in some decisive battles. Why, then, did these wars often end in defeat?

Austria against Prussia, 1740–63

These wars found Austria completely unprepared initially and it emerged that the Habsburgs were not able to rid themselves of Prussia, their most formidable rival in the Holy Roman Empire. The main outcome of these conflicts was Prussia's rise to great-power status. Here I mention only two important battles (Soor 1745 and Leuthen 1757), in which a strange mixture of inactivity and lack of discipline led to the defeat of numerically superior armies.

Austria against France 1809

The same constellation proved fateful, even after a period of intense reforms and with the army under the command of one of the most capable military theoreticians of his time, Archduke Charles. In 1809, Austria returned to the fight against Napoleon and managed to raise a numerically superior army against the French who were assembled in Bavaria (Battle of Eggmühl/Regensburg); Charles, however, though a gifted author and reformer, was unable to concentrate his troops for a decisive battle and suffered a heavy defeat, having lost all energy and strength (Schmitthenner 1937: 101–3). The Austrian commanders were still lacking initiative and implanted in their troops an attitude of passive obedience, making them ready to be sacrificed in blind devotion but lacking in self-reliance and circumspection.

Königgrätz 1866

Rivalry with Prussia led to the famous showdown in 1866, when an unprecedented half a million troops went to war in one of the greatest battles of the nineteenth century. Here, both armies were of near-equal strength (260,000 Austrians, among them 40,000 Saxons, stood against 254,000 Prussians; Preil 1993: 66). The Prussian army enjoyed a substantial advantage in terms of infantry firepower, while the Austrians had a better artillery and cavalry at their disposal. But again, a slow and hesitant Austrian advance led to dispersion and attrition of the troops. Deep pessimism befell the commander but battle was joined, from a comparatively good position on the heights. When all was already lost, several suicidal offensives brought immense losses.

World War I

Austria–Hungary's decision to go to war in 1914 still puzzles observers. How could a state with such a weak army start this war and hope to survive? After just a few days, Plan B (attacking Serbia) had become unfeasible since Plan R (war with Russia) demanded the removal of important divisions to the eastern front. The architect of Austria–Hungary's strategy was the reformer and 'military genius' Franz Conrad von Hötzendorf, who was nevertheless dependent on the unclear command structure that had typified the Monarchy for centuries. After the first four near-suicidal offensives directed by Conrad against a better-equipped Russia in the autumn of 1914, the Habsburg army only narrowly escaped total destruction, but was able to regain some of its initial strength after the arrival of larger reserves. This enabled a further attack against the Russian army in Galicia in August 1915. But here, familiar problems arose: again, the result was extreme dispersion and wasting of strength, while frontal attacks led to an enormous loss of life. Generals and other officers were unable to show any initiative or to convince the troops by word or example. The war against Russia also brought mass desertions of Czechs and Ruthenes. After this disaster, the position of the Habsburg Monarchy – also against its formal ally, Germany – was thoroughly shattered and neither the economy nor diplomacy was able to improve it (Rauchensteiner 1994: 290–1; Kuzmics and Haring 2013).

Although the Habsburg army was reformed after every defeat, bringing changes in the principles and strategies of the conduct of war in its train, its primary character never changed: it had been defensive, slow, undecided and hesitant throughout the centuries. Education, training, logistics and organisation certainly played a role, but these factors cannot explain the extraordinary stability of this trait. Contemporaries were already able to see the institutional reasons for the Austrian dilemma.

When, in 1740, Maria-Theresa found herself at war against a coalition of France and the German states of Bavaria, Saxony and Prussia, she was virtually without an army, since neither the Austrian nor the Bohemian nobility had paid their taxes. It was the war that brought reform and taxation for the clergy and nobility too. But there was also, for instance, the Austrian *Hofkriegsrat* (Court War Council). Even the charismatic Prince Eugene, who had once been its president, was not able to reform this clumsy body. After defeat at the hands of Napoleon, its size was, for the first time, reduced (the number of councillors shrank from 31 to 11, that of the secretaries from 28 to 6 and that of the other personnel from 78 to 48; Allmayer-Beck and Lessing 1981: 52–3). As one of the Austrian generals with the greatest initiative (Radetzky) observed, the Austrian practice of sharing responsibility – at the army high command – among four of the Emperor's advisers meant that an efficient command structure was totally impossible (Radetzky, quoted in Regele 1957: 86). Estate dominance was slowly replaced by patrimonial bureaucracy and met with centrifugal, national resistance, and this bureaucracy opposed all attempts to provide sufficient money for an army of a great power.

A good example of the particular difficulties Austria faced when it tried to conduct a more active foreign policy, not shying away from war if that seemed necessary, is the case of the Franco-Prussian war in 1870–1. The representative of the international-relations school of 'offensive realism', Mearsheimer (2001: 292–3), is puzzled that Austria, just beaten at Königgrätz, did not seek revenge by forming a coalition with France against Prussia. Instead, the Habsburg Monarchy relied on the strategy called 'buck-passing' by Mearsheimer, which means that another great power has to shoulder the burden to defend not only its own interests but also those of the buck-passer who is endangered by the rise of a new hegemon. In Mearsheimer's opinion, both France (in 1866) and Austria–Hungary thought erroneously that each would be able to make it alone (apart from earlier animosities and Austria's fear of Russia, Prussia's presumptive ally at that time). How was it possible to miss what was probably the last opportunity to regain the great-power status lost to Prussia and to block her ascendancy in Germany? And to prevent the later dissolution of the multinational Habsburg empire, which indeed was seen as a looming danger in leading circles of the Monarchy, and in particular by Kuhn, the Minister of War? Lackey (1995) has reconstructed the critical moments in 1870, helping us to see things more clearly. There was a complex polygon of persons, groups and interests, along with the structural, recurring constraints of Austrian politics, that had already shaped a habitualised inability to take risky decisions in timely fashion. Conflicts and unclear responsibilities between the most influential actors hampered communication. Seeking revenge for Königgrätz met structural opposition from the liberal Austrian and Hungarian bourgeoisie. Their deputies sat in both governments and, in the person of the Minister of Finance, controlled the money necessary for equipping the army. The Hungarians, who did not want to provide the 200,000 horses seen as indispensable in the case of mobilisation, could not be trusted: they might have been inclined to erect their own empire between the Black Sea and the Adriatic. A parallel structure existed in the imperial Military Chancellery, which turned against what it regarded as the renewal of a painful German civil war with little prospect of victory. The parallelogram of divergent forces resulted in neutrality, and the short window of opportunity to keep the southern German states from joining Prussia vanished. Several passionate sessions of the Crown Council (*Kronrat*) led to absolute paralysis, and even a defensive mobilisation turned out to be impossible. The Austrian Prime Minister, being Polish, feared a Russian invasion of his homeland more than anything else. When Paris fell to the German troops at the end of January 1871, the Austrian Minister of War burst out in tears, knowing what an opportunity had been missed.

The extremely complex situation in which Austria–Hungary found itself after 1867 was characterised by a constellation not unlike that of the EU today. The external *Umwelt* of the Habsburg system, with its fast-changing conglomerate of states – old and new, big and small, most of them linked to the fragile internal structure of the Monarchy, made up of national groups sharing a language and ethnic origin – combined with a rapidly evolving balance of forces within, under pressure to overcome economic backwardness by unleashing market forces to make up for lost time. The 'realist' school of thought sheds light on this. Mearsheimer (2001: 71) has defined an indicator for national wealth (production of steel and energy) as a precondition for military strength: in 1816, Austria's share of European wealth represented 9 per cent, falling to 4 per cent in 1860 and rising to 8 per cent in 1913, still far short of the 40 per cent share of Germany or the 28 per cent share of Britain. Lieven (2000) points to the loss of dynastic control when Hungarian statehood was accepted, thus empowering a feudal parliament unwilling to sustain the common army, and opening citizenship to the German and Jewish middle classes, forcing them to assimilate through

'Magyarisation'. But Hungary was also the model for Czech and other Slavic attempts to gain autonomy and statehood. As Habsburg society became functionally democratised, in Elias's sense of the term, the more difficult it became to provide the financial means necessary for the military to keep up its great-power status. In 1906, only 0.29 per cent of Austria–Hungary's citizens were recruited for military service, against 0.35 per cent in the much more populous Russia, 0.47 per cent in Germany and 0.75 per cent in France (Stevenson 2006: 67). In absolute numbers, in 1914 the Dual Monarchy mobilised 415,000 troops against Germany's 761,000 and Russia's 1,200,000 (Bihl 2010: 53–4). But an even bigger problem was the fact that the 'awakening' of the 'unredeemed' peoples of the Monarchy also influenced her foreign policy: Hungary's hostility towards Serbia (leading, for instance, to new tariffs aimed at reducing imports of pigs from Serbia in the so-called *Schweinekrieg*) and her own 'minorities' contrasted with the we-feelings of Germans, Czechs, South Slavs, Romanians, Ruthenians and Italians, parts of whose nations were included in foreign states. Only a growing number of workers made their presence felt as a potentially loyal force in the first elections under the new electoral law, which granted voting rights to all male citizens aged twenty-four or more in the Austrian half of the Monarchy. But after the 1907 election, even the 87 Social Democratic MPs were split into a group of 49 of German orientation who formed their own *Klub* in the *Reichsrat*, while the others were also members of *Klubs* according to national (largely Czech) affiliation; 66 'Christlich-Soziale' and 30 'Katholisch-Konservative' formed a faction of 96, but there were also 82 Czechs, 79 German nationalists, 61 Poles, 37 South Slavs, 30 Ruthenians and 14 Italians (Andics 1980: 53). The previous tolerant policy of Count Taaffe, head of government from 1879 to 1893, had aimed at keeping all groups in a kind of 'tolerable discontent'. This did not change. In hindsight, looking back from today's Europe, this system looks much better than it would if seen from the perspective of the nation-state, which dismisses such conditions as 'sick'; according to Lieven (2000), the contemporary cacophony of multiculturalism, pluralism and democracy creates similar feelings, and ancient Austria seems here to be the true precursor of modern Europe and equally undemocratic. In Hungary, with its much more limited franchise (12 per cent of the population), which favoured the aristocracy and Hungarian gentry at the expense of the other nations (Croats, Germans, Romanians and Slovaks), the elections saw a huge majority (more than two-thirds; cf. Andics 1980: 53) of the electorate vote for the Independence Party. Here, the options of the Crown were divided between a possible coup to prevent Hungarian independence, as contemplated by the heir to the throne, Franz-Ferdinand, and the threat of a general franchise as in the Austrian part of the Monarchy – both feared and loathed by the aristocratically dominated Hungarian nation-state. The Social Democratic 'outsiders' had briefly seemed to develop into a pillar of the throne. But now, even the workers were nationally split.

This is the situation that leads many commentators on the sad fate of the Habsburg Monarchy to lay all the blame on the 'ruling' circles: in particular, the aristocracy and the top ranks of the army. Both are seen as the true culprits behind Austria's march into war. But we get a slightly distorted view of the factors contributing to the final tragedy if we blame only those who were professionally responsible for thinking in terms of war and armament and who were understandably frightened by the danger of 'encirclement'. It was their job to prepare for all kinds of scenarios. And in the world-view of the leading officers and commanders, in particular those who were well educated and who had trained in military academies to take up the duties of military staff (the scientification of war set new standards), the perspective involved looking back to the empire's long history of achievements, challenges and weaknesses of the system in a largely self-referential way. Against the so-called *Marasmus*, a standstill in all attempts to overcome these systemic weaknesses, a counter-movement was formed, whose leading exponent was Franz Conrad; he became the central figure in a circle of 'Young Turks' in the Austrian army, with a totally new philosophy of battle (cf. Zeynek 2009) that placed attack far above defence, as had been preferred in the older 'Baroque philosophy of battle'. But this movement came late and was unable to penetrate the spirit (or 'habitus') of the army as a whole. It remained piecemeal and created more promises, even illusions, than fulfilment. Besides that, it also clashed with the new realities of mechanised warfare.

Analysing novels, autobiographies and diaries, as well as qualitative administrative data and regimental histories, helps us to reconstruct the rise and failure of the Habsburg military habitus (Kuzmics and Haring 2013), culminating in defeat in World War I. This habitus was the result of an extremely complex, multilayered social process taking place on at least three levels. The first is the highest echelon of the political and military decision-making structure of the Habsburg Monarchy, where scarcity of resources and divergent interests created situations of ambivalence and indecision that shaped the organisational culture of hesitation and circumspection. Commanders and leading officers had to take these factors into account, even if their (now largely bourgeois) personalities were also heavily influenced by a feudal code of honour characteristic of the descendants of ancient warrior-societies. A second level was formed by the bureaucratic environment of officer training and education, and the organisation of the army itself, in which the state's financial neglect was partly compensated by a high rank in society, but where good manners and amiability often replaced professional skill and competence. A third level refers to the simple, common soldier who was, after reform towards a general draft in the year 1868, a member of one of at least twelve nationalities, but largely commanded by officers of Austro-German origin (according to military statistics, about 80 per cent; Déak (1991: 218–24) doubts this number and reduces it to 55 per cent). The problem of loyalty became severe, though, only after the terrible loss of blood and life in the Russian campaigns.

During the war, as in most cases before, the Austrian generals tried to save the substance of their armies for their ruler, and diplomats tried to prevent a catastrophe by negotiating for peace. What did not work, this time, was escape from an alliance with a bellicose nation-state that opted for continuation of the war without respect for the centrifugal national processes affecting its ally. Slowly, and with quiet determination, the Austrian army marched into its last war.

Europe's history of integration after World War II and its role as a 'survival unit' in historical–sociological explanations

In his essay on 'Changes in the We-I-Balance' (Elias [1987] 2010: 137–208; cf. Leonardi 2011), Elias developed his concept of a 'survival unit' in accordance with his process-sociological understanding of the development of human societies along three lines: control of violence, control of nature by economic means, and production and control of the means of orientation – that is, knowledge (Elias [1983] 2006). What we call a 'state' is only one stage in this process. States themselves do not come alone, but form 'systems' in which they cooperate and compete with each other. What constitutes the 'survival' aspect for their members? There is a certain hierarchy between different dimensions of survival. First, Elias lists the needs for physical safety, always endangered by war and natural disasters – the core of the survival function.

Second, he underlines the capability to act as a collective in order to persist in military, economic and scientific competition. Third, Elias mentions the function that a survival unit has for securing continuity and tradition in the memory of coming generations (Elias [1987] 2010: 137–208). The disappearance of a state or tribe can, thus, lead to a massive depletion of meaning, the deeds and suffering of previous generations become senseless, and a kind of 'collective dying' occurs, generating deep feelings of mourning.

These different layers of the 'survival' function correspond to equally differing forces that shape we-feelings, we-images, we-I-balances, forms of national habitus and we-identities. They are strong in the case of the various European nation-states and they are weak when it comes to Europe as a supranational entity. For it was exactly the nation-state – seen as atavistic by numerous contemporary commentators – that effected a deeply penetrating reciprocal adjustment of the personality structures of its members in a process of functional democratisation and inclusion of all social strata, also of the working class. Therefore, habitus formation lags behind the newly felt necessities of integration and makes adaptation more difficult.

New and higher-level survival units will rise if growing interdependence between units at a lower level makes them useful and necessary, replacing the more and more fictitious autarchy or self-sufficiency of nation-states. In the case of European unification, Elias ([1987] 2010: 137–208) saw three different options for a new stage of integration in the face of geopolitical competition between the super-powers of the USA and the Soviet Union, and new and rising great powers in the making (like China and India):

- Europe as a satellite of the USA
- Europe as a federation of states or a multilingual federal state
- Europe as the status quo of unconnected nation-states.

How do these possibilities figure in concrete historical–sociological explanations?

The political process tying together the sovereign states that call themselves a 'European Union' has become so familiar that the question of its causes has ceased to be asked. For many, Europe had to come together simply because it is a 'project of (for) peace'. Critics of the EU may, then, soon start to look like peace-breakers, but what is the truth behind this theory?

Perry Anderson's essay on the 'origins' of European integration, written 1995 and published as the first chapter of his book on the subject (Anderson 2009), starts with exactly this question. Why a united Europe, at all? It is, indeed, absolutely unclear why one of the worst wars in history was not followed by a vicious circle of poverty, hate and striving for revenge similar to the interwar period of the 1920s and 1930s. The various attempts at an explanation for this counter-intuitive development are therefore highly divergent.

Anderson lists four explanations and adds two of his own:

- The 'neo-functionalist' approach (Haas 1958; 'Uniting of Europe') focuses heavily on the economy, by concentrating on incremental growth of the transnational division of labour that makes step-by-step cooperation between states useful and necessary. (Elias's notion of growing networks of interdependency points in the same direction but is complemented by a violence-related aspect.)
- The 'neo-realist' interpretation (Milward 1984) also predominantly stresses the advantages of open markets for each single state. Here, the focus also lies on the interests of the working class (wealth and economic security) and its fuller integration into the nation-state, whose power is thereby strengthened rather than weakened.
- Anderson's own theory of 1995 aims (against Milward) at transcending the economic framework. He deals with the creation of the European Coal and Steel Community as an attempt to curb interstate rivalry between the European powers (Young 1998 is similar), in particular between France and Germany, and dependence on the USA, from which only the French wanted to liberate themselves under De Gaulle. Under the aspect of purely economic advantages, supranational integration beyond the stage of a customs union by establishing a European Commission would appear superfluous. Writing under the influence of the collapse of the Eastern bloc, Anderson stresses the unexpected, unanticipated character of the integration process and the unintentional consequences of planned politics. Among these, he singles out the peculiar European dilemma of the conflict between the intergovernmental mode of decision-making and the growing powerlessness of the broader masses in the face of the neo-liberal turn towards the 'single market', favoured by Thatcher's Britain and backed by the USA. Market-induced integration and secret diplomacy replace political integration and democracy.
- Following the totally unexpected breakdown of Soviet power and the opening up of new opportunities to extend the influence of the

European Community over Eastern Europe without military means (the preserve of the North Atlantic Treaty Organisation, NATO), new theories have portrayed Europe as an empire (Middlemas 1995; Münkler 2005, who rather sees it as a sub-system of the American empire).

- Partly as a reaction to the wars conducted by a US-led coalition in the Middle East, and partly as a formulation of the contrast between American neo-liberalism and the model of European welfare states, Anderson mentions theories that treat Europe as a peaceful moral hegemon in the making (Rifkin 2004, Leonard 2005, Habermas 2006, Zielonka 2006).
- Written in 2008, but before the financial crisis caused by the bursting of the American subprime bubble, Anderson's own judgement of further European integration steps (Maastricht 1993, Amsterdam 1997, Nice 2001, Lisbon 2007) contains three main theses. Geopolitically, the dynamics of expansion after the collapse of the Soviet Union has brought a huge shift in the power balance between Europe and the USA in favour of the latter: NATO dictated the speed and volume of the Eastern expansion. Economically, the trend towards a more federal union and a common currency administered by an 'unpolitical' European Central Bank, which Anderson had also described in his essay of 1995, strengthened the power of the market (liberalisation and privatisation, especially in the East, amounted to a true 'triumph of capitalism') and weakened the power of both state and suprastate, as Hayek (1939) had prophetically predicted (cf. also Moravcsik 2002, who praises this result). In terms of the development of the power balance between elites and the masses who – particularly in Southern Europe – suffered most from growing neo-liberal unemployment, Anderson sees a sharpening of the divide in the chances of participation of both the lower classes and the eastern and southern states, but also between a losing France and a winning Germany.

How can these theories be classified according to the dimensions characterising Europe as a process towards a new 'survival unit'? How do they compare with the traditional wisdom about internal and external aspects of state-formation processes – among them, for example, Habsburg Austria?

The first and possibly surprising impression is that the notion of Europe as 'peace project' has scarcely been used to explain the sixty-year-long integration process. The second finding, also quite interesting, is that many theories do not deal with the survival aspect of a European super-state at all; rather, they focus on the economy, and here, they deal less with the advantages that European unity brings in competition with other large survival units, but more with the reciprocal benefits that European nation-states enjoy by opening up their markets. The dimension of interstate political and military competition has also been neglected – although it has become more important after the sudden eastward expansion of the EU, which included more than 130 million new citizens. (Perry Anderson's own theory is an exception, and also Middlemas's (1995) and Münkler's (2005).) It seems that Elias's first option for the development of European unity – Europe as American satellite – is, in the eyes of most observers, regarded as either too painful to deal with or too trivial to bother with. But this is essentially the central dimension of a 'survival unit'. As Smith (2001: 134–5) has shown, after the disaster of World War II the USA was in a position to pacify Europe, not unlike the French King Louis XIV following the model of a court society: Europe and its former leading powers had to abdicate. Marshall Plan funding served a function similar to that of royal provision for proud former warrior–aristocrats, who metamorphosed into tame and vain courtiers. Military competition between European states was not wisely eliminated from below, but the Marshall Plan and NATO led to a peaceful order imposed from above. Like the court aristocracy that was allowed to bear a sword but not to use it, European states still possessed armies (even atomic weapons), but they no longer had any real possibility of utilising them without obtaining American permission (as became clear during the Suez Crisis of 1956). The American monopoly of violence complements European economic integration, a view that is shared and postulated by leading US strategic advisers (Drozdiak 2010). This seems to work quite well, except when the USA causes turmoil in the neighbourhood and European states have to clean up the mess.

If one now compares European unification with what we know about the Habsburg Monarchy's process of state formation, there are important differences but also some commonalities. The dynastic union of kingdoms and princedoms that became the Danube Monarchy was, first of all, the result of warlike competition between aristocratic elites. Elites can also be found to be responsible for the New Europe – that it is an elite project not only is Anderson's view but also is shared by detailed empirical analyses as well (Haller 2009). The difference lies in the fact that the pressure of military state competition (wars with Prussia and so on) also led, in the eighteenth century, to the transformation of Austria into real statehood, with the reform of administration and central taxation and the creation of a great-power army. In the process, the dynasty had to ally itself with the middle classes and the peasantry against their landlords. This meant compulsory schooling in various national languages, and even the creation of some of the nations. Loyalty towards dynasty and empire was strengthened by the hereditary charisma of the emperor, another factor that is not available in today's Europe. And Europe has an even more complex body of governance than the Monarchy: There is a European Commission, which functions as both supreme executive organ and also legislator, whose members are sent there by the nation-states. Its budget represents only roughly 1 per cent of European gross domestic product (GDP) and is not the result of direct taxation; a large share of it still goes to agriculture. As Anderson maintains, the European Council of Ministers and the European Council of the heads of government are arcane bodies of intergovernmental politics, little controlled by the European public sphere. The European Court of Justice watches over a fictitious constitution with judges sent by the states, delivering judgements in procedures lacking transparency. Today's EU decided, in the Treaty of Lisbon (2007/9), to cooperate more closely in terms of a Common Foreign and Security Policy (CFSP). Arguably, the wars in the collapsing Yugoslavia and in the Middle East contributed to its formulation (Fischer 2011: 26, 37). In terms of international law, these regulations still do not amount to a military alliance – unlike NATO – since

> (1) the collective mutual defence clause can be applied exclusively on EU territory, (2) the collective mutual defence clause of NATO will be as untouched as (3) existing obligations under International Law of individual member states, and (4) the selection of appropriate means will be left to individual member states. (Fischer 2011: 37; my translation)

Apparently, these limitations hollow out the mutual defence clause even in the case of armed aggression from outside, and it certainly does not replace NATO.

What do Habsburg Austria and contemporary Europe have in common? In some respects, the European Parliament lacks real power and acts largely ceremonially, not completely unlike diverse consulting bodies of the Dual Monarchy. Both can be seen as successful economic modernisers, the Monarchy was as multinational as Europe is, and both can be described as lacking democratic control from below. Habsburg

Austria has finally failed to be a great power; Europe is not sure that it aspires to be one. And as far as democratic control is concerned, Europe is now being advised to become a 'European Republic' (Guerot 2016) with a real parliament and centralised government. This should not only help to correct the democratic deficit, but also to secure a quicker process of decision-making. As will soon be clear, however, this republic would meet with some of the same centrifugal, national forces preventing efficient politics, as in the old Austria; sometimes, even the national actors are the same, when we hear of Hungarian or Czech resistance to European burden-sharing or of a new wave of authoritarianism in other countries of the vanished Habsburg world.

The big crises demanding determined political action of the EU as a 'survival unit' and the logic of centrifugalism

Soon after Anderson had completed his book on Europe, several crises shattered the trust in the EU's ability to cope with them: the global savings-and-loan meltdown of 2008 and the refugee crisis of 2015, which is still present at the time or writing. But even before 2008, the limits of the ability of European politics to influence the even more 'survival'-related wars in the Balkans (Croatia, Bosnia, Serbia) and in the Middle East had become visible. And before the refugee crisis of 2015, the topic of migration had long since turned toxic, with migration from east to west and south to north within Europe. The last two decades saw, not totally surprisingly, a substantial rise in nationalist and/or authoritarian political movements/parties throughout most of the Union. From the 49.21 per cent for Fidesz (2018) in Hungary to the 37.6 per cent for PiS (Law and Justice) (2015) in Poland, 26.0 per cent for the Freedom Party of Austria (FPÖ), 21.1 per cent (2015) for the Danish People's Party in Denmark, 13.20 per cent (2017) for the Front National in France, the roughly 13 per cent for rightist parties in the Netherlands and Sweden (<https://en.wikipedia.org/wiki/List_of_active_nationalist_parties_in_Europe> (last accessed 25 May 2018)) and, last but not least, the triumph for Brexit in Britain 2016, the message is clear. The landslide towards nationalist parties also affected the European Parliament, where they are represented in growing numbers but mostly still hide under the umbrella of larger factions. As will be seen, not only has the EU had serious problems in deciding and acting as a truly supranational unit, but every attempt at central crisis resolution has met with ever greater resistance, first, from the nation-states and, second, from their electorates.

The 'geopolitical', external side of European unification took centre stage when it came to the bloody dissolution of Yugoslavia, beginning with the secession of Slovenia in 1991. A consistent and uniform European policy on this issue could never be achieved (Privitera 2004). For some European states – France, Britain, the Netherlands – German diplomacy, aided by a weak and small Austria, seemed to repeat the fatal strategy of 1914. France and Britain, first supported but later deserted by the USA, wanted to keep Yugoslavia intact, and saw Germany's intervention as an attempt to extend its hegemonic influence over the Balkans. The struggle, increasingly bitter since the Bosnian war with British and French newspapers sometimes falling back on the rhetoric of 1914, could be resolved only by US diplomatic and military intervention. Here, European indecision resulted from a conflict that looks familiar when we compare it with the situation of the late Monarchy. And in 2003, when the US decided to form a 'coalition of the willing' for wars in Iraq and Afghanistan, Europe was totally split and unable to form any coherent policy. It is easy to see that a European parliament with real powers could have provided a stage for the demonstration of overwhelming national passions, but the idea that it could have helped to formulate a coherent policy is less plausible than a regression to the feuds and emotions of last century.

Another dimension of the European survival unit was involved when the US housing bubble burst in 2008. It soon became clear that the European banking sector was affected even more deeply than America itself. European sovereign debt turned into the new subprime (Swedberg 2012), with countries like Greece, Ireland, Spain and Portugal suffering the most. But also, most other states were pressed to bail out their endangered banks, deemed 'too big to fail', in order to overcome the credit crunch (Jackson 2009). The ensuing policy of austerity led to youth unemployment rates of 50 per cent and more in countries like Greece or Spain. It was only the establishment of the European rescue funds (European Stability Mechanism) in 2012, with 620 billion euro, that banished the looming danger of state collapse. The creation of the Asset-backed Securities Purchase Programme (ABSPP) of the European Central Bank helped to keep interest rates for state debt low and manageable. But, as German critics fear (Sinn 2015), this mechanism will lead to the massive redistribution of wealth from North (in particular, Germany) to South. As soon as such measures and countermeasures can be attributed to identifiable subjects and peoples, there will be more cartoons portraying the German Chancellor with a Hitler-style moustache, and articles demanding war reparations in trillions of euros. If discussed in a real European parliament, the publicity of such utterances can scarcely be exaggerated. Democracy may be served, peace between states possibly less so. These quarrels may well surpass the passions of the *Ausgleich* negotiations held every decade between Austria and Hungary.

The European consequences of the refugee crisis that began in 2015 might be even more fateful for the cohesion of the Union. A common European distribution system for refugees has apparently failed, in spite of arguments for it (Altemeyer-Bartscher et al. 2016). The discussion has so far led to the so-called Visegrád states – the Czech Republic, Slovakia, Hungary and Poland – taking up entrenched positions. It seems that the attempt to enforce EU policy from above has done more than anything else to generate resistance, which may also be based on resentment about quite different developments. But the general revival of nationalism, be it a late stage in the formation of an Eastern nationalism, which had risen in the Habsburg countries as a bid for protection against the hegemonic Germans or Hungarians (as Gellner 1983 saw it), or be it a more recent phenomenon in old Western democracies like France and Britain, must certainly be linked to the simultaneity of mass migration and the cut-throat competition in the workplace experienced by sections of the lower classes. How changes in the structures of big enterprises (ownership, organisation, technology) affect the living conditions of people when capital becomes mobile (cf. Pixley and Flam 2018) – that is, transgresses borders – has been shown in some detail by Meek (2017). He describes the sequence of events in which a traditional, patrimonial–capitalist chocolate-producing company like Cadbury (the epitome of British chocolate for centuries) turned into an anonymous corporation dominated by shareholder interests, was finally sold to an American-based multinational firm and moved its factory from England to Poland. Leaving the company town of Somerdale/Keynsham and taking the equipment to Skarbimierz in Silesia in Poland, the corporation had to dismiss its employees in Britain whose parents and grandparents had worked for Cadbury for many generations and who had enjoyed good salaries, healthcare, job security, paid holidays and generous pension schemes. Because of all this, the workers had developed a deep sense of loyalty towards their company. Many of the dismissed were to turn into glowing advocates for Brexit, as Meek found out in the interviews he conducted with former employees. When the factory moved into a Special Economic Area in Poland, with long-lasting tax exemption and European money guaranteed, the Polish workers were paid only a small fraction of the English wages and remained without a permanent contract – with one month's notice, they could be fired at any time. They were not allowed to form trade unions and their jobs were endangered both by Ukrainian competitors on the labour market and by the further shift of capital to even cheaper countries like Romania. While many Poles left their country for Britain and found themselves thoroughly rejected there, the sentiment of colonial dependence and humiliating insecurity befell many workers staying in Poland. The propaganda of the Party for Law and Justice against cosmopolitanism and multiculturalism fell on fertile soil, and the fact that it was the only party advocating a policy of romantic national self-aggrandisement was helpful too. The corresponding we-feelings also profited from remembrance of the danger posed by Germany and Russia, who had indeed tried in the past to extinguish both Polish identity and Poland herself. Grief, mourning and resentment are, thus, the companions of a simple economic procedure of moving capital and labour from A to B. If this analysis is correct, it will be clear that not the supranational EU but rather the 'atavistic' nation-state can confront a multinational corporation on the move. Even if the hopes of British and Polish employees for support from their own state are exaggerated, it is still more realistic to assume that help will come from the nation-state rather than from the EU, which is light years away from any social union – not least because intra-EU inequality is only slightly smaller than global inequality.

It was E. Gellner (1983: 129) who once formulated the 'Wrong Address Theory favoured by Marxism': like Shi'ite Muslims, who thought that the Archangel Gabriel had erroneously delivered his message to Mohammed instead of to Ali, Marxists assume a terrible postal error for delivery of the revolutionary message, intended to go to *classes* and instead arriving at *nations*. As Austrian theoreticians of the national question knew (Bauer 1907, Bernatzik 1912), the national question at the turn of the twentieth century was as much a product of the modern forces of mass mobilisation for the market as a legacy of the past. The Habsburg Monarchy paid for it dearly, not only because of the dark forces it unleashed (Snyder 2015), but also for a more trivial reason: like the EU of today, it aspired, but did not manage, to be really democratic. The more democratic it wanted to be, the more it risked immobilism, and finally, attempts to solve that problem ended in failure.

References

Allmayer-Beck, J. C., and E. Lessing (1981), *Das Heer unter dem Doppeladler: Habsburgs Armeen 1718–1848*, Munich: Bertelsmann.

Altemeyer-Bartscher, M., O. Holtemöller, A. Lindner, A. Schmalzbauer and G. Zeddies (2016), 'On the Distribution of Refugees in the EU', *Intereconomics: Review of European Economic Policy* 51(4): 220–8.

Anderson, P. (1974), *Lineages of the Absolutist State*, London: Verso.

Anderson, P. (2009), *The New Old World*, London: Verso.

Andics, H. (1980), *Der Untergang der Donaumonarchie: Österreich-Ungarn von der Jahrhundertwende bis zum November 1918*, Munich/Augsburg: Wilhelm Goldmann.

Bauer, O. (1907), *Die Nationalitätenfrage und die Sozialdemokratie*, Vienna: Wiener Volksbuchhandlung Ignaz Brand.

Bernatzik, E. (1912), *Die Ausgestaltung des Nationalgefühls im 19. Jahrhundert: Rechtsstaat und Kulturstaat. Zwei Vorträge gehalten in der Vereinigung für staatswissenschaftliche Fortbildung in Cöln im April 1912*, Hannover: Helwingsche Verlagsbuchhandlung.

Bihl, W. (2010), *Der Erste Weltkrieg 1914–1918: Chronik – Daten – Fakten*, Vienna/Cologne/Weimar: Böhlau.

Bloch, M. ([1939/40] 1982), *Die Feudalgesellschaft*, Frankfurt am Main/Vienna: Propyläen.

Clark, C. (2012), *The Sleepwalkers: How Europe Went to War in 1914*, London: Allen Lane.

Deák, I. (1991), *Der K.(u.) K. Offizier 1848–1918*, Vienna/Cologne/Weimar: Böhlau.

Drozdiak, W. (2010), 'The Brussels Wall: Tearing Down the EU-NATO Barrier', *Foreign Affairs* 89(3): 7–12.

Elias, N. ([1939] 2000), *The Civilizing Process*, Oxford: Blackwell.

Elias, N. ([1983] 2006), 'Über den Rückzug der Soziologen auf die Gegenwart (I)', in Norbert Elias, *Aufsätze und andere Schriften II, Gesammelte Schriften*, vol. 15, Frankfurt am Main: Suhrkamp, pp. 389–408.

Elias, N. ([1987] 2010), *The Society of Individuals* (*Collected Works*, vol. 10), Dublin: UCD Press.

Fischer, K. H. (2011), 'Der Vertrag von Lissabon: Die neue außen- und sicherheits-politische Dimension der Europäischen Union – ein politischer Stresstest', in F. Algieri, A. H. Kammel and J. Rehrl (eds), *Integrationsprojekt Sicherheit: Aspekte europäischer Sicherheitspolitik im Vertrag von Lissabon*, Baden-Baden: Nomos, pp. 25–52.

Gellner, E. (1983), *Nations and Nationalism*, Oxford: Blackwell.

Good, D. F. (1984), *The Economic Rise of the Habsburg Empire, 1750–1914*, Berkeley/Los Angeles: University of California Press.

Guerot, U. (2016), *Warum Europa eine Republik werden muss: Eine politische Utopie*, Bonn: J. H. Dietz.

Haas, E. (1958), *The Uniting of Europe*, Stanford: Stanford University Press.

Habermas, J. (2006), *The Divided West*, ed. and tr. Ciaran Cronin, Malden, MA: Polity Press.

Haller, M. (2009), *Die europäische Integration als Elitenprozeß: Das Ende eines Traums?*, Wiesbaden: Verlag für Sozialwissenschaften.

Hayek, F. A. von (1939), 'The Economic Conditions of Inter-state Federalism', *New Commonwealth Quarterly* 5: 131–49.

Heer, F. (1981), *Der Kampf um die österreichische Identität*, Vienna/Cologne/Graz: Böhlau.

Hochedlinger, M. (2003), *Austria's Wars of Emergence: War, State and Society in the Habsburg Monarchy, 1683–1797*, London/New York: Pearson Education.

Ingrao, C. W. (1994), *The Habsburg Monarchy 1618–1815*, Cambridge: Cambridge University Press.

Jackson, J. K. (2009), *The Financial Crisis: Impact on and Response by the European Union, CRS Report for Congress.* Available at: <www.crs.gov> (last accessed 25 May 2018).

Judson, P. M. (2017), *Habsburg: Geschichte eines Imperiums, 1740–1918*, Munich: C. H. Beck.

Kann, R. A. (1982), *Geschichte des Habsburger Reiches 1526–1918*, Vienna/Cologne/Graz: Böhlau.

Kennedy, P. (1990), *The Rise and the Fall of the Great Powers: Economic Change and Military Conflict from 1500 to 2000*, London: Fontana.

Kuzmics, H., and R. Axtmann (2007), *Authority, State and National Character: The Civilizing Process in Austria and England, 1700–1900*, Aldershot/Burlington: Ashgate.

Kuzmics, H., and S. A. Haring (2013), *Emotion, Habitus und Erster Weltkrieg: Soziologische Studien zum militärischen Untergang der Habsburger Monarchie*, Göttingen: V&R Unipress.

Lackey, S. (1995), 'The Habsburg Army and the Franco-Prussian War: The Failure to Intervene and its Consequences', *War in History* 2(2): 151–79.

Leonard, M. (2005), *Why Europe Will Run the 21st Century*, London: Atlantic.

Leonardi, L. (2011), 'Changes in the We-I Balance and the Formation of a European Identity in the Light of Norbert Elias's Theories', *Cambio: Rivista sulle trasformazioni sociali* I(2): 168–75.

Lieven, D. (2000), *Empire: The Russian Empire and its Rivals*, London: John Murray.

Mann, M. (1993), *The Sources of Social Power*, vol. II: *The Rise of Classes and Nation-States, 1760–1914*, Cambridge: Cambridge University Press.

Mearsheimer, J. J. (2001), *The Tragedy of Great Power Politics*, New York/London: W. W. Norton.

Meek, J. (2017), 'Somerdale to Skarbimierz', *London Review of Books* 39(8): 3–15.

Middlemas, K. (1995), *Orchestrating Europe: The Informal Politics of the European Union, 1973–95*, London: Fontana.

Milward, A. S. (1984), *The Reconstruction of Western Europe, 1945–1951*, London: Methuen.

Moravcsik, A. (2002), 'In Defence of the "Democratic Deficit": Reassessing Legitimacy in the European Union', *Journal of Common Market Studies* 40(4): 603–24.

Münkler, H. (2005), *Imperien: Die Logik der Weltherrschaft - vom Alten Rom bis zu den Vereinigten Staaten*, Berlin: Rowohlt.

Pixley, J., and H. Flam (2018) (eds), *Critical Junctures in Mobile Capital*, Cambridge: Cambridge University Press.

Preil, A. (1993), *Österreichs Schlachtfelder 4: Trautenau 1866, Nachod 1866, Skalitz 1866, Königgrätz 1866*, Graz: Weishaupt.

Privitera, F. (2004), 'The Relationship between the Dismemberment of Yugoslavia and European Integration', in J. S. Morton, P. Forage, S. Bianchini and R. Nation (eds), *Reflections on the Balkan Wars: Ten Years after the Break-up of Yugoslavia*, Houndmills/Basingstoke/Hampshire: Palgrave Macmillan, pp. 35–54.

Rauchensteiner, M. (1994), *Der Tod des Doppeladlers: Österreich-Ungarn und der Erste Weltkrieg*, 2nd edn, Graz/Vienna/Cologne: Styria.

Regele, O. (1957), *Feldmarschall Radetzky: Leben/Leistung/Erbe*, Vienna/Munich: Herold.

Rifkin, J. (2004), *The European Dream: How Europe's Vision of the Future Is Quietly Eclipsing the American Dream*, New York: Jeremy P. Tarcher/Penguin.

Schmitthenner, P. (1937), 'Regensburg 1809', in *Der Genius des Feldherrn*, ed. Deutsche Gesellschaft für Wehrpolitik und Wehrwissenschaften, Potsdam: Sanssouci, pp. 93–124.

Sinn, H.-W. (2015), *Der Euro: Von der Friedensidee zum Zankapfel*, Munich: Hanser.

Smith, D. (2001), *Norbert Elias and Modern Social Theory*, London: Sage.

Snyder, T. (2015), *Black Earth: The Holocaust as History and Warning*, New York: Tim Duggan.

Stevenson, D. (2006), *1914–1918: Der Erste Weltkrieg*, 2nd edn, Düsseldorf: Artemis & Winkler.

Swedberg, R. (2012), 'How European Sovereign Debt Became the New Subprime: On the Role of Confidence in the European Financial Crisis (2009–2010)', in J. Pixley (ed.), *New Perspectives on Emotions in Finance: The Sociology of Confidence, Fear and Betrayal*, London/New York: Routledge.

Van Creveld, M. (1998), *Die Zukunft des Krieges*, Munich: Gerling.

Young, H. (1998), *This Blessed Plot: Britain and Europe from Churchill to Blair*, London/Basingstoke/Oxford: Macmillan.

Zeynek, T. (2009), *Ein Offizier im Generalstabskorps erinnert sich*, ed. P. Broucek, Vienna/Cologne/Weimar: Böhlau.

Zielonka, J. (2006), *Europe as Empire: The Nature of the Enlarged European Union*, Oxford: Oxford University Press.

5

Europe in Crisis: The History, the Players and the Stakes

Dennis Smith

A political experiment in crisis

DURING THE SECOND decade of the twenty-first century, the European Union (EU) has been debating its future development. This debate was triggered by a combination of factors, including: the sluggish performance of the European economy; the spread of resistance to Brussels amongst member states; the rise of populist parties expressing discontent with shrinking wage packets, diminishing social rights, increased unemployment and rising immigration; and, not least, the prospect of losing one of the most powerful member states, the UK.

This chapter draws upon but also goes beyond a number of analyses by the author over the past few years (Grundman et al. 2000, Smith 2012a, Smith 2012b, Smith 2014a, Smith 2014b, Smith 2015, Smith and Wright 1999a, Smith and Wright 1999b). To understand what is at stake, we need to locate our uncertain present in the context of Europe's past. A convenient place to begin is the extraordinary case of Brexit (the voluntary withdrawal of the UK from the EU), a strange coinage now familiar to all. It took the UK three applications, in 1961, 1967 and 1973, before gaining entry to the Common Market, and another two years to stop fretting about it. A major difficulty was that, in President de Gaulle's view, Britain did not fit into the European project. He once compared the Common Market to a coach and horses. The Germans supplied the horsepower while the French sat in the coach, giving directions. De Gaulle saw no place for the British either inside the coach or tethered between the shafts. His verdict: 'l'Angleterre, ce n'est plus grand chose' (as quoted in 'Theresa May is in Denial about Britain's Declining Power over Brexit in the Age of Trump', *Independent*, 2 June 2017. Available at: <http://www.independent.co.uk/voices/brexit-trump-manchester-attack-britains-declining-power-a7769811.

html> (last accessed 16 February 2018); see also Beloff 1963, Lundestad 1998, Major 1995, Mander 1963, Milward 1992).

However, the new Europe was an exciting cause, especially amongst the young. This mood was cultivated by events such as the annual European Schools' Day international essay competition. The present writer attended the London award ceremony in 1963 as a laureate, along with others from 'the Six' – France, Germany, Italy, Belgium, the Netherlands and Luxembourg – but also from Norway, Sweden, Switzerland, Ireland and the UK. The status given to the event was shown by the receptions at Lancaster House, the Mansion House, the House of Lords and County Hall, Westminster. Some of the laureates were taken on a coach tour on the continent, going down a mine, through a steel works, across a vineyard, into the parliament chamber at Strasbourg, round the sights of Luxembourg, into the Rotterdam docklands and so on. The Common Market was definitely on the youth agenda in 1963.

Ten years later, Britain, under Edward Heath's leadership, joined the Common Market. Two years after that, in 1975, Harold Wilson, Heath's successor, held a referendum, which registered popular, in addition to parliamentary, consent for British membership. This signalled the start of at least three decades during which most British citizens thought about 'Europe' as little as possible, and rather passively accepted the new arrangements without reflecting deeply on the institutional changes that came along. Turbulent episodes in the House of Commons – for example, over the Maastricht Treaty signed in 1992 – were heard by most of the electorate as echoes from another world. Media reporting typically treated political storms in Westminster as entertaining diversions rather than existential battles about the destiny of the nation (see Ward 1994).

The situation changed after 2008 due to the sovereign debt crisis, the widespread imposition of austerity, the political campaigns of the United Kingdom Independence Party (UKIP), enlivened by Nigel Farage's robust rhetoric, and the demonisation of migrants from, in turn, Poland, Romania and North Africa. The Conservative government, elected in 2015 with its first overall majority for nearly two decades, decided to hold another referendum in 2016, on the UK's membership of the EU. The referendum was set up as advisory rather than binding. When Prime Minister David Cameron started the referendum process, he evidently expected to win quite comfortably, and informed his EU colleagues of this fact. But by a narrow margin (52:48) the voters opted to leave the EU. Britain's political and business establishment was overwhelmingly opposed to this. So were voters in

Northern Ireland and Scotland. However, the population of England and Wales was split down the middle. The government chose to treat the result of this advisory consultation as, in effect, an instruction from the people and, after some months of infighting and dithering, Theresa May, David Cameron's successor, triggered the legal process intended to culminate in the UK leaving the EU.

This was a huge shock to the political and business establishments of both Britain and the EU. In June 2016, Britain was the second most powerful member of the EU, having displaced France from that position in the wake of the post-2008 recession. Equally significant, negotiations were under way early in 2016 in connection with the proposed Transatlantic Trade and Investment Partnership (TTIP). If negotiations for TTIP had reached a successful conclusion, this would have brought into being a single trading area stretching from America's Pacific coast to the EU's eastern border. In other words, at that moment it was possible to envisage a near future in which Britain was the strategic centre of a very large transatlantic EU/US free trade area in which London and New York counterbalanced Frankfurt, Brussels and the eurozone. This outcome would have strengthened the City of London, which was, in effect, not only the chief financial hub for most EU trade but also Wall Street's virtual Siamese twin, so closely interwoven were the business affairs of the British and American stock exchanges.

But prospects for realising this scenario were shattered by two events. One was Britain's Brexit vote in June 2016 and the other was Donald Trump's election to the US presidency in November 2016. The success of the UK Leave campaign put additional wind in the sails of Donald Trump, who made a point of befriending the most effective campaigner for Britain to leave the EU. That was Nigel Farage, leader of UKIP. Trump repeatedly referred to Farage as an example of the pragmatic, patriotic, anti-immigrant spirit the future President wanted to strengthen in American government. Trump's electoral victory was followed in February 2017 by the indefinite deferment of plans for TTIP.

Many people in Britain, especially outside the business world, were pleased to see the back of TTIP, which seemed to threaten a decisive shift away from parliamentary democracy towards rule by global corporations. But opinion was mixed. So it was with Brexit. Almost half the electorate had voted to remain and saw their preferences overruled, and, in many cases, their prospects and interests damaged, by the referendum's result. That included millions of disappointed young people who had looked forward to enjoying the freedom that EU membership gave them to travel, study and work abroad. Also dismayed were trade unions, political parties and voluntary associations that valued the legal and financial support the EU gave to their constituents and clients, including many older and less well-off people. Many of them felt let down by the vote's outcome. However, a high proportion of senior citizens in the Midlands and the North disliked foreign intrusion in British affairs, and resented the influx of immigrants, which had reached high levels. They likewise abhorred the London-based establishment that had encouraged those things. Such sentiments were encouraged and expressed by UKIP.

After June 2016, activists who had campaigned hard during the referendum were trapped in an uncanny liminal condition, like a quarrelsome group of close relatives waiting in the corridor outside an intensive care unit. So-called Remainers were waiting to see whether they would soon be forced to mourn an untimely death, the end of Britain's EU membership. But others, the Leavers, were demanding to know why their eagerly anticipated baby, post-Brexit Britain, was being kept so long in the incubator. Meanwhile, a large part of the population did not feel strongly either way. They wanted the matter sorted out so the uncertainty would end and other urgent matters like health, welfare, social care, housing and education could get higher up the government's agenda.

British politics became clogged up with Brexit, a condition destined to prevail for several more months. This would not have mattered very much if it were only the UK's problem, but it was very much the EU's problem also. Any withdrawal from the EU by a member state would be a politically damaging reversal of the union's core narrative of growth and consolidation. Once that happened, others might be tempted to jump ship or threaten to do so. Membership of the EU might begin to look as optional as belonging to the Automobile Association – or the League of Nations. Europe might even find itself on a road that led back towards the interwar years or worse (see Hilary 2014, Shipman 2016, Shipman 2017).

Between the wars

Between the two world wars, Europe, and the West more generally, had a paradoxical aspect. Europe continued to parade the imperial grandeur it had cultivated during the previous century but in fact the continent was profoundly fragmented. The dynastic, courtly and still semi-feudal regimes based in St Petersburg, Vienna, Constantinople and Berlin had all been overthrown by 1918, as had the writ of the Spanish empire in Latin America during the previous century. On mainland Europe, new nationalities were struggling out of the egg while a gruesome contest of ideologies enforced by violence set Fascist Italy and Nazi Berlin against their neighbours, including Soviet Russia. The main contenders tried out their weapons and tactics during the Spanish civil war (1936–9). Ironically, while the UK's imperial rivals crumbled, the British monarchy was magnified. The boundaries of its empire were pulled across the Middle East into territory previously held by the Ottomans, just as the EU's boundaries were later sucked towards the east and southeast following the collapse of the Soviet bloc and Yugoslavia.

The American and British states both tried to distance themselves from the dynamic struggle under way on the European mainland during the 1920s and 1930s. One reason was that Whitehall and Washington each had major long-term projects in play that were liable to become disruptive and dangerous if they got out of hand. The British establishment was, little by little, discovering how to scale down, partially decommission and ultimately dismantle an enormous empire. Meanwhile, the Americans were working out how to run corporate capitalism. In the USA, the owners and senior managers of large-scale business enterprises engaged in extraction, manufacture and distribution all wanted to ensure that their expensive investments were both protected and made profitable. This meant manœuvring to achieve the right physical and legal infrastructure, effective cooperation from government, politicians and labour leaders, and a national population educated into respecting corporate America and consuming the flow of commodities and services that it provided. As is well known, all this was the objective of intense political struggle, during and after the crash of 1929, the New Deal and World War II.

Meanwhile, on the other side of the Atlantic, the British establishment was dealing with the other side of the coin. The British Queen had become the Empress of India in 1876, turning her immediate successors into king–emperors. But it became increasingly anachronistic to have such garlanded figures, well suited to travel by elephant or horse-drawn carriage, acting as titular heads of one of the world's leading urban–industrial democracies in the age of Henry Ford. Edward Elgar, composer of several rousing 'pomp and circumstance' marches, made valiant musical efforts to bestow gravity upon these arrangements. Some of this music is still heard annually at the Albert Hall in London on the

Last Night of the Proms. But an increasingly embarrassing disjunction became evident during the 1920s and 1930s between Britain's imperial pomp and its democratic urban–industrial circumstances.

The political heirs of Cecil Rhodes were keen to preserve and exploit the British empire but Ireland's violent, and ultimately successful, revolt (1916–22) against rule from London made two things clear. One was that the British, with their new democratic franchise and recent war memories, did not have the political will or muscle power to hold down their colonies by authoritarian strategies dependent on repeated and widespread resort to force. Second, Britain's authority in the world, and even its continued survival as an independent power in wartime, depended on the voluntary contribution of fighting forces from the so-called white dominions (including Australia, New Zealand and Canada) and, equally important, from India, Africa and the Caribbean. The price for this help, explicit or implicit, was an increasingly rapid march towards freedom, not just for the dominions but also for exploited peoples on all continents under British lordship (see also Smith 2018).

The game and the stakes after World War II

After World War II the global initiative rested mainly with the West, where the key players were two new super-powers, the USA and the Soviet Union, each keen to assert their international clout and dignity, and two recently dethroned global players, both anxious to protect themselves from dishonour and insignificance, especially at the hands of either of the two new superpowers. One of these players was the UK. The other was a cluster of European polities, the Six, led by France and Germany, who founded the Common Market in 1957 with strong American encouragement.

Alan Milward (1992) has argued that the postwar European movement was less about supranationalism – that is, subordinating the nation-state – than it was about using interstate collaborations to advance the interests of specific nation-states, especially France. This was a key insight. National assertion took two forms. One was General de Gaulle's dream of a Western Europe jointly managed by its political leaders, a *Europe des patries* led by France. The other form was the plan developed by Jean Monnet, a leading French diplomat and businessman, who wanted to ensure a progressively more complex mutual entanglement of the industrial, agricultural, financial and bureaucratic dealings between France, West Germany and other member states of the European Economic Community (EEC). The resulting treaties and institutions were heavily influenced by French *dirigiste* ideas, notably during the period when Jacques Delors presided over the European Commission (1985–95). In effect, the French state was a kind of godfather to the Commission and remained so until after the 2008 credit crunch when, somewhat reluctantly, Berlin, France's long-standing continental rival, established itself in the European control room that Paris had fashioned for itself and occupied for the previous half-century.

But the EU was more than a game of thrones. Alan Milward's (1992) careful demonstration of the reconstitution of strong bases for resurgent European nation-states after 1945 must be put in the broader context of the American government's determination to create a large, peaceful and prosperous marketplace in Europe. Without such an effort, and complementary moves to build up rapidly expanding commercial environments in Southeast Asia, especially Japan, American business would have found itself without outlets for the massive productive capacity it had developed during the war years. That might well have meant economic stagnation, high unemployment, social unrest and, perhaps, increasingly violent political movements in the American homeland.

The European movement, then, was not just about rescuing the European nation-state but also about preserving the interests of American business and its corporate allies abroad. After the initial pro-business push in the late 1940s and early 1950s, Europe's leaders continued in the same direction. Germany, France, the Benelux countries and Italy provided an arena progressively freed from tariffs, tolls and other transaction costs, especially after the British, led by the commissioner Lord Cockroft, pushed hard to create the so-called 'single market' in the early 1990s. Large business corporations, many of them American, benefited from this increasingly large free trade area (see Smith 1999, Sutton 2007).

Keith Middlemas has researched in detail the dense networks of lobbyists feeding into and off the honey pot of Brussels with its civil servants, diplomats and MEPs (Members of the European Parliament), all making decisions that affected the bottom line of business corporations and other special interests. Almost all those involved were in it for the long haul, committed to the day-by-day business of perpetual persuasion. Lobbyists dug in and prepared for 'periods of low-key surveillance and monitoring followed by intensely fought battles', which often resulted in merely 'marginal gains' (Middlemas 1995: 456).

In effect, Brussels became the centre of a political complex whose currency consisted of favours exchanged and influence garnered and spent. In that sense, it was, and is, like a court society, although Middle-mas does not use this term. Compare the words of Jean de la Bruyère (1645–96), an experienced courtly operator on the seventeenth-century Paris–Versailles circuit:

> Life at court is a serious, melancholy game, which requires us to arrange our pieces and our batteries, have a plan, follow it, foil that of the adversary, sometimes take risks and act on impulse. And after all our measures and meditations we are in check, sometimes checkmate. (quoted in Elias 1994: 475)

La Bruyère might have been describing the modern Versailles that is Brussels. All actors involved in both cases were 'civilised' in the sense of being careful, realistic and calculating, striving to conceal their own emotions while reading those of others. In other words, they expressed the new Europe's 'Euro-civilizing aspect' (Middlemas 1995: 684).

Courtly practices are the essence of diplomacy, which itself is often a means of softening or displacing conflict: sometimes burying or disguising it, sometimes making it less violent, sometimes achieving agreements that encourage cooperation or mutual tolerance, sometimes failing to do so. Institutions and social structures are shaped by such transactions, as well as by the underlying conflicts partially contained or transformed by them. To understand the EU, we need to disinter the lines of conflict and tension within and around it.

Two triadic relationships are key to understanding the development of the EU. One is the triad that links together the state, big business and ordinary citizens ('the people'). Within Europe, a covert battle seems to be under way between government and business for the upper hand within the commanding heights of the capitalist political economy. This is being played out on several fields of combat, including political campaigning, taxation, privatisation, lobbying and corruption. The key question is: which kind of citizenship and human rights will have priority in the programmes of governments and the EU? Will they give first place to the interests of big business or will they put the needs of citizens for employment, accommodation, healthcare and so on at the top of the agenda? The default condition in the EU is a compromise between these approaches that leaves many citizens, consumers and traders broadly content, although the most enthusiastic advocates of market principles and social rights are somewhat dissatisfied.

The other triadic relationship is between the EU, the USA and Russia. Both before and after the Cold War, a long-term transatlantic struggle has been under way between the EU and the USA for priority in prestige, authority and clout within the West and globally. This struggle may be seen, historically, in, for example, De Gaulle's suspicion of 'Anglo-Saxons' on both sides of the Atlantic, disagreements over Vietnam, disputes over the Iraq and Afghan wars, debates within the World Trade Organisation, and contests for influence in North Africa and the Middle East (see Davidson 2016, Zielonka 2007, Zielonka 2014, Zielonka 2018).

Six phases of Europe

Since 1939, the EU and its original founders and supporters have passed through six phases: *catharsis*, *genesis* and *sclerosis* up until the end of the Cold War in 1989; and, since 1989, *hubris*, *nemesis* and, most recently, *crisis*. These will be explained in sequence.

Catharsis

During World War II, at least 60 million people were killed, about half of those in Europe. In fact, the whole period from 1914 to 1945 was a kind of Thirty Years' War, a miserable period of prolonged uncertainty. Many of the survivors were traumatised. Others lost their taste for or belief in ideologies, which treated war or bloody class struggle as acceptable or even necessary mechanisms for political change. In October 2012 the European Union, as it officially became in 1991, was awarded the Nobel Peace Prize. This is a reminder that, since its inception, the EU has provided a welcome refuge from war and political oppression.

Genesis

Countries on both sides of the Iron Curtain were under external discipline after 1945, and not just the so-called Eastern bloc. Washington, like a conquering monarch, turned Europe's bloody warrior chiefs into servile courtiers. France and Germany's long revenge cycle, stretching back to the early nineteenth century, was taken off the battlefield, toned down, and relocated in the council chamber and counting house. This was the Euro-pacification that preceded the Euro-civilising process. Norbert

Elias's *The Court Society* (Elias 1994), mainly about seventeenth-century France, captures the essence of this postwar pacification–civilisation process: a decisive military victory followed by the establishment of a strong centralising court (NATO headquarters), where courtiers were given permission to joust (NATO exercises) but also had to bow down before the (American) throne. Marshall Aid provided a useful royal treasure chest, helping to win compliance. The Coal and Steel Community (1951) was a precursor to the European Community (1957), which led in turn to the European Single Market Act (1986).

By the late 1950s, these developing structures had survived an attempted Fronde-like uprising (Suez 1956) and the European courtiers had regained a great deal of control over their lives, developed a new multinational bureaucracy and learned to trust other members of their shared club. In 1973, three 'northern' democracies (UK, Ireland and Denmark) joined the Common Market, followed a few years later by three 'southern' ex-dictatorships: Greece (1981), Spain (1986) and Portugal (1986). The latter three states were, so to speak, inherited from the Americans, who had experienced 'imperial overstretch' and were keen to pass over to the EU some of their diplomatic responsibilities as a democratic beacon for the world.

Sclerosis

The general postwar yearning for peace, stability and prosperity turned the Common Market into a friendly club where old adversaries settled down to cosy deal-making. But the downside was a hardening of institutional tissue, or 'Eurosclerosis', a term invented in 1985 by Herbert Giersch, a leading German economist (see Giersch 1985). This condition was due to the European desire for peace at all costs and the readiness of negotiators to buy their way out of trouble rather than change their ways. As a result, there was a reduction of flexibility and capacity to adapt. This mattered by the early 1970s. By then, the long postwar boom was over, costs were rising, unemployment was increasing and growth rates were falling. It became clear that peace and stability were no longer delivering the steady upward curve in citizens' living standards that had been enjoyed in previous decades. Giersch pointed out in 1985 that European nations were facing many rising costs: from raw materials, energy, welfare-state expenditures and the demands of vested interests. The EU's response was the Single European Act of 1986, intended to open up trade within the EU.

But this initiative was knocked off course by two massive developments. One was the 'big bang' (1986), which opened up the City of London to American finance houses and helped to create a vast reservoir of private and public borrowing capacity, available to politicians and private consumers across Europe. This reduced the pressure on European governments, businesses and vested interests to address their own inefficiencies and rigidities seriously. The second development was the unexpected collapse of the Soviet Union, which meant the end of the Cold War and the reunification of Germany. Much of Europe's political dynamism after 1989 came from the challenge of responding to German reunification. The EU leadership eventually agreed that the best response was to draw the new Germany deep inside the European project, which, in turn, became more ambitious.

Hubris

Before 1989, the EU was buoyed up by its credit reservoir and politically contained between the strong and apparently stable walls of the USSR and the USA. The eastern wall collapsed in 1989, although the American alliance remained firm, at least until 2016. After 1989, lobbyists and consultants from the West swarmed across Central, Eastern and Southeastern Europe, promoting packages for healthcare, education, management services and other functions to help fill the vacuum left by the wholesale collapse of state socialist administrations. The Maastricht Treaty (1993) and other innovations tried to maintain the pre-1989 state of approximate balance between state and market but raised the bar on both sides of this equation. On the one hand, monetary union was introduced, with plans for stricter national budgetary discipline. On the other hand, a strong ideal of social citizenship was promoted, reinforced by the demanding Copenhagen criteria (1993) for new member states. But could the new EU build a dynamic, business-friendly economy, provide substantial social rights for citizens and, at the same time, expand its membership, bringing in several countries newly 'released' from the socialist bloc?

Nemesis

The tide of apparent success during the 1990s was initially turned by American humiliations in the early twenty-first century. Basically, Washington failed to deliver on its vow to avenge 9/11 by asserting its mastery in the Middle East and eliminating its enemies. American forces eventually killed Osama bin Laden but otherwise its response made the USA look much weaker and less determined than before. That perception of American weakness overflowed into the financial sector. Lehman Brothers collapsed on 15 September 2008, just before the US presidential election, triggering a widespread credit crunch and the eurozone crisis. The huge reservoir of credit that had kept the EU and its member states afloat since the 1970s gurgled down the plughole, although eventually quantitative easing provided a partial and temporary substitute (see Tett 2009).

Crisis

The European Central Bank and the European Council protected the euro currency at the cost of Europe's citizens, forcing millions into unemployment and less secure employment with the prospect of smaller pensions, lower standards of healthcare and reduced social rights. National governments stepped in to recapitalise the banks, increasing their own national debts, and then cut their own public spending so that these national debts could be reduced as soon as possible. The banking crisis humiliated the EU leadership, forcing it to request assistance from the International Monetary Fund in 2010. Ironically, the violent rage and public disturbances caused by extreme austerity measures in Greece helped the EU to win support from anxious voters throughout Europe for its fiscal treaty imposing mandatory budgetary discipline upon national governments in the eurozone.

The EU, then, created a more powerful European Central Bank, the European Semester, the 'six pack', the 'two pack', the Macroeconomic Imbalances Procedure and the Fiscal Stability Treaty (all introduced in 2010–12), as well as the European Stability Mechanism (October 2012), Outright Monetary Transactions (OMTs) and Long-Term Refinancing Operations (LTROs). Belts were tightened across Europe. The promises made by the EU during the optimistic 1990s were abandoned in the new age of austerity. EU citizens became acquainted with humiliation and resentment, and were prepared to express these feelings at the ballot box and on the streets (see Smith 2015).

Mandarins and warriors

Jan Zielonka argues that the EU, in the early twenty-first century, has not achieved the ever closer union it vowed to pursue but instead has the look of a neo-medieval empire. One reason for this was the impact of the Berlin Wall's collapse. Between 1995 and 2013, EU membership almost doubled as the union inherited nation-states with diverse political, cultural and religious traditions, recently liberated from the Soviet Union and ex-Yugoslavia. As a result, the EU became politically fragmented, with polycentric governance and a sociopolitical life characterised by diversity, fuzziness and a tendency to become intermittently incoherent. In 2007, Zielonka suggested that these characteristics were, in many respects, benign and had survival value both for individuals and for the EU as a whole. By 2014 he was less confident. The analysis is beguiling. But are there other patterns and regularities behind the fuzziness?

Perhaps there are. For example, can we not discern at least four roles, personas or, perhaps, masks that are available for big business operators and political practitioners in the EU? Players may adopt more than one of them in the course of a career or even during an afternoon. There are the *high priests*, most notoriously in Brussels with its sternly rule-enforcing governmental approach. Also in play are *cavaliers* such as Silvio Berlusconi, actually nicknamed *Il Cavaliere*, who became adept at rule-breaking political clientelism and crowd-pleasing adventurism. Romania and Hungary have provided other prominent examples. So has Greece.

Turning from the realm of government and the people towards business and the market, we find parallel tendencies. Consider the punctilious *puritans*, otherwise known as ordo-liberals, who are based in Frankfurt and Berlin. They demand scrupulous adherence to market principles as they understand them. Finally, big business and finance have their *buccaneers*, all mainly concerned with bottom-line success before correct protocol. Deliberate deception on a large scale is not unknown in the realm of big business (witness the LIBOR scandal). We will come back to these distinctions in a moment.

Meanwhile, the transformation of the EU over the past half-century since the 1960s may be described by using the distinction between social integration, which is, crudely, about people getting on with each other, and system integration, which is about having institutions that work relatively smoothly and effectively. We will shortly draw together these ideas about different roles and types of integration, but first we need to define these two concepts of integration slightly more formally.

Briefly, *social integration* means maintaining solidarity through cooperative social interaction between people, whether as individuals or groups, including nations; and *system integration* means smoothly coordinating the different institutions, including families, governments and markets, that people use to maintain or transform their ways of life. This is done by instilling a readiness to comply with the appropriate rules, procedures, rights, expectations and obligations in people that enter the relevant roles: for example, in the spheres of work, consumption, market trading, political activity and government.

During the half-century leading to the 2010s, system integration advanced in the EU and sociopolitical integration retreated, yielding before divisive sociopolitical differentiation. The EU began as a relatively small political organisation with tightly interwoven sociopolitical integration, embodied in the central alliance between old enemies, France and West Germany. The Common Market tolerated wide divergence between members in their institutional practices, especially before the Single European Act came into force in 1986. Since the mid-1980s, the EU has become a much larger organisation that is much less tolerant of institutional divergence across member states. It is striving for an ever higher degree of system integration, especially in the eurozone.

However, while achieving an ever more integrated system of budgetary coordination amongst member states since 2008, the EU became, so it seemed, a much less close union overall in terms of sociopolitical integration, as noticed by, for example, Zielonka. This change was especially evident with the deterioration of relations between the European Commission and the so-called Visegrád countries (Hungary, Poland, the Czech Republic and Slovakia), the election of insurgent populist MEPs and, not least, the spectres of Grexit (the expulsion of Greece from the EU) and Brexit, which haunted the scene during the 2010s.

We can drill down more effectively into some of the underlying conflicts just mentioned if we now keep the promise just made to draw together the distinctions just explored. This is done in Figure 5.1, labelled collaboration, rivalry and alienation in the EU. It identifies two spheres of operation along the horizontal axis, and two codes of behaviour and judgement along the vertical axis. As can be seen, the two spheres of operation within the EU are the political and the economic, which clearly overlap in practice. The two codes of behaviour and judgement are, first, the way of the mandarin, which specifies rights and rules orientated towards maintaining and advancing system integration, and, second, the way of the warrior, a code emphasising strength and guile in the sphere of social integration, including social differentiation. These two codes, that of the mandarin and that of the warrior, also evidently overlap in practice.

Figure 5.1 Collaboration, rivalry and alienation in the EU

KEY: ➔← = zone of collaboration ↓ = zone of rivalry ↘↙ = zone of alienation ↑ ↗↖		**SPHERES OF OPERATION**	
		A **POLITICAL:** STATE/PEOPLE	**B** **ECONOMIC:** BUSINESS/ MARKET
CODES OF BEHAVIOUR AND JUDGEMENT	**1** **THE WAY OF THE MANDARIN:** RIGHTS AND RULES (System integration) 'Doing things right'	➔ ← 1A *HIGH PRIEST* ↓ *Brexit?* ↘	 1B *PURITAN* *Grexit?* ↓ ↙
	2 **THE WAY OF THE WARRIOR:** STRENGTH AND GUILE (Social differentiation) 'Getting things done'	↗ ↑ *Grexit?* 2A *CAVALIER* ➔	↖ *Brexit?* ↑ 2B *BUCCANEER* ←

The conjunction of these two axes and their subdivisions (2 × 2) produces the four boxes labelled as high priest, puritan, cavalier and buccaneer. High priests and puritans, both mandarins, make a virtue of being rule-makers, rule-implementers and rule-followers. They have a tendency to present themselves as bearing the mandate of heaven. The way of the mandarin encompasses two kinds of rules and rights that coordinate the EU: first, those that specify universal human expectations as embodied in EU citizenship – for example, gender equality, the prohibition against discrimination on grounds of ethnicity, religion, sexual orientation and so on; and second, the procedures, protocols and standards set out in European law and its various bureaucratic codes regulating institutional behaviour. These rights and rules, applicable to all, are intended to make effective system integration possible: doing things right, systematically and transparently for everybody's benefit.

By contrast, cavaliers and buccaneers, both warriors, are rougher types, happiest in a free-for-all where the devil takes the hindmost. In their dreams, perhaps, they make and break empires. The warrior sees all others as potential rivals or allies. He or she thinks and behaves on the basis that people are differentiated according to whether they are clever or less clever, useful or less useful, and pragmatically effective or not at getting the kinds of reward that most people want, such as power and money. Warriors try to avoid or minimise some of the restrictions imposed upon them by the universalistic mandarin code. In return, the warrior code is generally regarded as subversive by leading high priest and puritan types, although some of them find themselves drawn into following it on occasion. Strength, guile and, perhaps, a willingness to employ bullying and deception enable high-achieving warriors in government, politics and business to outmanœuvre or overwhelm rivals and opponents. The implementation of the warrior code creates a hierarchy of talent and success, not the level playing field valued by the proponents of universal rights and rules. It differentiates the strong from the weak, and the crafty from the less imaginative.

Both of these codes depend for their implementation upon the bedrock of social integration created by the EU during its first three decades of existence until the late 1980s. Since that time, the high priests in the European Commission and the ordo-liberal puritans in Frankfurt and Bonn (and now in Berlin) have, between them, arduously stitched together procedures and protocols, all embodied in the *acquis communautaire*, the body of EU legislation that, so to speak, attempts to institutionalise the enthusiastic commitment evident in the Common Market's early years. It is a kind of Bayeux Tapestry that embodies the story of the EU, especially its achievements, and prescribes how those achievements should be honoured and maintained in daily practice. The idea is, in effect, to maintain the benign effects of the cooperative behaviour of those early years, even though the initial conditions for strong social integration bringing cohesion and solidarity have faded away to a great extent: for example, the recent memory of world war, and the small number of member states.

Turning to the warrior code, norm-breaking cavaliers such as Alexis Tsipras, Prime Minister of Greece, and disrespectful buccaneers such as Nigel Farage, originally a commodity trader in the City of London, have also built their campaigns upon ground gained by the EU's past successes. They have positioned themselves to free-ride gainfully on the social and system integration achieved by the mandarins and their followers. Farage and Tsipras have used EU institutions to provide platforms and hiding places, rather as a restless courtiers preparing to revolt might use dance floors and pillars in a Tudor court to advance their plans. The leaders of

Syriza and UKIP either were very lucky or chose their opponents well: respectively, Wolfgang Schäuble and Jean-Claude Juncker. These are thoroughly committed advocates of the EU rulebook, men who could easily be caricatured as inflexible and unreasonable.

We will return to these two cases shortly, but before that, notice that the field of play set out in Figure 5.1 contains three zones. One is the *zone of collaboration*, which is strongest in groups who adhere to the same code, whether in the same sphere or different ones. Examples include the Eurogroup where informal deal-making occurs amongst eurozone finance ministers. Another is the virtual college of five presidents (of the Council, Commission, Eurogroup, European Central Bank and European Parliament), whose members recently co-authored the plan for completing economic and monetary union by the early 2020s (Juncker et al. 2015).

A complementary collaboration has developed between two other groups: on the one hand, cavalier politicians keen to use their muscle to dominate or cut back the thickets of state administration, favouring their own supporters while withholding state support from others; and, on the other hand, buccaneering business operators who see the wasteland created by austerity as a good opportunity to make money by offering privatised services in areas such as transport, health, education and care for the aged.

The *zone of rivalry* also covers both the political and economic spheres. In each sphere, a tug-of-war has been going on. Within the economic sphere, puritans and buccaneers are in competition. There is a contest between London and Frankfurt for access to trading opportunities and for control over the type and extent of market regulation. The Bundesbank would like to attract financial business that currently goes to the City of London. For its part, the European Central bank has reservations about London's operations in the eurobond market. There is a parallel contest within the sphere of political governance, between high priests and cavaliers: more specifically, the European Commission and the governments of certain member states, including not only Britain and Greece, but also the Visegrád countries, Romania and Italy.

The most dramatic action has occurred in the *zone of alienation*. Here, differences of code (mandarin versus warrior) between rivals are reinforced by differences of sphere (political versus economic): for example, setting parts of the City of London against the European Commission, and pitching Frankfurt bankers and their political spokespersons against Greek politicians. It is, perhaps, understandable that it is within this zone that the spectres of Grexit and Brexit have risen up. Both spectres have been encouraged by the virulent rhetoric of Farage and Schäuble, which has given expression to deep and long-standing prejudices between mutually hostile interests.

Schäuble became the classic exemplar of neo-Calvinist insistence on strict compliance with all the EU's procedures and obligations, a mantra that has legitimised an almost visceral recoil by many Germans and, indeed, other northern Europeans from the supposed moral inadequacies of Greek politicians and citizens. For his part, Farage of UKIP expressed buccaneering contempt for the whole EU hierarchy and its institutions. Farage was trained in the commodities markets and, as a politician, the commodity he has been promoting is resentment, a mood that is infectious and can easily become a style.

There is no space here to explore in detail the contrasting outcomes, so far as they are known, of Grexit and Brexit. Commentary soon becomes outdated. But, briefly, by 2018 Grexit had come to mean, in effect, not Greece's exit from the EU or the euro but that country's final escape from detailed supervision by Brussels. This outcome, difficult to envisage in 2012, was nearing completion by early 2019. Brexit has been even more difficult to read but two possibilities seem to be as follows: a calamitous 'crashing out' of the EU by the UK without any negotiated agreement; or some arrangement that would preserve the previous relationship between the UK and the rest of the EU to a very high degree, packaged up in a way that could be presented as a Brexit, allowing at least the less ideological and more opportunistic Brexiteers inside Westminster to save face and claim victory (see Smith 2014b).

Dangers and opportunities

Finally, some observations may be made about the dangers and opportunities that may lie ahead for Europe. The balance of forces set out in Figure 5.1 suggests that the power of veto, and the disposition to deploy it, are widely dispersed across the EU. This provides a kind of stability. Perhaps, if either the warriors (buccaneers, cavaliers) or the mandarins (high priest, puritans) gained the undisputed upper hand, this might conceivably lead to a rise in annual GDP rates of growth. But such increased growth, if it occurred, would have to be balanced against likely losses in terms of either freedom or social justice. More specifically, a substantial UK withdrawal from EU internal politics, especially the 'crashing out' scenario, might well weaken the buccaneering element within the EU.

This might seriously disrupt the existing balance as set out in Figure 5.1, perhaps with large but unpredictable consequences.

However, the deeper, long-term challenge is to recover and boost political and cultural dynamism across Europe; or, perhaps, to recapture that dynamism from existing populist movements and re-engage it in the cause of rebuilding Europe. How might the latter-day European movement tap into the interests of young people trying to carve out ways of earning and living? Can it regenerate the kind of enthusiasm that was evident amongst the Schools Day prize-winners in 1963 mentioned earlier? By pandering to xenophobia and anti-Muslim prejudice, European politicians are turning their backs on a stream of humanity that contains many highly civilised, educated and ambitious young people coming into Europe, eager to work, get on and put down roots. Given the right encouragement and an inspiring vision, many of these newcomers could turn into enthusiastic and highly productive Europeans in the same way that young European migrants became American in the nineteenth century.

Meanwhile, in the absence of that kind of renaissance, the EU seems like a kind of 'pushmi-pullyu', as in *The Story of Doctor Doolittle* (Lofting 2017): a sort of llama with heads at each end – a tug-of-war on legs. Seen from one direction, it is trying to shore itself up through integrating and centralising initiatives, as set out in the so-called five presidents' report, which recommended: a stronger macro-economic imbalance procedure, a beefed-up European stability mechanism, a system of competitiveness authorities (national bodies 'in charge of tracking performance and policies in the field of competitiveness'; Juncker et al. 2015: 7), a capital markets union, an advisory European fiscal board, a banking union, a euro area treasury and a European strategic investment fund. Logical, perhaps, but where is the great vision that justifies the painful discipline this orgy of corset-making is preparing us for?

From the other side, we see disruptive, centrifugal, delegitimising challenges such as: the continuing anti-refugee campaign having an impact across the union; the vocal anti-Brussels resentment at street level caused by EU-enforced austerity programmes, especially in Greece, Cyprus, Spain, Portugal and Italy; the increased representation of anti-EU populist parties in the European Parliament following the 2015 elections; defiance of the Commission's authority by Visegrád countries and others; independence movements in Catalonia, northern Italy and Scotland; and the risk of a highly disruptive exit from the EU by Britain.

Unfortunately, the energy of disruption has a tendency to become the energy of collapse. The past quarter of a century provides ample evidence of this. Consider how *perestroika* (restructuring) and *glasnost* (openness), worthy innovations in themselves, were quite soon followed by the breakup of the USSR and the Soviet bloc in Central Europe. This process coincided with the disintegration of Yugoslavia, triggering wars across Southeast Europe throughout the 1990s. After 9/11, the turbulence continued throughout the Middle East and North Africa, undermining stability in Afghanistan, Pakistan, Iraq, Libya, Syria, Georgia and Ukraine during the first decade and half of the twenty-first century.

In other words, the western part of the Eurasian continent and its close neighbours around the Mediterranean, Red Sea, Persian Gulf, Caspian Sea and Black Sea became a very large disaster area. As a result, the EU lost the solid outworks that gave it protection in depth during the Cold War. By the late 2010s, it seemed to stand almost alone amongst the ruins, a large but lonely survivor rather like the British empire proved to be for three decades following the scything down of Europe's other dynastic empires in 1918 (Smith 2012a in Dennis and Kalekin-Fishman 2012).

We will understand Brexit more clearly if we recognise that the crumbling of empires, federations, states and institutions has been relentlessly at work for well over a century. During and after World War I, St Petersburg, Berlin, Vienna and Constantinople all lost their empires and their old ruling classes. The Cold War regime restored a kind of tense stability for about four decades. However, after 1989, the disintegration continued, a process that threatened millions with degradation and the disruption of their social identities and ways of life. Across the West and beyond, attempts have been made to escape, adjust to and resist the effects of collapse. These include efforts to build up new political or economic structures that can, if possible, reclaim the territory, resources and influence being lost. This has produced centralised leaderships of a forceful kind, often murderous but not always rational or effective. Hitler's Third Reich and Stalin's Russia clearly stand at one end of the spectrum.

The argument returns directly to Brexit by noticing that the crumbling of the British empire occurred in counterpoint to the sequence just described. While the great land empires of Europe were releasing their captive nations after 1918, London held on carefully to its possessions while discovering, little by little, how to scale down its enormous empire, how to instil some order into an apparently unavoidable process of imperial collapse.

Dublin was London's great teacher. Ireland's successful revolt against rule from London (1916–22) showed Whitehall that the British people, with their new democratic franchise and recent war memories, would not allow their government to spill blood and spend money holding down their most troublesome possessions by massive resort to force (as explored in Smith 2018).

After 1945, Britain was forced to face up to its post-imperial demotion. Joining the Common Market in 1971 gave its ministers, diplomats and other civil servants the security and activity that came from being an influential member of an increasingly powerful and independent multistate organisation.

However, ever since World War I, there have been repeated attempts by some parts of the British establishment, especially in the Conservative Party, to go forward by looking through the rear-view mirror and taking the UK's past as the best guide for its future, even though Britain's circumstances had radically changed.

But parts of the British establishment have been attempting for over a century to compensate for Britain's old top-down dynastic empire's failing capacity to command obedience or even allegiance from its overseas subjects. These enthusiastic imperialists tried to reformulate the enterprise through: a cat's cradle of trading deals between 'kith and kin' in the Anglo-sphere at home and abroad; and, a politically influential and mutually supportive club of nations, the Commonwealth, that had, so to speak, grown up in the world together. One recent manifestation has been the various proposals of the European Research Group in the House of Commons, which have been influential in guiding the approach taken by Prime Minister Theresa May during the long Brexit negotiations in Brussels.

At the same time as these ambitions were being formulated by supporters of the UK's minority Tory government, the EU was facing its own first major failure in Europe-building. The eurozone crisis after 2008 was followed by the migration crisis during the 2010s. They both stimulated aggressive challenges to the authority of Brussels from a number of member states. The response of Brussels has been to increase central monitoring and discipline in fiscal and budgetary matters.

In dealing with Brexit since 2016, the EU has been formidably correct and polite. Brussels has been able to make political life difficult in 2019 with the so-called 'backstop' proposal, and will almost certainly, if Brexit goes ahead, make things increasingly troublesome over the coming years. The backstop was an arrangement designed to keep the UK in a customs union with the EU until a satisfactory agreement on their future trading and security relationship had been signed. Special conditions applied to Northern Ireland, which is party to the so-called Good Friday Agreement that is vital to maintaining peace after decades of violence.

Some campaigners for Brexit had given the impression that leaving the EU would be a bit like ending one's subscription to the Automobile Association. They said it would not be unduly difficult or painful. It will be both these things because Brexit has triggered a confrontation between two well-established enterprises, one in London and the other in Brussels, that both fear encroaching collapse. In both cases, a proud establishment and its historic project are under threat.

The leadership of British Conservatism is wrestling with its dismal electoral record over the past two decades and hoping, somehow, to rescue and restore the political fortunes of the Conservative Party while at the same time unleashing its postcolonial yearning to pull away from Europe to reconstruct those longed-for worldwide networks so they are fit for the twenty-first century.

On the other side, the EU's governing establishment is increasingly coming under threat from the huge cloudbank of resentment and anger that has built up across the EU because of the non-collegiate, even cruel, way in which the eurozone crisis was handled by a European Commission captured by the puritan self-righteousness of ordo-liberals (following a hyper-rigid form of Thatcherism) in Frankfurt and elsewhere; and the continuing demographic influx from beyond its borders has intensified that resentment and anger amongst EU citizens who fear renewed humiliation, this time not just from 'above' (the Commission) but also from 'outside' (immigrants).

It seems likely that Brexit may not work or deliver in the way or to the extent that its main sponsors hope. Specifically, the British Tory party may come out of the Brexit confrontation in a much worse state than the European Commission but both will be badly damaged. Since 2016, the Conservative Party has done huge harm to itself, not least by losing its majority as a result of an ill-advised snap election in June 2017 that left the Conservatives as a minority government depending on the votes of Northern Irish Democratic Unionist Party (DUP).

Reflecting on the Brexit machinations, it is instructive to recall the assessment made late in 2018 by Sir Ivan Rogers, the UK's one-time representative to the EU, and an insider par excellence. He provided his analysis at the University of Liverpool's Heseltine Institute for Public Policy on 13 December 2018 (see Rogers 2018; quotations in the following three paragraphs are from this source). Sir Ivan argued that Britain was facing its biggest political crisis for at least two generations; that this would undermine public respect for the political class; and that Britain faced a medium-term future of internal division and conflict with the EU, especially if certain lessons are not learned very quickly. These may be briefly summarised.

Leaving the EU would be a major regime change, with massive political, legal, economic and social consequences. For example, 'the solidarity of the club members will ALWAYS be with each other, not with [the UK] ... [and] ... This may be the first Anglo-Irish negotiation in history where the greater leverage is not on London's side of the table.' The UK will be regarded as 'an opponent and rival, not just a partner, now'. The EU members' pooling of sovereignty gives them enhanced agency within a world order dominated by large nation-states (such as China and the USA) with a view to 'adding to their "power of agency" in a world order in which modestly sized nation-states have relatively little say' if they do not take a collective approach. On the EU side, then, there is tremendous global clout while, outside the EU, the UK will 'struggle to achieve even observer status in the setting of policies which will have a major impact on our national life'.

Meanwhile, UK politicians have not recognised or admitted how complex, lengthy and tough the transition will be. Nor have they clarified where they want to end up. By triggering Article 50, which began the withdrawal process, very quickly after the referendum, the UK sacrificed a lot of bargaining power about how the process would be organised and sequenced. The UK lost further flexibility as a result of Prime Minister Theresa May's early statements about her non-negotiable red lines. The highly public quarrels in the UK parliament and at the party conferences provided Brussels with more information that helped them shape a very challenging offer to the UK negotiators, especially when the latter came to realise that they would not be ready to leave by March 2019, the appointed time, and would need a transition period. As a result, the EU was able to make sure that, if the British wanted a period during which they could adjust to being outside the EU as well as agree new free trade arrangements with Brussels, they would first have to sign a withdrawal treaty containing 'a permanent legal all-weather backstop'.

The UK ministers who conducted the negotiations walked into a trap that was partly of their own making. They set themselves an unachievable deadline for making a complete regime change after forty years of EU membership. Not surprisingly, the European Commission, determined to protect and preserve the integrity of its regulatory system with its four freedoms, was able to exploit the advantage of dealing with a harassed and conflicted UK leadership facing a steep cliff edge with the sound of ever louder ticking in their ears. Similar dynamics may be expected during the extended negotiations over a free trade agreement, especially as the next UK general election looms.

Meanwhile, Theresa May has made some damaging choices in formulating her negotiating position. She has prioritised the ending of free movement of people, even though it greatly diminishes the value of a British passport when travelling in the EU, and she has emphasised getting as near frictionless trade in goods as she can achieve while neglecting the interests of the service sector, including finance, resulting in a major loss of access in a vital export market. Market access into the EU will diminish under any feasible form of Brexit, and making up the loss will require a considerable effort lasting several years and entailing considerable disappointment and suffering.

Not least, there are striking internal contradictions in the position asserted by the Brexiteers, whom Mrs May has been at pains to pacify. They have not grasped the fact that the more you pull down tariff and non-tariff barriers and open up trade to companies based in other countries, the more you restrict your own capacity to give special advantages to businesses based in your own country. In other words, if you sign deals to open up your national markets to traders from elsewhere, you are willingly sacrificing some of your national sovereignty. It is difficult to combine both approaches. Beginning with the former ambition, you are liable to move to the latter. Sir Ivan traces a line from Joseph Chamberlain's Imperial Preference schemes, which failed to be implemented seriously, through to his son Neville's protectionist schemes in the early 1930s.

As Sir Ivan sees it, if the withdrawal agreement made by Theresa May survives, or if Britain withdraws from the EU under some other arrangement, the UK service sector is likely to face exclusion from the EU single market, where they have enjoyed a large trade surplus. Many more traders in this field will relocate away from the UK into the EU. Brussels is likely to bargain hard with the UK, which will be desperate to restore access for its service industries. The cost is likely to be borne by British interests outside London, such as fishing communities, which have provided very strong support for Brexit in the provinces. There will be a heavy political price to pay by the leaders of the Brexit campaign.

Three recent commentaries mix optimism and pessimism. Fintan O'Toole (O'Toole 2018) grasps the shaping power of the imperial stiff upper lip and its wartime formulation, the Dunkirk spirit, both barely containing British resentment at having their victory in 1945 undercut by their empire's disintegration. In response, the British have behaved like a victimised colony. Anthony Barnett (Barnett 2018) also picks up the constrained self-image of the British, or, more especially, the English, comforted by the Falklands victory but progressively shorn of influence and recognition as the strong and stable two-party order of the immediate postwar decades faded into the populist media-driven sloganising of Blair and Cameron. Their revenge was the Brexit vote, soon followed by the Trump victory, both signalling a demand for change.

Barnett hopes the restless anti-establishment mood might be captured for progressive causes. Jan Zielonka (Zielonka 2018) has a similar hope, observing the populist, or, as he calls it, counter-revolutionary, upsurge across the European continent. He hopes for the gradual evolution of a more subtle and flexible democratic order built around cities and regions networked amongst themselves, as well as being dynamically linked into companies, non-governmental organisations, neighbourhoods, national representative bodies and the existing European Parliament. However, Brexit would make that more difficult and might even presage the disintegration of both of the two unions involved: the European Union and the United Kingdom.

From mid-2017, Mrs May repeatedly decreed that Friday 29 March 2019 would be the definitive point of UK departure from the EU. But on 21 March she went to Brussels to ask for an extension of the Article 50 deadline: a major and highly public humiliation for her. The EU laid down its terms: the UK had to agree to the withdrawal deal by 12 April or participate in the European Parliamentary elections of May 2019 as the price for getting an even longer extension. Mrs May tried to diminish her own humiliation: first, by accusing British MPs of refusing to enter into constructive dialogue with her (a misrepresentation or, at least, exaggeration that surely lost her potential parliamentary votes); and, second, by engineering a vote on her 'deal' on the symbolic date of Friday 29 March, hoping, presumably, to blame the Labour opposition for voting against it, as they duly did with only five exceptions. But so did all DUP members and many diehard Tory Brexiteers.

This was the third time she had tried to get the House of Commons to agree to her withdrawal agreement. She lost by 58 votes. On two earlier occasions, she had lost by 230 votes (15 January) and 149 votes (12 March). A government source commented, perhaps sardonically, that at least the trend was in the right direction. This time, Mrs May said she would resign, clearing the way for another Tory leader, if her deal was passed. This hardened the opposition of Labour, keen not to risk being forced to endure several months under the whip of some born-again Thatcherite before the scheduled 2022 general election.

Even after four months of delay and prevarication, Mrs May appeared inclined to bring her plan back to parliament for a fourth time in early April 2019. In the mean time, MPs had, with the Speaker's acquiescence, voted to give themselves control of parliamentary business for a short period, allowing them to propose their own ideas about the future relationship with the EU. However, by that time, nearly six million people had subscribed to a petition demanding revocation of Article 50; about a million people had marched through London demanding a second referendum (23 March 2019); and it had become perilous for MPs to be seen in the streets just outside the Houses of Parliament, where competing demonstrations were ongoing, with pro-Brexit speakers in full voice, including Nigel Farage and Stephen Yaxley-Lennon (alias 'Tommy Robinson'), the latter now speaking on the UKIP platform.

In conclusion, recall that, in 2015, David Cameron, a pragmatic EU-tolerant sort of prime minister, rather conventional in taste, tried to arrange a pleasant life for himself and engineer a succession of middle-of-the-road Tory types running his party by getting rid of the nagging, troublesome UKIP challenge. He expected that a EU referendum held under his benign authority would do the trick. It would, he hoped, confirm the UK's EU membership under acceptable conditions and, ideally, deliver several years of peaceful Tory hegemony in the UK. That project is not going well.

Nearly half a millennium before, in the early sixteenth century Henry VIII, a pragmatic Rome-tolerant sort of king, rather conventional in taste, tried to devise a pleasant life for himself and engineer a succession of Tudor monarchs running his realm by getting rid of Papal diplomats trying to tell him who he could or could not marry. That eventually led, directly or indirectly, to: the Protestant Reformation in England challenging Catholicism; a heightened preoccupation with the soul (or self) among the population; the proliferation of extremist sects on all sides; the Gunpowder Plot (1605); confrontation between government and parliament; a civil war that thundered through England, Scotland and Ireland; the execution of Charles I; a puritan protectorate under Oliver Cromwell, administered through provincial military governors; and, eventually, after several decades of turmoil, the establishment of a parliamentary party system whose two poles were, on the one hand, the metropolitan interests clustering around the royal court and the City of London, and, on the other hand, the middling landowners and trading townsfolk across the shires, in places like Somerset, Yorkshire, Durham and Devon.

In the Brexit trauma, some echoes of those Tudor and Stuart times could be heard. But it is too early to say that David Cameron's lurch for a peaceful and prosperous life will have equally profound consequences. It is also too early to say it will not. Time will tell but, surely, British politics will never be the same again, especially for the Conservative Party. Theresa May resigned as Tory leader on 7 June 2019. Her successor, Boris Johnson, became British prime minister on 23 July 2019. Prime Minister Johnson declared he was prepared for a 'no deal' Brexit. He said the UK would leave the EU by the end of October 2019, if necessary without a withdrawal agreement. This was evidently intended to appeal to the electorate's strong desire to be finished with the whole business, to get it over and done with, to move beyond Brexit into the promised sunny uplands after three years hovering between anxiety, frustration and boredom. But could Boris Johnson deliver such an outcome?

References

Barnett, A. (2018), *The Lure of Greatness: England's Brexit and America's Trump*, London: Unbound.

Beloff, N. (1963), *The General Says No: Britain's Exclusion from Europe*, Harmondsworth: Penguin.

Davidson, C. (2016), *Shadow Wars: The Secret Struggle for the Middle East*, London: Oneworld.

Dennis, A., and D. Kalekin-Fishman (eds) (2012), *The Shape of Sociology*, London: Sage.

Elias, N. (1994), *The Civilizing Process*, Cambridge: Polity.

Giersch, H. (1985), 'Eurosclerosis', *Kieler Diskussionsbeitrage 112*, October 1985, Kiel: Institut für Weltwirtschaft.

Grundmann, R., D. Smith and S. Wright (2000), 'National Elites and Transnational Discourses in the Balkan War: A Comparison between the French, German and British Establishment Press', *European Journal of Communication* 15(3): 199–320.

Hilary, J. (2014), *The Transatlantic Trade and Investment Partnership: A Charter for Deregulation, an Attack on Jobs, an End to Democracy*, Brussels: Rosa Luxemburg Stiftung.

Juncker, J.-C., with D. Tusk, J. Dijsselbloem, M. Draghi and M. Schulz (eds) (2015), *Completing Europe's Economic and Monetary Union* (Five Presidents' Report), 22 June. Available at: <https://ec.europa.eu/commission/sites/beta-political/files/5-presidents-report_en.pdf> (last accessed 17 February 2018).

Lofting, H. (2017), *The Story of Doctor Doolittle: Being the History of his Peculiar Life at Home and Astonishing Adventures in Foreign Parts*, London: Andesite Press.

Lundestad, G. (1998), *'Empire' by Invitation: The United States and European Integration, 1945–1997*, Oxford: Oxford University Press.

Major, J. (1995), *The Autobiography*, London: HarperCollins.

Mander, J. (1963), *Great Britain or Little England?*, Harmondsworth: Penguin, 1963.

Middlemas, K. (1995), *Orchestrating Europe: The Informal Politics of the European Union, 1943–95*, London: Fontana.

Milward, A. (1992), *The European Rescue of the Nation State*, London: Routledge.

O'Toole, F. (2018), *Heroic Failure: Brexit and the Politics of Pain*, London: Apollo.

Rogers, I. (2018), 'Full text: Sir Ivan Rogers on Brexit'. Available at: <https://news.liverpool.ac.uk/2018/12/13/full-speech-sir-ivan-rogers-on-brexit/> (last accessed 9 January 2019).

Shipman, T. (2016), *All Out War: The Full Story of How Brexit Sank Britain's Political Class*, London: William Collins.

Shipman, T. (2017), *Fall Out: A Year of Political Mayhem*, London: William Collins.

Smith, D. (1999), 'Making Europe: Processes of Europe-formation since 1945', in D. Smith and S. Wright (eds), *Whose Europe? The Turn Towards Democracy*, Oxford: Blackwell in association with *Sociological Review*, pp. 235–56.

Smith, D. (2012a), 'Dimensions of World Making: Thoughts from the Caspian Sea', in A. Dennis and D. Kalekin-Fishman (eds), *The Shape of Sociology*, London: Sage, pp. 113–33.

Smith, D. (2012b), 'Norbert Elias and the Court Society', in M. Fantoni, (ed.), *Europa delle corti/The Court in Europe*, Rome: Bulzoni, pp. 415–35.

Smith, D. (2014a), 'Coping with the Threat of Humiliation: Contrasting Responses to the Crisis of the Eurozone in Greece and Ireland', in N. P. Petropoulos and G. O. Tsobanoglou (eds), *The Debt Crisis in the Eurozone: Social Impacts*, Cambridge: Cambridge Scholars, pp. 84–108.

Smith, D. (2014b), 'When the Peloton Hit the Mud: Displacement Struggles and the EU Crisis', in J. E. Fossum and A. J. Menendez (eds), *The European Union in Crises or the European Union as Crises?*, ARENA Report Series, Oslo: ARENA Report, pp. 157–83.

Smith, D. (2015), 'Not Just Singing the Blues: Dynamics of the EU Crisis', in V. Guiraudon, C. Ruzza and H.-J. Trenz (eds), *Europe's Prolonged Crisis: The Making or the Unmaking of a Political Union*, London: Palgrave Macmillan, pp. 23–43.

Smith, D. (2018), *Civilized Rebels: An Inside Story of the West's Retreat from Global Power*, London: Routledge.

Smith, D., and S. Wright (1999a), 'The Turn Towards Democracy', in Smith and Wright, *Whose Europe? The Turn Towards Democracy*, Oxford: Blackwell in association with *Sociological Review*, pp. 1–18.

Smith, D., and S. Wright (eds) (1999b), *Whose Europe? The Turn Towards Democracy*, Oxford: Blackwell in association with *Sociological Review*.

Sutton, M. (2007), *France and the Construction of Europe, 1944–2007: The Geopolitical Imperative*, Oxford: Berghahn.

Tett, G. (2009), *Fool's Gold: How Unrestrained Greed Corrupted a Dream, Shattered Global Markets and Unleashed a Catastrophe*, London: Little Brown.

Ward, I. (1994), The Best of All Possible Worlds? Maastricht and the United Kingdom', *The Indiana International & Comparative Law Review*, 5(1): 75–99.

Zielonka, J. (2007), *Europe as Empire: The Nature of the Enlarged European Union*, Oxford: Oxford University Press.

Zielonka, J. (2014), *Is the EU Doomed?*, Cambridge: Polity Press.

Zielonka, J. (2018), *Counter-Revolution: Liberal Europe in Retreat*, Oxford: Oxford University Press.

6

Constitutionalism, Judicialisation and Human Rights in the Integration of European Society

Paul Blokker

SOCIOLOGY IS INCREASINGLY showing an interest in constitutions and constitutionalism. This is certainly not to say that sociologists did not engage with matters of a constitutional nature before. It can, however, be argued that in recent years a renewed interest has emerged, not least due to the significantly changing nature of constitutions and constitutionalism, not in the last place as a result of apparent constitutional qualities inherent in legal regimes beyond state borders (Blokker and Thornhill 2017; Brunkhorst 2014; Chernillo 2014; Teubner 2012; Thornhill 2017).

Modern societies have, from early on, been perceived as closely related to the idea of the Constitution as their central dimension, an observation often followed by a reference to Article 16 of the Declaration of the Rights of Man and of the Citizen of 1789: 'A society in which the observance of the law is not assured, nor the separation of powers defined, has no constitution at all.' The significance of the constitutional dimension remained evident throughout the nineteenth and twentieth centuries, not least in national independence struggles, but it can be argued that it is most prominently after World War II that constitutionalism – conceived of in a very distinctive, legalistic manner – becomes understood as an essential component of the overall constitution of modern, democratic societies.

The postwar period is of special interest from a historical–sociological point of view: one can observe a clear break with the earlier prevalent understanding of modern constitutions as deeply grounded in local political communities or the people, an idea expressed clearly in the works of scholars such as Savigny or Hegel (cf. Madsen and Thornhill 2014: 1). After 1945, constitutionalism becomes increasingly understood as a universalistic political programme, in which national societies become intimately part of an international scheme of legal norms and principles.

The postwar period stands out in the novel imagination of democratic orders as strongly grounded in judicial institutions, the rule of law and constitutional frameworks, in a narrative that identifies an independent and depoliticised constitutional and rights-based order as the most robust antidote to totalitarianism. The distinctive societal role of constitutions becomes the guarantee of order and stability, not least by means of a deliberate narrowing of the space of politics through juridification of some of its most essential aspects (such as human rights, cf. Ferejohn 2002), but also due to the fact that national constitutional orders in Europe are increasingly embedded in international legal regimes,[1] such as the human rights regime of the European Convention of Human Rights on the one hand, and the (economic) legal norms of the European integration project on the other. The new understanding of constitutionalism, often labelled 'legal constitutionalism' (Blokker 2013; Sajó and Uitz 2017) or 'new constitutionalism' (Hirschl 2004; Gyorfi 2016), entails, in the words of Gyorfi, a limiting of the constitutional imagination, in that a distinctive constitutional model becomes the general blueprint for all countries to follow, without much deeper reflection on its local relevance or potential alternatives (Gyorfi 2016: 30–3).

A major expression of this narrowing of the constitutional imagination regards the active promotion of a legal–constitutional model in the European context. This is not only due to a specific approach to post-totalitarian transition (as in Germany and Italy) or the latter's reflection in the EU enlargement policies (as in the cases of the Mediterranean countries in the 1970s and 1980s and the East–Central European countries in the 1990s), but also a result of the specific development of European integration itself, in which courts with a strong constitutional character have played an increasingly prominent role (Ferejohn 2002: 42). Such courts limit the 'capacities of national political institutions to make and implement domestic and international policy' (Ferejohn 2002: 42). The European trajectory of integration takes a specific and, it will be argued, one-sidedly legalistic form in which judicial institutions and actors are upfront (at least until the 2007 crisis), and in which legal and constitutional instruments are utilised to build up a European order further. As argued by Kate Nash,

For more than 50 years – albeit in fits and starts – legal constitutionalism, the view that rights are de-politicised by referring disputes over their interpretation to constitutional courts, and that other branches of the state must defer to judges' decisions, has been the dominant model through which human rights are to be achieved in Europe. As a result, there is now effectively a kind of European constitution. (Nash 2016: 1296)

A conspicuously absent dimension on the European level is that of *constituent power*, understood as the decisive manifestation of the expression of a collective political will underpinning a novel political order. In the postwar years, and increasingly so from the 1960s onwards, the European constitutional edifice stands out in its increasingly autonomous development, grounded in self-constituted principles of direct effect and primacy of EU law, and visible in increasingly powerful judicial institutions, even if at the same time displaying a pluralistic and relatively fragile nature (cf. Thornhill 2012: 355).

The European constitutional project is different from national experiences with constitutionalism, not least in that – if taken from a sociolegal or legal–pluralist perspective – it is less comprehensive, of a more partial or sectorial nature, and partially leans on, but also finds its limits in, domestic constitutional orders (as, for instance, is expressed in Article 4(2) of the Treaty on European Union). One widely used way of classifying the European situation is 'constitutional pluralism'. This may also mean that distinctive areas of European integration are constitutionalised much more extensively than others (for example, the market), while the more comprehensive, federal mission of the unification of European society through law remains a strongly contested one, not least due to the remaining tensions between national constitutionalism grounded in national sovereignty and European constitutionalism endorsing significant transfers of sovereignty to the transnational level. Such tensions play out in a dialectical relationship between claims for the supremacy and autonomy of European law vis-à-vis claims for fundamental rights protection and constitutional identity embedded in national law.

This chapter suggests that a historically and politically informed sociological analysis of the constitutional project is of much use in bringing out the fragility and tensions of the European project, which in recent times in particular have become highly apparent. I first briefly introduce a sociological approach to constitutions and constitutionalism in more general terms, and subsequently discuss the multifaceted process of constitutionalisation and judicialisation of postwar Europe in a political–sociological fashion. A prominent emphasis is on the depoliticising and at the same time contested nature of the process.

The final part reflects on contemporary issues related to the problematic dimensions of the constitutionalisation and judicialisation process, including a backlash against universal rights and supranational law in many European societies.

The sociology of constitutions

In a general sense, interrelations of sociology and law have been conceived in two different ways. One view is that law is a, or even *the*, precondition for the constitution of social life. A second view understands law as a specific institutional sphere within larger modern society (Schluchter 2002: 258). While these two conceptions are not mutually exclusive, the present account will lean towards the former observation, which is prominent in the recent sociological–constitutional revival.

It is clear that constitutionalism, understood as manifesting itself both at the national and at the inter- and transnational levels, is now an increasingly important object of inquiry for sociologists.[2] Traditionally, sociological researchers tended to show a lack of interest in constitutionalism, even if early sociological and philosophical works proposed some form of theory of constitutional legitimacy (Thornhill 2017: 494).[3] Since the 1980s, one has been able to speak of a certain revival of sociological interest in constitutions. This is not least due to the fact that, in the latter half of the twentieth century, it became undeniable that constitutional law is to be understood as a primary dimension of the constitution of modern society: that is, a distinctive understanding and implementation of constitutionalism forms now the 'preferred system of sociopolitical organization' (Thornhill 2017: 494). The recent history of modern (democratic) societies indicates the emergence of constitutionalism as an (almost) universally accepted legal foundation for national government. Most prominently in recent 'waves' of democratisation – for instance, in Southern Europe in the 1970s and 1980s, and in East–Central Europe from the 1970s onwards – constitutionalism has played a highly conspicuous role. Recent processes of democratic transition or systemic restructuring have usually revolved around the consolidation of political systems based on strong and enforceable constitutional norms. Indeed, there now exists an effective expectation that all national polities will be formed and obtain legitimacy as constitutional states.

This recent rise of constitutionalism means that, globally, states tend to converge around a relatively uniform, *legal–constitutional* model

(Klug 2000). In particular, first, most transitional and post-transitional states are marked by deep interaction between domestic and international legal norms, such that domestic constitutional law is often backed by international norms. Partly for this reason, second, most states ascribe a high degree of importance to the judicial branch, especially to Constitutional Courts or Supreme Courts, which acquire responsibilities for constitutional review of statutes and for ensuring conformity between domestic and international law. This is particularly upfront in the experience of European integration. As a result, many new constitutions involve a repositioning in the classical relation between the branches of government, and the growing force of the judiciary means, in the formation of constitutions, that the classical functions of the constituent power are diminished in scope and, after their formation, that the formal authority of legislatures is weakened.

The emergence of a universal legal–constitutional model of society is equally related to a tendency towards *judicialisation* in modern societies, which includes a 'profound shift of power away from legislatures and toward courts and other legal institutions around the world' (Ferejohn 2002: 41). Judicialisation further refers to a growing importance of legal norms in social and political interaction, not least in the form of human rights, shifting political demands and claims away from representative and participatory democratic institutions to the legal arena.

There are, of course, exceptions to the diffusion of a strictly legalistic constitutional model. In Europe, some states that originally endorsed strong judicial power – for instance, Hungary and Poland – have since reacted strongly against this constitutional model. Generally, recent decades have none the less witnessed a remarkable *constitutional revolution*, which, globally, has been strikingly similar in its institutional results. Indeed, in addition to defining the structure of new states, the model of constitutionalism marked by a strong judicial emphasis has even been able to penetrate polities (such as the UK) that are traditionally resistant to notions of higher-order judicial power.

Sociologists have been applying various approaches to study the emergence of legal constitutionalism and judicialisation, including Luhmannian perspectives (Kjaer 2014; Thornhill 2011; Teubner 2012), Bourdieusian analyses (Madsen 2014; Vauchez 2015), critical–theoretical works (Brunkhorst 2014) and conflict–theoretical endeavours (Blokker 2017; Klug 2017). The analysis below will draw on all these approaches and will particularly emphasise political conflict and contestation over legal constitutional and human rights arrangements. Unlike some socio-logical studies, the approach taken here is less informed by the conviction that the legal–constitutional mode of societal integration is necessarily of a stable and lasting form. Rather, the intuition is that it consists of a rather one-sided form of integration, in which the contestable, and hence politi-cal, nature of the whole arrangement is downplayed. The analysis here follows Klug (2017) in stressing the relation between the legitimacy of a constitutional settlement and the capacity of constitutions to mobilise, channel and coordinate power (Klug 2017: 67). It is driven by the idea that constitutions fulfil a number of functions (constitutive, self-limiting, regulatory but also symbolic, self-governing and emancipatory; cf. Tuori 2015), and that the current predominance of legal constitutionalism stresses some functions (self-limiting, regulatory) over others (in particu-lar symbolic, emancipatory and self-governing). In a pluralistic language, this means that, in the European context, economic and judicial constitu-tionalisation has taken the lead, but without adequately addressing issues of a symbolic, self-governing and emancipatory nature. Emphasis is put on how the contemporary order has been constituted, but also on the extent to which it is contested, subject to internal tensions, and portrays a depoliticising thrust (cf. Blokker 2017). Contestability tends to be inten-sified through the rise of constitutional pluralism, seen as the increased prominence of constitutional arrangements beyond the nation state.

New constitutionalism in postwar Europe

The postwar European context is important for a sociological explora-tion of constitutionalism in two ways. First, the diffusion of the distinc-tive legal–constitutional model at the level of national democratic states is highly evident in postwar Europe. Second, beyond the national level, an unprecedented unfolding of distinctive dimensions of constitution-alisation of transnational law can be observed.

The reconstruction of West European states after 1945 – notably, Italy and Germany – was importantly grounded in the development of constitutional orders, which displayed a very distinctive idea of consti-tutional democracy and constitutionalism: that is, as based in higher law orders, with independent and hierarchically superior constitu-tional courts (an idea pioneered by Hans Kelsen), and with relatively strong powers of judicial review. This European, Kelsenian narrative of constitutionalism emphasises the orderly, stabilising dimensions of constitutions, in which law becomes an instrument to mould society according to a specific design (cf. Blokker 2017; Gyorfi 2016). From a sociological perspective, what stands out is a more general process of judicialisation, in which legal norms and judicial institutions have gained greater prominence in modern societies. A key dimension of judicialisation is the idea that it is only by means of higher law and the role of 'guardians of the constitution' in the form of constitutional courts that societies can be stabilised. Such a process cannot, however, be understood without taking into account a profound shift in the democratic and constitutional imaginary of European societies, away from a self-understanding of democracy as an expression of popular and parliamentary sovereignty, and towards a more abstract ideal of 'jurisgovernment' or 'juristocracy', in which important dimensions of politics are turned into juridified norms that are increasingly beyond political control.

The trend towards judicialisation is prominent in postwar Europe. As argued by Olechewski, '[a]fter the end of World War II, the central-ised Constitutional Court system embarked on a triumphant takeover throughout much of Europe' (Olechewski 2014: 90). The Austrian Constitutional Court, which had already briefly existed in the inter-war years, was re-established after 1945, and similar courts emerged first in Bavaria, and then inspired the Federal Constitutional Court of West Germany. The Italian Constitutional Court, which became oper-ative in 1956, is equally an example of this constitutionalist approach (Olechewski 2014: 90–1; Gyorfi 2016).

The postnational process of European integration also clearly reflects a complex form of judicialisation, evident in growing constitutionalisa-tion of the treaties of the European project, and in the prominence of the European Court of Justice as a (quasi-)constitutional court, which, through its activism, furthers the process of integration and postnation-alisation of European society (cf. Olechewski 2014: 78). By now, the EU is widely understood as having a 'material constitution', largely created through judicial action, rather than, as in the classical modern-state ver-sion of constitutionalism, through political action grounded in constitu-ent power. An equally important development is the emergence of an extensive human rights regime in Europe, with significant constitutional dimensions, guarded by the institutions of the Council of Europe (CoE).

The diffusion and institutionalisation of a distinctive, legal–constitutional narrative does not, however, mean a lack of contestation and resistance to this narrative, and therefore it is equally important to account for manifestations of critique of and resistance to this model, now widespread throughout Europe. Significant tensions underlie the legal–constitutional model. One such tension is that between a universalist and a particularist understanding of the law, where a radical emphasis on the former ultimately denies the essentially contested nature of law, while a radical emphasis on the latter denies any abstract principles with a transcendental claim, beyond the political will of a specific political community. A further, not unrelated, tension is that between constituent and constituted power. In more concrete terms, this includes the well-known and widely debated tension between democratic self-government (and the possibility for radical, constituent politics) on the one hand, and the idea of the rule of law and political self-constraint (and even post-constituent politics) on the other. This also relates to the constitutional dimensions of legal regimes beyond the national level, as manifest in the European integration project as well as in the human rights regime grounded in the European Convention of Human Rights (ECHR).

The constitutionalisation of European law

The early process of European integration was largely based on a managerial, technical approach to law and came about as an intergovernmental effort prioritising economic integration. Initially, the legal structure was largely understood as being of an international kind, as with the Treaty of Paris (1951), which established the European Coal and Steel Community (ECSC), rather than as an overarching, autonomous and supranational constitution of sorts. The nature of the Treaty of Rome (1957) has been described as 'functionalist' rather than political: that is, the telos was not a political union, but rather the facilitation of incrementalist integration on the basis of economic objectives (Christiansen and Reh 2009: 23; cf. Tuori 2015). The initial integration steps ignored the issue of democratic legitimacy, which was regarded as sufficiently guaranteed through national governments and parliaments, and the fact that member states ratified the treaties (Tuori 2015: 41). As observed by Boerger and Rasmussen, the 'idea of creating a European federal state based on a European constitution was neither politically viable nor wished for by national governments' (Boerger and Rasmussen 2014: 201).

An 'integration method', based on technocracy and 'managerial problem-solving', took hold and consisted in 'functional integration of sectors such as agrarian policies or external trade and environmental protection whose regulation is administered by a small bureaucracy' (Möller 2015: 233).[4] Kaarlo Tuori points to the 'functional primacy of economic constitutionalization' in the early years of European integration, in which the promotion of the establishment of the common market was prioritised (Tuori 2015: 45, 47). And in the words of Hauke Brunkhorst, a functional economic constitution consisting of the structural coupling of the legal and economic system was adopted and further expanded through a process of 'unspectacular evolutionary incrementalism' (Brunkhorst 2014: 47, 42). There seems to be a rough consensus that this managerial, incrementalist and sectorial-functionalist method remained a dominant form of integration until the 1970s, and, even if a transfer of sovereignty by the member states was an intrinsic part of the process, national governments and courts in general acted in benign neglect of the process of integration, as well as the increasingly prominent role of the European Court of Justice, or at least did not strongly resist them, even if the 'doctrines of the European Court were not widely accepted in national legal and political communities' (Alter 2001: 1). This situation of relative acquiescence has been labelled a 'quiet revolution' (Rasmussen 2013: 1192). From the 1960s and 1970s onwards, juridical as well as political constitutionalisation processes became visible, not least as a result of judicial activism by the supranational European Court[5] (Brunkhorst 2016: 693–5), and, in reaction, the increased contestation by national courts, who challenged the European Court on the grounds of rights and democratic legitimacy (Thornhill 2012: 357). The nature of the European legal structure changed radically due to two phenomena in particular. First of all, the international dimension of EU law was increasingly being replaced by the development of autonomous EU law, distinct from both international and state law, resulting in the expansion of a 'juridical constitution' (Tuori 2015: 53). This strengthening of the supranational level is equally evident in the self-empowerment of the European Court. Second, by the 1970s, the political dimension of European integration became increasingly prominent, and one could speak of the development of a 'political constitution'.

Regarding the first tendency, that of *juridical constitutionalisation*, it is widely recognised that two judgements of the European Court of Justice in the 1960s de facto constituted the EU legal order in a constitutional sense, and can be seen as prominently resulting from 'judicial activism': that is, the active creation of law by judges shaping primary features of EU law, adding up to a 'constitutionalisation of the treaties' (Shaw 2017: 369). Boerger and Rasmussen claim that the exercise of the European Court established a 'legal order of proto-federal character' (Boerger and Rasmussen 2014: 199). The 'constitutional moment' created by the European Court consisted of cases 26/62 of 1963 and 6/64 *Costa v. ENEL* of 1964, the first leading to the formulation of the principle of *direct effect* ('capacity of a norm of Union law to be applied in domestic court proceedings'), the second leading to *primacy* of EU law ('capacity of that norm of Union law to overrule inconsistent norms of national law in domestic court proceedings'; de Witte 2011: 323).

From the 1960s onwards, the European Court steadily worked on carving out an autonomous, supranational EU legal order, not least by increasingly invoking human rights and emphasising the rule of law in the EU context, and by the 1980s, the Court explicitly invoked the idea of constitutionalism in the case of *Les Verts* of 1986, in which it relates to the 'basic constitutional charter, the Treaty'. This self-empowerment of the European Court and its active transformation of the European constitutional order were provocative and 'extremely controversial', not least because many politicians and legal scholars understood the Treaty of Rome in traditional international treaty terms (Alter 2001: 2). The process of juridical constitutionalisation, driven by the European Court in particular, included an increasing reference to, and development of, a human rights jurisprudence, which the Court in part developed to counter criticism from national courts. But whereas human rights can be understood as an expansion of the juridical constitution, they are also part of a process of *political constitutionalisation*, not least due to the relation of human rights to democracy, democratic legitimacy, and self-government (cf. Brunkhorst 2014: 55), as well as a result of the role of rights in the process of integration of European society as such, providing individual entitlements (Madsen 2014: 260).

This is a second tendency in the constitutionalisation of European law that can be identified in particular from the 1970s onwards. It may be described as one of growing political constitutionalisation and includes, next to the expansion of human rights, the strengthening of supranational political institutions (the Parliament) and EU citizenship. The deepening of political constitutionalisation indicated a more overt realisation of a latent political project. According to Tuori, the 'embryos of democratic legitimation of European policy-making' were already inserted in the Treaty of Rome, in terms of the creation of the Council (guaranteeing the national legitimatory dimension) and of the Assembly (the European Parliament as the supranational legitimatory dimension) (Tuori 2015: 41). The European Parliament became of real supranational significance only in 1979, when the first direct elections to the European Parliament were held. With the introduction of European citizenship in the Maastricht Treaty (1992) (granting, inter alia, local voting rights for EU citizens resident in states other than their home country), the political constitution was further strengthened. In 2000, a European Bill of Rights, the European Charter of Fundamental Rights, was adopted and subsequently made legally binding with the Lisbon Treaty of 2009.

The political constitutionalisation process should be understood as a reaction to economic and juridical constitutionalisation and its deep lack of democratic legitimisation (Tuori 2010: 21). Economic constitutionalisation is predominantly grounded in a specific 'output' claim towards legitimacy: that is, providing socioeconomic wealth for the wider European citizenry. Juridical constitutionalisation builds on a Weberian formal–rational type of legitimacy or, in the European case, 'autolegitimation' (Tuori 2010: 22). Both forms of legitimacy tend to negate a third, crucial type of legitimacy: that is, direct democratic or 'input' legitimacy, connecting the members of a political community to the political institutions. The attempt to constitutionalise the European integration project politically should hence be understood against the backdrop of the increasingly perceived democratic deficit of the project (Tuori 2010: 21). The most far-reaching attempt to constitutionalise the EU politically was the much-discussed Convention on the Future of Europe (2001–3), which produced a full-blown draft Constitution. The attempt backfired, however, in that the European public, in the form of the French and Dutch voters in ratificatory referenda in 2005, did not perceive the Constitution as a convincing instrument to diminish the democratic deficit nor to address the social dimension of the largely market-driven European project. The most prominent outcome so far of political constitutionalisation is hence a European Bill of Rights in the form of the Charter of Fundamental Rights, without, however, providing any comprehensive democratic dimension.

The emergence of human rights in Europe

A significant dimension of political constitutionalisation is, as mentioned above, the increasing importance of human rights in the postwar context. Human rights has gained 'serious political and social momentum' only since the end of World War II, by means of a 'firmer national entrench-ment of constitutional democracy, human rights, and the rule of law, and their better protection in much more effective international institutions' (Greer 2006: 2, 8; cf. Madsen and Verschraegen 2013). But while the polit-ical momentum in the postwar period was evident, and the human rights narrative has become difficult to refute altogether, this did not mean that human rights have lost their deeply contestable nature, something that became particularly visible in the construction of the CoE (Greer 2006: 17–24) but is equally manifest in contemporary contexts.

On the one hand, the ideal of human rights as a core element of a uni-fied Europe had strong support in the immediate postwar years (Bates 2011: 19), but, on the other, the concrete institutionalisation of such an ideal was much more cumbersome, as is visible in the history of both the CoE and the European integration project. The 'rights revolution' in early postwar Europe was a complicated, differentiated process of European unification. The CoE and its legal institutions – the European Convention for the Protection of Human Rights and Fundamental Free-doms (ECHR) and the European Court of Human Rights (ECtHR) – constituted a regional human rights project that was separate from the European integration project, which remained largely an economic one (despite attempts to form a political community, cf. De Búrca 2011). The EU became an explicit human rights actor only much later: that is, by the 1990s (Madsen 2013: 147–8). By the early 1970s, the European Court increasingly started to refer to human rights in its own judgements, and not only to those human rights relating to national constitutional tradi-tions and to the court's 'discovery' of 'unwritten general principles of Community law', but increasingly and explicitly to those of the ECHR (Madsen 2014: 260). Madsen understands this as a process of a 'general orientation towards human rights in the two European courts [the Euro-pean Court and the ECtHR], so that they began to take human rights seriously as real legal entitlements and thus as law' (Madsen 2014: 261).

From a sociological point of view, this differentiation indicates a key and persistent divide in the postwar European reconstruction of society: that is, a partial focus on economic and legal integration in the integration project, while a more explicit but highly contested, and only gradually institutionalised, normative–political project constituted a separate effort (Madsen 2013: 147). The original split might shed some light on the persistent weakness of this normative–political dimension, even if, by the early twenty-first century, the two European projects have started to converge.

In the wake of World War II, the CoE, the ECHR and the idea of a distinctive European court were proposed as pillars of a new European order, grounded in the ideas of universal human rights and understood as means to integrate European society (Madsen 2013: 149). The European Convention could be understood as a regional version of the United Nations Declaration of Human Rights (1948), concretising the idea of securing human rights by means of international law (Huneeus and Madsen 2018). The idea was aimed against the Fascist past, as well as against the emerging Communist presence (cf. Huneeus and Madsen 2018: 141).

The human rights project remained highly fragile and contested key dimensions, such as those regarding the acceptance of the jurisdiction of the new court and the right to petition, which in later years were to emerge as the key underpinnings of the project, remained initially optional for the participating states (Huneeus and Madsen 2018: 141). For at least two decades, the Convention, as well as the status of the ECtHR, remained rather weak, and the human rights project consisted, in large part, of trying to gain robust acceptance of its key dimensions by key players such as France, the UK and Italy, an acceptance that was achieved only in the 1960s (the UK) and the 1970s (France and Italy). Madsen, indeed, describes this period as one of 'prolonged negotiation of the ECtHR and its institutional set-up' (Madsen 2013: 152). The 1970s saw a radically changed geopolitical context, not least due to the process of decolonisation, but also in terms of a shift in attention towards authoritarian and Communist regimes. In this new context, the ECtHR became a much more activist and progressive player, endorsing a view of human rights in a series of landmark decisions that stressed the 'practical and effective' nature of human rights, in potential defiance of member states of the CoE (Madsen 2013: 153).

In the 1970s, the European Court, as alluded to in the preceding section, also started to develop its own doctrine of fundamental rights in the context of the European Communities, not least by drawing on the ECHR (Madsen 2013: 154; Thornhill 2016: 384). The growing importance of the European Court in human rights promotion also reflected a shift in the human rights narrative, away from an exclusive focus on gross fundamental rights violations in cases such as torture and genocide, towards more 'ordinary' cases regarding the social and socioeconomic rights of European citizens, rendering human rights relevant for the 'evolving societal fabric of Europe' (Madsen 2013: 154; Huneeus and Madsen 2018: 148). The 1970s can hence be seen as a period of convergence and consolidation of the idea of human rights in the project of European unification, perhaps most dramatically playing out in the human rights struggles in East-Central Europe.

The human rights system in Europe became more robustly consolidated in the 1990s, when the ECtHR turned into a permanent court (by means of the adoption of the so-called Protocol 11 in 1998). As the main guardian of the ECHR, the ECtHR has increasingly taken up an assertive stance regarding constitutional law, or a 'role of policing national systems' (Sadurski 2012: 3–4), with a particular emphasis on basic fundamental rights protection of individuals, but increasingly also regarding issues of constitutional design, touching on issues of the design of democratic governance (Altwicker 2015). The ECtHR has developed an ambitious approach to both rights protection and democratic consolidation. The latter is particularly part of the agenda of the increasingly active Venice Commission, or Commission of Democracy Through Law, part of the CoE. Altwicker argues that the two dimensions together – of individual rights as well as constitutional design – enable the Convention to function as 'minimum constitutional guarantees', 'safeguarding a minimum standard of constitutionality in the Council of Europe (CoE) states' (Altwicker 2015: 333). Any European state seeking democratic and international legitimacy has a strong incentive to join the CoE (as verified in the rapid enlargement of the CoE after 1989), while now a condition of CoE membership is the acceptance of the compulsory jurisdiction of the ECtHR.

By the end of the 1990s, the EU developed its own European Charter of Fundamental Rights (or EU 'Bill of Rights'), labelled the 'most comprehensive and modern human rights catalogue in Europe' (Hoffmeister 2015), not least in preparation for the looming EU membership of East-Central European, post-Communist countries. The European Charter was elevated to legally binding status with the Lisbon Treaty (2009). Human rights are hence now a comprehensive part of the European integration project, and importantly strengthen the European legal order; they equally play a significant role in expanding that order. A significant dimension of the strengthening of human rights institutions was the 'attempt to develop a moral–political justification of the EU that could serve as an instrument of further unification, internal democratic audit, and, not least, in the demarcation vis-à-vis the surrounding "non-EU" world' (Madsen 2013: 156).

In an optimistic assessment of the constitutionalisation and judicialisation processes characterising postwar Europe, some authors have argued that it is the story of the development of a 'vibrant tradition of democratic constitutionalism' and the transformation of an 'international treaty governing economic cooperation [into] a quasi-constitutional polity granting individual rights and public inclusion' (Cichowski 2007: 1). In the words of Chris Thornhill, the 'EU evolved as a polity that drew legitimacy from rights *instead of* a national people: rights stood in for constituent power' (Thornhill 2016: 381). In his view, the

> logic of internal rights-based self-constitutionalisation in the EU illuminates general legal–sociological patterns in modern society. It is now quite widely the case that the legal system assumes constructive political functions, and inclusionary structures to support collectively binding laws are increasingly produced in highly autonomous, self-authorized legal acts. (2016: 381)

In the light of widely diffused scepticism about the European project and equally widespread critiques of the main institutions of the European constitutional edifice, not least in the form of the recently exploded wave of populism, one wonders to what extent this legalistic utopia of a human-rights based, apolitical form of supranational democracy is a sustainable one. This is particularly compelling if one takes seriously sociological questions relating to the democratic and societal legitimacy of the European project.

The contemporary backlash against European legal constitutionalism

It is paradoxical that the consolidation of a human rights regime in Europe, which has seen the convergence of the CoE and the EU on human rights protection, has not lasted for long, and is now faced with an ever stronger national resistance against the ECtHR on the one hand, and more generally against the EU's constitutional and rule of law order, on the other. As Huneeus and Madsen state, '[t]he post-Cold War era of democratisation and resulting honeymoon of human rights is coming to an end and a new world order less attuned to the liberal project of international law seems to be emerging' (2018: 156).

A clear instance of an increased scepticism and critical attitudes to a European-wide constitutional order can be observed in recent developments with regard to the ECtHR. While its authority radically increased from the late 1990s onwards, turning it into a 'high profile and influential international court with de facto supreme jurisdiction over European human rights' (Madsen 2016: 141), in recent years forms of resistance to the Court's rulings and a more general political and popular backlash have become visible. In the second decade of the twenty-first century, a more general critique has come to the fore, in particular driven by the UK and Russia, denying the Court's authority. A generalised critique of the Court has become visible, not least in the so-called Brighton Declaration of 2012, in which all forty-seven member states subscribed to a process of limitation of the ECtHR's powers (Madsen 2016: 144). A more generalised 'bashing' of the court appears to be a relatively novel development, and in certain ways in line with a more general political and popular anti-legalist *Zeitgeist*. The UK is clearly one of the main critical forces, having moved away radically from its positive stance in the 1990s, when the ECHR was 'internalized' by means of the Human Rights Act (1998). The Conservative Party has engaged in a 'classically national–populist' rhetoric (Nash 2016: 1299), arguing against interference in national affairs by the Strasbourg Court, while strongly emphasising the popular sovereign and historical right of the UK to define the substance of its 'own' human rights and even threatening to leave the ECHR altogether. Among other founding members, such as the Netherlands, such a critique has become equally prominent (Oomen 2016).

With regard to the European Court, these more radical forms of critique seem less diffused, even if an increased national resistance by some of the 'new' EU member states is noticeable, in particular Hungary and Poland, and increasingly also Romania. Critique of and resistance to the European Court have been prominent since the emergence of the Court as an independent, supranational actor. This is particularly evident in the so-called *Solange* cases, in which the West German Federal Constitutional Court scrutinised the democratic and human rights qualities of the EU law system. Some argue that a narrative of domestically guaranteed human rights has often been used by national courts as a form of national resistance against the supranational project (cf. Thornhill 2016: 374). In the last four decades or so, relevant instances of resistance have involved, among others, the Czech, Italian and Polish Constitutional Courts. In general, resistance to the European Court has so far appeared to be largely of an intrajudicial nature, and has only rarely involved political actors or the wider society.

A radical change, however, has now become visible in a number of the post-Communist member states, in particular Hungary, Poland and, to a lesser extent, Romania. With regard to Hungary and Poland, the challenge consists in far-going constitutional and legal changes implemented by what are often labelled as populist governments (in Hungary since 2010 and in Poland since 2015). These challenges are interpreted by European institutions, in particular the European Commission, as fundamental breaches of the rule of law as understood in the EU Treaties, in particular the fundamental values of the EU as stipulated in Article 2 of the Treaty on European Union (including the 'rule of law and respect for human rights'). A strong critique of a universalist understanding of EU law, and distinctive notions such as 'judicial independence' and the 'rule of law' as such, is evident in both Hungary and Poland, where governments claim a national–sovereign right to engage in far-reaching judicial and constitutional reform, along the lines of local understandings of 'illiberal democracy' (in Hungary) or a 'Fourth Republic' (in Poland). What is striking in both cases is the wholesale critique of the legal or 'new' constitutionalism as promoted by the EU in the enlargement process, as well as by the CoE (in particular through its Venice Commission), and as implemented in both countries in the post-1989 period. The post-1989 constitutional regimes in East-Central Europe have, to various extents, involved strong, independent apex courts, powerful forms of judicial review, and relatively rigid constitutional documents with rather extensive fundamental rights protection, a trend that is now strongly countered in most, if not all, post-Communist societies (Blokker 2013). Hungary and Poland are spearheading a strong societal critique of the post-1989 trajectories of legal constitutionalism, executing radical reforms of constitutional courts and the wider judicial system, while engaging in extensive 'court packing' (peopling these courts with party-affiliated judges). Furthermore, both ruling parties extensively engage in the construction and articulation of an alternative understanding of the law and of constitutionalism, along Conservative and strongly anti-liberal lines, challenging the 'legal cosmopolitan' view prevalent in European institutions.

Conclusions

The postwar project of integration through law has taken the distinctive form of a diversified legal–constitutional project, in which national judicial institutions have been reinforced, while powerful new supranational institutions have been created as 'guardians' of a de facto pluralistic European constitution. The project has to be understood as sui generis, in that it differs from the various national constitutional trajectories in terms of comprehensiveness, as well as its pluralist nature, and has resulted in only a partial constitutionalisation of European society. This means that, from early on, an economic constitution took precedence, while juridical (direct effect and supremacy of EU law) and political constitutionalisation (the expansion of a dual human rights regime) became more prominent only later, not least in order to add normative–political substance to the idea of the unification of European society through law. According to some observers, this has resulted in a European order, which is to be understood as a protective framework for European democracy, grounded in a 'common heritage of the European constitutional tradition as it has emerged in the second half of the 20th century' (Kumm 2006: 517). As Mattias Kumm, for instance, argues, it consists of the 'idea that legally constraining the relationship between Member States is an effective remedy against the great evils that have haunted the continent throughout much of the 19th and first half of the 20th century' and that

> legal integration can be seen as a mechanism which tends to immunise nationally organized peoples from the kind of passionate political eruptions that have led to totalitarian or authoritarian governments and/or discrimination of minorities that have characterized European history in the 19th and 20th century. (Kumm 2006: 514–15)

Constituent power is to be understood as a largely normative but not sociological concept, which, in this reading, holds particularly true on the European, transnational level (Kumm 2016). European integration through law can, on this view, indeed continue as a legal project, without a robust democratic, participatory dimension. A not dissimilar view is endorsed by Chris Thornhill in his recent work. According to Thornhill, the lack of a sovereign people in the European context is compensated for by a 'legal/political system', which is able to 'produce principles of inclusion *ex nihilo*, at a high level of inner, auto-constituent abstraction' (Thornhill 2016: 381). Human rights substitute for constituent power, in this view, allowing European integration through law to proceed without the need for either extensive, collective input from society or full-blown democratically legitimated politics.

The theoretical denial of the need for sociological and democratic legitimacy in the European integration project may be more or less robust, but needs to be able to withstand the test as constituted by historical and political trends that have by now gained such momentum that they cannot be dismissed as mere temporary interruptions of an otherwise forward-moving project of legal integration, grounded in public reason and benign neutrality. The fundamentals of the European legal project have to be scrutinised in a self-reflexive and historicised manner (cf. Schulz-Forberg and Stråth 2010), so as to provide due acknowledgement of the deeply political and conflictive origins of the project, as well as of its current deficits.

Notes

1. The Netherlands is the most radical example of this; see van Leeuwen (2012).
2. Some parts of this section are based on Blokker and Thornhill (2017).
3. In particular, the works of Max Weber stand out in their contribution to a sociology of constitutions (see Schmidt 2012: 245ff.; Thornhill 2017).
4. It should be recognised that, even if, in the early years, a predominantly managerial approach seems undeniable, the key impulse for European integration had come from the federal idea. Indeed, key actors in the European integration process, such as Jean Monnet, the first President of the High Authority (the predecessor of the European Commission) (1952–5), and Walter Hallstein, first President of the European Economic Community (EEC) Commission (1958–67), actively promoted a highly political idea of the law. The political ideal of a legally integrated Europe understood law as a way towards uniting Europe (Rasmussen 2013; Möller 2015), in particular into the direction of a federal legal order for Europe. The federal view made clearly much more extensive demands of a political nature, not least regarding national sovereignty.
5. Throughout the chapter, the 'European Court' refers to the European Court of Justice, whereas ECtHR refers to the European Court of Human Rights.

References

Alter, K. J. (2001), *Establishing the Supremacy of European Law: The Making of an International Rule of Law in Europe*, Oxford: Oxford University Press.

Altwicker, T. (2015), 'Convention Rights as Minimum Constitutional Guarantees? The Conflict Between Domestic Constitutional Law and the European Convention on Human Rights', in A. von Bogdandy and P. Sonnevend (eds), *Constitutional Crisis in the European Constitutional Area*, Baden-Baden: Nomos, pp. 344–63.

Bates, E. (2011), 'The Birth of the European Convention on Human Rights', in J. Christoffersen and M. R. Madsen (eds), *The European Court of Human Rights Between Law and Politics*, Cambridge: Cambridge University Press, pp. 17–42.

Blokker, P. (2013), *New Democracies in Crisis?: A Comparative Constitutional Study of the Czech Republic, Hungary, Poland, Romania and Slovakia*, London and New York: Routledge.

Blokker, P. (2017), 'Politics and the Political in Sociological Constitutionalism', in P. Blokker and C. Thornhill (eds), *Sociological Constitutionalism*, Cambridge: Cambridge University Press, pp. 178–208.

Blokker, P., and C. Thornhill (2017), 'Sociological Constitutionalism: An Introduction', in Blokker and Thornhill (eds), *Sociological Constitutionalism*, Cambridge: Cambridge University Press, pp. 1–32.

Boerger, A., and M. Rasmussen (2014), 'Transforming European Law: The Establishment of the Constitutional Discourse from 1950 to 1993', *European Constitutional Law Review* 10(2): 199–225.

Brunkhorst, H. (2014), *Critical Theory of Legal Revolutions*, London: Continuum.

Brunkhorst, H. (2016), 'Constituent Power and Constitutionalization in Europe', *International Journal of Constitutional Law* (14)3: 680–96.

Chernillo, D. (2014), 'Concepciones de sociología en la sociología constitucional contemporánea', *Economía Política* 1(2): 101–29.

Christiansen, T., and C. Reh (2009), *Constitutionalizing the European Union*, London: Macmillan.

Cichowski, R. A. (2007), *The European Court and Civil Society: Litigation, Mobilization and Governance*, Cambridge: Cambridge University Press.

De Búrca, G. (2011), 'The Road Not Taken: The European Union as a Global Human Rights Actor', *American Journal of International Law* 105(4): 649–93.

De Witte, B. (2011), 'Direct Effect, Primacy, and the Nature of the Legal Order', in P. Craig and G. de Búrca (eds), *The Evolution of EU Law*, Oxford: Oxford University Press, pp. 323–62.

Ferejohn, J. (2002), 'Judicializing Politics, Politicizing Law', *Law and Contemporary Problems* 65(3): 41–68.

Greer, S. (2006), *The European Convention on Human Rights: Achievements, Problems and Prospects*, Cambridge: Cambridge University Press.

Gyorfi, T. (2016), *Against the New Constitutionalism*, Cheltenham, UK, and Northampton, MA: Edward Elgar.

Hirschl, R. (2004), 'The Political Origins of the New Constitutionalism', *Indiana Journal of Global Legal Studies* 11(1): 71–108.

Hoffmeister, F. (2015), 'Enforcing the EU Charter of Fundamental Rights in Member States: How Far are Rome, Budapest and Bucharest from Brussels?', in A. von Bogdandy and P. Sonnevend (eds), *Constitutional Crisis in the European Constitutional Area*, Baden-Baden: Nomos, pp. 204–47.

Huneeus, A., and M. R. Madsen (2018), 'Between Universalism and Regional Law and Politics: A Comparative History of the American, European, and African Human Rights Systems', *International Journal of Constitutional Law* 16(1): 136–60.

Kjaer, Poul F. (2014), *Constitutionalism in the Global Realm: A Sociological Approach*, London and New York: Routledge.

Klug, H. (2017), 'Towards a Sociology of Constitutional Transformation: Understanding South Africa's Post-Apartheid Constitutional Order', in P. Blokker and C. Thornhill (eds), *Sociological Constitutionalism*, Cambridge: Cambridge University Press, pp. 67–94.

Klug, Heinz (2000), *Constituting Democracy: Law, Globalism and South Africa's Political Reconstruction*, Cambridge: Cambridge University Press.

Kumm, M. (2006), 'Beyond Golf Clubs and the Judicialization of Politics: Why Europe Has a Constitution Properly So Called', *American Journal of Comparative Law* 54: 505–30.

Kumm, M. (2016), 'Constituent Power, Cosmopolitan Constitutionalism, and Post-positivist Law', *International Journal of Constitutional Law* 14(3): 697–711.

Madsen, M. R. (2013), 'Human Rights and European Integration: From Institutional Divide to Convergent Practice', in N. Kauppi (ed.), *A Political Sociology of Transnational Europe*, Colchester: ECPR Press, pp. 147–65.

Madsen, M. R. (2014), 'International Human Rights and the Transformation of European Society: From "Free Europe" to the Europe of Human Rights', in M. Madsen and C. Thornhill (eds), *Law and the Formation of Modern Europe: Perspectives from the Historical Sociology of Law*, Cambridge: Cambridge University Press, pp. 245–74.

Madsen, M. R. (2016), 'The Challenging Authority of the European Court of Human Rights: From Cold War Legal Diplomacy to the Brighton Declaration and Backlash', *Law & Contemporary Problems* 79: 141.

Madsen, M. R., and C. Thornhill (2014), 'Introduction: Law and the Formation of Modern Europe – Perspectives from the Historical Sociology of Law, in Madsen and Thornhill (eds), *Law and the Formation of Modern Europe: Perspectives from the Historical Sociology of Law*, Cambridge: Cambridge University Press, pp. 1–25.

Madsen, M. R., and G. Verschraegen (2013), 'Making Human Rights Intelligible: An Introduction to a Sociology of Human Rights', in M. R. Madsen and G. Verschraegen (eds), *Making Human Rights Intelligible: Towards a Sociology of Human Rights*, London: Bloomsbury, pp. 1–24.

Möller, K. (2015), 'From the Ventotene Manifesto to Post-democratic Integration: A Reconstructive Approach to Europe's Social Dimension', in H. Brunkhorst, C. Gaitanides and G. Goezinger (eds), *Europe at a Crossroad: From Currency Union to Political and Economic Governance?*, Baden-Baden: Nomos, pp. 228–46.

Nash, K. (2016), 'Politicising Human Rights in Europe: Challenges to Legal Constitutionalism from the Left and the Right', *The International Journal of Human Rights* 20(8): 1295–308.

Olechowski, T. (2014), 'The Beginnings of Constitutional Justice', in M. Madsen and C. Thornhill (eds), *Europe: Law and the Formation of Modern Europe. Perspectives from the Historical Sociology of Law*, Cambridge: Cambridge University Press, pp. 77–95.

Oomen, B. M. (2016), 'A Serious Case of Strasbourg-bashing? An Evaluation of the Debates on the Legitimacy of the European Court of Human Rights in the Netherlands', *The International Journal of Human Rights* 20(3): 407–25.

Rasmussen, M. (2013), 'Rewriting the History of European Public Law: The New Contribution of Historians', *American University International Law Review* 28(5): 1187–221.

Sadurski, W. (2012), *Constitutionalism and the Enlargement of Europe*, Oxford: Oxford University Press.

Sajó, A., and R. Uitz (2017), *The Constitution of Freedom: An Introduction to Legal Constitutionalism*, Oxford: Oxford University Press.

Schluchter, W. (2002), 'The Sociology of Law as an Empirical Theory of Validity', *Journal of Classical Sociology* 2(3): 257–80.

Schmidt, R. (2012), *Verfassungskultur und Verfassungssoziologie: Politischer und Rechtlicher Konstitutionalismus in Deutschland im 19. Jahrhundert*, vol. 1, Berlin: Springer.

Schulz-Forberg, H., and B. Stråth (2010), *The Political History of European Integration: The Hypocrisy of Democracy-Through-Market*, London: Routledge.

Shaw, J. (2017), 'The European Union and Global Constitutionalism', in A. F. Lang and A. Wiener (eds), *Handbook on Global Constitutionalism*, London: Edward Elgar, pp. 368–82.

Teubner, G. (2012), *Constitutional Fragments: Societal Constitutionalism and Globalization*, Oxford: Oxford University Press.

Thornhill, C. (2011), *A Sociology of Constitutions: Constitutions and State Legitimacy in Historical-Sociological Perspective*, Cambridge: Cambridge University Press.

Thornhill, C. (2012), 'The Formation of a European Constitution: An Approach from Historical-Political Sociology', *International Journal of Law in Context* 8(3): 354–93.

Thornhill, C. (2016), *A Sociology of Transnational Constitutions: Social Foundations of the Post-National Legal Structure*, Cambridge: Cambridge University Press.

Thornhill, C. (2017), 'The Sociology of Constitutions', *Annual Review of Law and Social Science* 13: 493–513.

Tuori, K. (2010), 'The Many Constitutions of Europe', in K. Tuori and S. Sankari (eds), *The Many Constitutions of Europe*, London: Ashgate, pp. 3–27.

Tuori, K. (2015), *European Constitutionalism*, Cambridge: Cambridge University Press.

van Leeuwen, K. (2012), 'On Democratic Concerns and Legal Traditions: The Dutch 1953 and 1956 Constitutional Reforms "Towards" Europe', *Contemporary European History* 21(3): 357–74.

Vauchez, Antoine (2015), *Brokering Europe: Euro-lawyers and the Making of a Transnational Polity*, Cambridge: Cambridge University Press.

7
Islam and the European Crisis: Reciprocal Discrimination and Co-radicalisation

Natalie J. Doyle

FOR SEVERAL DECADES, there have been tensions around the presence of Muslim minorities in European societies. These tensions were aggravated when the wave of fundamentalism rolling across the Muslim world came to be associated with terrorist attacks in the West, most dramatically in the USA in 2001, then in Europe in 2004 and 2005. The appearance in recent years in the Middle East of a new terrorist actor, the self-proclaimed Islamic State, and the violent attacks committed in its name in Britain, France and Germany since 2015 have fuelled the fear that Europe now faces in Islamism[1] a particularly dangerous form of right-wing political extremism, sometimes labelled 'Islamofascism'.[2] This extremism has been presented as a phenomenon threatening Europe's very cultural identity and commitment to liberal democracy. The discussion of Islamofascism has, however, been met by a rival discourse indicting European societies for their intrinsic 'Islamophobia'. In the wake of postcolonial theory, some have argued that modern European political culture and its key principles, first and foremost the secular state, are, by definition, culturally biased against Islam.

The two terms, Islamofascism and Islamophobia, have in fact become interconnected. Even though they point to important questions about the place of Islam in the pluralistic and democratic world, they have both been put to ideological use. As first stated in a report produced for the European Commission, Islamophobia is a nebulous and contested notion (Cesari 2005). It does not constitute a legitimate scholarly concept. Yet, as Turner and Roos argue (2016), it is still useful to describe the predicament of Muslims living and working in European societies, where they are now the subject of fear and hostility. Despite its controversial nature — for example, the criticism that the term has been appropriated by Islamist groups to delegitimise any critical discussion of Islam – it should still be retained as an effective political tool to address a specific form of discrimination targeting Muslims. It provides social activists with a linguistic device that highlights this discrimination and counters the pseudo-scholarly, political rhetoric used to give legitimacy to the anti-Muslim hostility often underpinning this discrimination. This rhetoric has distorted a valid inquiry into the parallels between Islamism and Fascism, reducing it to simplistic indictments of the Islamic faith that have found fertile ground in Europe.[3]

The purpose of this chapter is not to analyse the diversity of forms that hostility towards Islam assumes in Europe but to reveal the flaws in the notions that have colonised discussions of the problems associated with the integration of Muslims into European societies. I argue that the notions of Islamofascism and Islamophobia stand in the way of critical thought being able to analyse a new threat to social cohesion in European societies: the risk of co-radicalisation between Islamic neo-fundamentalism and extremist, neo-nationalist politics. This risk is heightened by a profound civilisational crisis, transcending cross-cultural diversity and concerning the place of religion in social life and the formulation of collective identity. Linked to globalisation, this crisis is ultimately motivated by a loss of political control that has become apparent as a result of the impact of the global financial crisis on the European financial system, worsened by the neo-liberal ideology entrenched in the project of regional economic integration.

All discussions of Islamofascism and Islamophobia are haunted by another very ambiguous notion, that of radicalisation, which has now become ubiquitous in all discussions of Islam. It is thus important, from the onset, to clarify what radicalisation has come to designate.[4] The term became prominent in the field of terrorism studies, in which it initially played a positive role (Neuman 2008, quoted in Sedgwick 2010: 480) in the aftermath of the attacks of 11 September 2001; it allowed a rational discussion of the phenomena that fed terrorist violence when such a lucid approach ran the risk of being discredited by the moral outrage that was unleashed by the American neo-Conservative rhetoric of the 'war on terror'. As Sedgwick has convincingly argued, this came at a cost. First of all, 'radicalisation' came to take the place of the term 'extremism', and, in tune with the individualistic interpretation of liberalism that has accompanied contemporary economic globalisation, it then put all the emphasis on the individual, his ideology[5] and social networks, to the detriment of any consideration of the wider sociological and geopolitical context in which some individuals choose to act violently upon their sociopolitical grievances. It then encouraged the complex social, political and cultural phenomena at play in Muslim-majority countries to be conflated in public opinion and reduced to simplistic common denominators: Islam and violence.

In particular, it fed ignorance of the historical responsibilities behind the advent of Islamism that include Western colonial and postcolonial interference. This seems to have allowed Islam to be essentialised and conflated with the political ideology of Islamism. This ideology is, in fact, both political and religious. Its analysis therefore cannot be totally dissociated from a discussion of broader historical questions about Islamic religious movements and their place in the political history of the Middle East, including the vexed question of their fraught relationship to modernity. At the same time, equating the Islamist ideology with all forms of Islamic faith paradoxically amounts to giving in to Islamism's rewriting of history and the imaginary construct underpinning the Jihadist ideology: the neo-Ummah, the perfectly unified Muslim cosmopolitan community supposedly victimised by the West whose plight justifies terrorist action (Khosrokhavar 2009: 190–6).

The term 'radicalisation' is problematic for a second reason. It designates an extremist pole situated on a continuum of expression with respect to opinions and values; but the term has validity only if the so-called 'moderate' centre is defined, a centre around which a collective consensus can be achieved with respect to what presumably constitutes legitimate manifestations of religious belief. In Europe, the definition of this centre is precisely what all discussions of the Muslim faith have eluded and this is very apparent in the way the adjective 'radical' and the noun 'radicalisation' have been adopted in official political discourse. Sedgwick (2010: 484) shows that those who become 'radical' are presented as constituting a threat but without the nature of this threat being clearly defined. It is a threat to the democratic expression of political conflict but it is not limited to the use of violence. Values to do with such things as gender relations or sexuality are often also invoked as being a central aspect of this threat to liberal democratic culture, together with the very nebulous notion of European identity (Doyle 2013).

This is symptomatic of the fact that the term 'radicalisation' has been used to pursue different agendas that have not been clearly delineated (Sedgwick 2010: 485–7): a security agenda to do with the need to protect state institutions and individual citizens from violent attacks, a foreign-policy agenda that clearly overlaps with the security agenda in so far as the Jihadist terrorist actors active in Europe have links to the Arab world, an agenda of sociocultural integration in the context of immigration from Muslim-majority countries and, more recently in 2015–16, of an unprecedented influx of refugees triggered by the Syrian war. The integration agenda and that of security noticeably overlap in Europe in so far as all discussions of social integration have now been successfully reframed by a new political phenomenon, neo-nationalism, which has rendered the definition of what constitutes a threat essentially hazy.

Neo-nationalism, which first surfaced in the early 1990s, has long been confused with the classical European extreme right, but it responds in fact to two trends that were unknown to that political tradition (Gingrich and Banks 2006). These trends became apparent in the last two decades of the twentieth century, and much more visibly inter-twined since the onset of the crisis of the European financial system based on the euro: namely, globalisation and European integration. Neo-nationalism – which, for some time, has inspired the electoral plat-forms of so-called populist parties in France, Belgium, the Netherlands, Austria, the UK and Scandinavia – has promoted an interpretation of the social and economic problems besetting Europe (de-industrialisa-tion, high youth unemployment, growing inequality) that focuses on cultural issues and scapegoats migrants (Eger and Valez 2015).

The emergence of neo-nationalism was facilitated by a range of factors, including the so-called democratic deficit of the EU and the reluctance of political and intellectual elites to address the question of immigration, long the poor cousin of European policy-making dedi-cated, in the first instance, to the construction and regulation of the single market. Immigration matters have been a major issue since the 1980s, but their connection to the symbolically sensitive question of national state sovereignty guaranteed that only intergovernmental arrangements were pursued whilst the powers of European institutions to intervene in the area were severely curtailed. At some point, though, it actually became electorally advantageous for national governments to devolve decision-making to the EU, as a way to circumvent liberal forces at the domestic level (such as a national courts and pro-immigrants advocacy group) in an attempt to pursue restrictive immigration. This 'venue shopping' approach to immigration policy (Hadj-Abdou 2016: 114) saw the Amsterdam Treaty of 1997 establish a formal communi-tarisation of immigration policy. Even if policy-making at the supra-national level was still limited by the requirement of unanimity in the Council and restrictions placed on the power of the European Court of Justice to intervene in the area of immigration, the Amsterdam Treaty initiated the process that saw supranationalisation prevail with the 2009 ratification of the Lisbon Treaty.

The decision to use European integration to avoid national political debates had unintended consequences, however. When member states in Western Europe chose to communitarise immigration matters, they unwittingly became caught in the long-term dynamics of the logic of liberal legalism[6] that dominates at EU level and imposes the primacy of rights-based considerations: 'The communitarisation of migration polies is [thus] increasingly constraining governments in ways [the member states] did not anticipate' (Hadj Abdou 2016: 115). The rights of immigrants have, in effect, been strengthened even if the policy regime of European directives to do with legal immigration – on family reunion – or illegal immigration – on the forced return of irregular migrants – remains restrictive overall. As Hadj Abdou (2016: 117) puts it, using the traditional metaphor of the 'European house', 'the doors are not open but national governments are no longer the only ones possessing the key'. At the same time, the EU does not have a coherent stance. It constantly has to arbitrate between a range of conflicting interests, including those of national politicians facing electorates largely hostile to immigration or those of the European Commission, which tends to promote both the economic benefits of immigration and the consideration of rights (Hadj Abdou 2016: 107).[7] Added to this fundamental tension is the fact the European Commission's pursuit of expert governance gives think tanks and lobby groups greater influence. Policy has, as a result, remained incoherent, perhaps deliberately so.

This incoherence, coupled with the encroachment of EU law, has encouraged the popular perception that national political leaders no longer steer the ship. The background to this perception is, of course, the radical transformation of Western societies that has been induced by globalisation, in its current neo-liberal form. The neo-liberal ideology[8] applies the principles of classical liberalism on a global scale – that is, outside of the political framework that used to be considered self-evident, the nation-state – and thus removes the sphere of individual rights and contracts from the domain of national states. It makes of these the desired normative framework of a new social utopia: the creation of a presumably homogenous and self-regulating postnational space of freedom. Mass population movements from the South to the North – and not just the desirable mobility of the highly skilled – are central to the major social transformation encouraged by the neo-liberal ideology, first and foremost the restructuring of the labour force in the West (Castles 2010).

International migration has been central to this complete transformation of the world of work: in the EU across member states, with the North–South wealth divide now mirrored by that between the older member states of the West and those of the formerly communist East. In developed countries widely, unregulated work has also become a substantial part of the 'new economy', constituting a pull factor for migrants and allowing immigration to become the tree that hides the forest: the radical transformation of the labour market and the appearance within it of a new form of ethnic segmentation (Castles 2010: 1578). This segregation now stands in the way of the sociocultural integration of immigrants in European countries facilitated in the earlier Fordist era by a common working-class identity that was fostered by a diversity of institutions across Western Europe: trade unions, political parties, sport associations, municipal government initiatives and so on.

Immigration has now acquired in European public debates what the French political philosopher Marcel Gauchet (2016: 339) calls a 'phantasmic status', something demonstrated by the fact that the neo-nationalist anti-immigration discourse often draws the greatest support in those geographical areas where there are, in fact, very few immigrants. In imaginations, it is now associated with the neo-liberal representation of the world underpinning the cosmopolitan utopia of globalisation. This representation is based on a principle of freedom whose logical conclusion is a radical form of universalism, one that considers that only individuals exist on the planet that have an absolute right to mobility. As a result, immigration triggers an irrational fear: that all the cultural structures now familiar to European societies can simply be wiped out by this definition of freedom, empowered by the legal notion paradoxically seen as central to European civilisation: human rights. Such is the underlying significance of the myth of Islamisation. It echoes the fundamental depoliticisation of European societies, under the influence of an understanding of freedom reduced to the free circulation of goods and people, together with that of services and capital as stipulated by the EU (Doyle 2014).

The forces of globalisation, which first appeared in the 1980s, encountered in the European economic institutions created in the late 1950s an ideal terrain for a kind of experiment: the construction of a great market; that is, a presumably self-regulating social space, as open as possible to external capital flows and totally devoted to both the principle of competition and that of individual rights. This experiment was facilitated by the inner transformation of European societies that saw individual emancipation grow considerably from the 1970s onwards as the last remnants of traditional hierarchy and vertical authority were dismantled, in education, the family and the private sphere of gender relations. In this respect, contemporary neo-liberal 'economism' constitutes a much more complex phenomenon than the 'Great Transformation' analysed by Karl Polanyi, with which it is tempting to compare it (Castles 2010: 1576). British liberalism in the nineteenth century was not pursued outside of a geographically circumscribed social and political framework. This also means that neo-nationalism constitutes a different and much more ambiguous phenomenon: it is, in part, an attempt to re-embed the economy (which fits into Polanyi's argument) but paradoxically also to defend a European way of life presumably defined by the pursuit of individual freedom and self-realisation in all areas of life, including the redefinition of gender and sexual identities. This has become increasingly apparent in the way a presumed incompatibility between the notion of European identity and Islamic faith is invoked to justify opposition to immigration.

Contemporary hostility towards immigration has long been analysed through the prism of racism – which was facilitated by the historical connection of immigration to decolonisation for the UK, France, Belgium or the Netherlands – as well as the memory of the Nazi regime's mass murder of European Jews. Islamophobia is thus often considered as a form of racism.[9] In contemporary Western culture, the term 'racism' seems to be used in a way that overlaps considerably with the notions of ethnocentrism and xenophobia, and thus no longer clearly connects with the belief in a hierarchy of races that was used to justify European colonialism and also underpinned Nazi antisemitism. In this respect, the notion of racism was caught up in the rise of identity politics from the mid-1970s, which, through the notion of universal rights, reshaped the definition of progressive politics, as first deplored by Eric Hobsbawm (1996). Ever since, the notion of racism has made it hard in Europe to have an open public debate about immigration, even though population flows into Europe have grown steadily over the last twenty years at least and their impact needs to be discussed publicly (Castles et al. 2014: 116–18).

For some countries, such as France, Belgium and Germany, the new flows encouraged by globalisation have added to a pre-existing problem of social integration: that concerning the migrants who first arrived in Europe in the two or three decades following World War II (Castles et al. 2014: 102–11). These migrants, who came mostly from Muslim-majority countries to serve the needs of a growing economy, defied expectations as they remained in Europe after the economic crisis of the mid-1970s. Because of their predominantly working-class profile, they were the first to bear the brunt of intensified global economic competition in the 1980s and the ensuing restructuring of the labour market. The countries that experienced this first wave of immigration thus saw the appearance of a segregated Muslim population enlarged by family reunion, a minority often dependent on welfare and culturally disenfranchised. Its socioeconomic profile today contrasts with that of the skilled immigrants attracted by the USA's selective immigration program (Pew 2017b).

The problem is well known and has encouraged an interpretation of the appeal in Europe of the neo-fundamentalist, radical interpretation of Islam (namely, Salafism) that focuses exclusively on the problem of sociocultural exclusion.[10] This interpretation, which speaks of an 'Islamisation of radicalism' (Roy 2015) and stresses the nihilism of those young people drawn to Salafism, has in France triggered a vigorous debate in the media. Gilles Kepel (2016), in particular, has argued that speaking of radicalism having been Islamised obscured the connection that exists between what is happening in Europe and what is happening within Muslim-majority countries, specifically the challenge that the spread of Salafism is posing for pre-existing Islamic traditions. He sees in the idea a consequence both of the fear of academics of being accused of 'Islamophobia', and of the influence exercised by the idea of radicalisation whose limitations were outlined above. This debate translates empirically into the question of what kind of link exists between pietist Salafism and its political variant on the one hand, and Jihadism on the other. Mainstream Salafis do not support violent Jihad but there is a lack of 'firebreaks between mainstream Salafist and Islamist groups and movements and some Salafi groups thus can act as gateways to terrorism' (Rabasa and Bernard 2014: 31). This overlap has encouraged perceptions of the pietist form of Salafism as a Trojan horse for political Islam or even Jihadism.

As Khosrokhavar (2018: 9–10) argues, neither the argument on the Islamisation of radicals or that on 'the radicalisation of Islam' can, in fact, account for the appeal of Jihadism in Europe. The situation varies between countries: whilst violent radicalisation in France generally precedes the adoption of a radical interpretation of Islam or conversion, in other European countries a hardening of religious attitudes comes first. This has led a number of commentators to argue that pietist Salafism should be given greater acceptance in European societies as it can act as a protection against violent radicalisation (Haenni and Amghar 2010, Roex 2014). This utilitarian argument, coupled with that of liberal tolerance, however, does not address the question of how Salafism is increasingly seen by European societies as threatening their sociocultural cohesion. Kepel's critique of the view that radicalism has become Islamised thus points to the problematic evolution towards fundamentalism of Muslims' religious views in Europe – which, even if it is not a necessary condition for violent radicalisation, remains a major challenge for European societies.

There is a significant generational dimension to the problem. To integrate into European societies, the first generation of the Muslim migrants that settled in Europe often distances themselves from visible religious practice. They also remained generally divided along ethnonational lines and adhered to traditional religious customs and attitudes. By contrast, the second (or third) generation was caught up in the global revival of religious movements and the appearance of what Roy (2004) has called 'globalised Islam', which assumed a fundamentalist form. Claiming greater legitimacy to represent Islam, these movements have inspired a re-Islamisation of Muslim minorities that has merged with the aspiration to greater recognition of their religious identity on the part of a new generation of young people who have grown up in Europe and become more conscious of their right to have their specific cultural identity publicly acknowledged. Whilst it remains a minority phenomenon, the visibility of Salafism in some urban areas, especially when it comes to the style of dress adopted by its female followers,[11] has encouraged the view that the integration of Muslims in European societies as a whole has been a failure, a view that has been promoted by some politicians, obscuring the fact that many Muslims have, in fact, successfully integrated and achieved social mobility.[12]

The idea that here has been a complete failure of integration is now a major theme of neo-nationalism, which draws on a powerful trope of conspiracy theories: 'the population replacement' presumably tacitly encouraged by business and political elites and contributing ultimately to the full Islamisation of Europe. The refugee crisis provoked by the Syrian war, the humanitarian decision taken in 2015 by Angela Merkel to let refugees into Germany without prior consultation with European partners and in the absence of a coordinated resettlement policy, only added fuel to the fears stirred by neo-nationalist parties.

As indicated in a survey conducted in 2017 by Chatham House, immigration from Muslim countries is now rejected by majorities in all but two of the ten states surveyed (Austria, Belgium, France, Germany, Greece, Hungary, Italy, Poland, Spain and the UK). In the two countries where it is not opposed as vehemently (Spain and the UK) there is still no strong disagreement with the idea that Muslim immigration should be curtailed.

Merkel's stance on the refugee crisis allowed neo-nationalist ideas to spread across Europe and take hold, even within Germany that was long thought to have been immunised against extreme right-wing populism by its Nazi past (Offe 2018). At the last federal election *Alternative für Deutschland* thus became the third largest party in Germany, gaining 12.3 per cent of the vote, a meteoric rise if one considers that at the last election the party did not even reach the threshold for representation in parliament. This success only confirmed the crisis of the party systems in Western Europe, which became visible during the course of 2017 in the Netherlands, France, Germany and, most recently, Italy. These elections demonstrated the incapacity of established parties to secure a governing majority (Social Democratic parties being the most affected by the loss of faith), and the disproportionate influence exercised by neo-nationalist, populist parties that now dictate the terms of the political debate. In Central Europe too, notably in Hungary and Poland, the reassertion of Europe's presumably Christian civilisational identity has played a major role in neo-nationalist politics.

The capacity of neo-nationalism to influence policy in Western Europe has become very apparent in the second decade of the twenty-first century (van Spanje 2010). In the Netherlands, Denmark, Sweden and France, government departments in charge of the social integration of immigrants started assuming cultural objectives that were much broader than the social goal of combatting segregation: that of redefining the notion of citizenship and national identity primarily in terms of liberal social values and individual rights to do with gender and sexual orientation (Sedgwick 2010: 486–7). At that point, these rights became the shibboleth allowing a presumably genuine national cultural identity to be posited and an outsider group to be rejected because of its religious views. These were presented as constituting a threat to a European way of life, in continuity with that represented by Islamist terrorism. Since 2010, the economic crisis and further terrorist attacks have only aggravated this tendency to define national identity in terms of progressive social values to do largely with the sphere of personal life, even though these values are far from being embraced wholeheartedly by the majority population, even in Western Europe.

This redefinition of national identity has fed into a vicious circle of reciprocal discrimination between Muslims and non-Muslims. Research has demonstrated that immigrants from Muslim-majority countries experience discrimination in a range of European countries, especially in the sphere of employment, as demonstrated through the use of fictitious curricula vitae (Adida et al. 2016: 7–8). The notion of Islamophobia has been used to explain this discrimination but on the basis of the assumption that the discrimination was essentially inspired by religious difference, as opposed to plain xenophobia, an assumption that was never put the test. An original in-depth empirical study of discrimination in France pursued by American and French social scientists challenged this hypothesis through a number of surveying techniques, including ethnographic interviews and experimental games (Adida et al. 2016: 54–76). These techniques contrasted attitudes towards Senegalese Muslims and Senegalese Christians, which allowed the question of religious identity to be isolated from other factors (social, economic and cultural).

The study's design is not without flaws. The choice of Senegalese people allowed the study to use a population in which individuals differed only in their religion and thus to isolate the variable to do with Islam in ways that convincingly demonstrate the fact that simply being a Muslim in France does predispose to greater discrimination. The Senegalese, however, are not representative of the majority of French Muslims, whose cultural roots are largely in North Africa, and as a result the study cannot consider the possible causes behind this discrimination at the macro-historical level (for example, the postcolonial legacy) and focuses exclusively on the micro- and meso-levels, the individual experience of Muslims and the attitudes they encounter within the firms in which they work. Clearly motivated primarily by the concern to provide quantitative, 'scientific' evidence, the study ignores many important elements needed for a comprehensive qualitative interpretation of the quantitative data. It has, however, two merits. First, it proves the existence of a form of discrimination motivated purely by the rejection of a specific religious identity, which discussions of Islamophobia have sought to highlight and which is by no means limited to France. Further, by distinguishing between what it calls the irrational component of discrimination, based on cultural distaste, and a presumably rational one, based on the assessment by employers that Muslim employees will not integrate totally in the workplace (because of restrictive religious practices such as fasting or the non-consumption of alcohol), it confronts head on the question of shared responsibility for Islamophobia.

The authors do not shy from highlighting the way in which a significant proportion of French Muslims has been cutting itself off from mainstream French society: both Muslim and non-Muslim citizens are implicated in a failure of social integration, a point that often gets drowned out in the discussion of Islamophobia, which easily becomes a discourse of victimisation. The phenomenon is again not restricted to France. In his comprehensive analysis of the appeal of Jihadist terrorism in Europe, Khosrokhavar (2018: 102–7) speaks of a 'double alienation' apparent in Great Britain, Germany and Belgium too. On the one hand, Muslims experience frustration at the fact that they do not have equal opportunity in the field of employment On the other, the non-Muslim population is itself increasingly frustrated by the fact that a non-negligible proportion of European Muslims have ideas and attitudes far from theirs with respect to what citizenship entails: respect for the rule of law and the principle of equality between men and women.

To illustrate his point, Khosrokhavar quotes the results of a 2016 study from Münster University (Detlef et al. 2016): 50 per cent of the German Muslim respondents believed that German nationals of Turkish background are considered and treated as second-class citizens, 50 per cent considered that Islam is the only true religion, 47 per cent considered their religious beliefs more important than Germany's law, 36 per cent thought that only Islam offers ways to resolve major contemporary problems, 33 per cent believed that women should be veiled, 20 per cent that the threat the West represents for their religion justified the recourse to violence . . . Similar surveys in France, Belgium and Great Britain point to an estrangement between Muslims and non-Muslims: the offspring of Muslim migrants feel rejected as citizens but have adopted ideas and types of behaviour that can only deepen their marginalisation, encouraging non-Muslims to stop seeing them as fellow citizens.

At the same time, as Khosrokhavar stresses, if one estimates that 25 per cent of Muslims in Europe are attracted to a fundamentalist understanding of Islam, the remaining 75 per cent are, in fact, making their way towards full sociocultural integration. This has been demonstrated by the survey conducted by the European Union Agency for Fundamental Rights (2017): across the fifteen countries considered, a great majority of Muslim respondents (76 per cent) felt highly attached to their country of residence and had a higher level of trust in public institutions – greater, in fact, than that of the general population, which suggests a substantial degree of cultural integration. There was, however, a drop in trust in the police and the legal system for the second generation, which confirms the generational dimension of the problem.

The existence within this generation of individuals hostile to the values of citizenship is fuelling the perception that the very social fabric of European societies is threatened by Islamisation. Demographics are often invoked by neo-nationalist parties to justify the need to combat such a threat. Muslims clearly constitute a growing share of the European population. According to a Pew Centre demographic study (2017a), the Muslim population in Europe grew considerably between 2010 and 2016 from 3.8 per cent to 4.9 per cent (from 19.5 million to 25.8 million) through births, but even more so, through migration: 2.5 million Muslims came for employment or education, while 1.3 million more Muslims received (or are expected to receive) refugee status. The proportion of Muslims will continue to grow, although uncertainty over future immigration policies, as well as the number of future asylum seekers, makes different scenarios possible. With a medium pattern of migration and a stabilisation in the rate of refugees, the Muslim population is set to represent 11.2 per cent of the population by mid-century. Whilst such a proportion still only represents a minority and does not justify fears regarding the demise of Europe's cultural heritage, the cultural impact of such a fast influx of Muslim migrants cannot be ignored, especially for smaller countries like Sweden, which took in a large number of refugees and does not have any historical experience of immigration.

By and large, however, migration and the need to manage its sociocultural consequences have not given rise to a full public debate, be it at the national or the European level; the field was claimed early on by neo-nationalist parties, and over past decades mainstream parties in Western Europe have reiterated the benefits of immigration (demographic and economic). As we have seen, the latter have been promoted by the discourse of European bureaucrats on the needs of European competitiveness in the global market. An underlying issue, Europe's demographic decline – which, in countries like Germany and Italy, has reached alarming proportions, also attracts selective attention. This decline results from a variety of factors, but in public debates, most of the attention is focused on the decline of fertility as an individual choice and explained with respect to the sociocultural transformation of gender roles in European societies and greater female participation in the workforce, not the broader political and socioeconomic context. Differences in birth rates across countries, however, show that the demographic decline strongly involves policy decisions: government welfare support, especially for child care and preschool education, is a crucial factor. France's birth rate has thus long outstripped that of all other countries to a large extent because of the public provision of such services and also greater employment flexibility. These are two areas in which Germany to a large extent lags behind, as a result of the political culture that has made of 'fiscal frugality' a national virtue and one that German elites have pushed the rest of Europe to adopt, alongside its neo-mercantilist economic policy (Mitchell 2015: 266).

The impact of the socioeconomic context is thus also important, although harder to demonstrate. The fertility rate across Europe has slowed down since the onset of the financial crisis, probably due to a high rate of unemployment and poor prospects of stable employment for the younger generation. This is also true of France but it is too early to know conclusively if this is primarily due to the fact that the state has started to roll back family social benefits as part of its attempt to reduce the budget deficit, to conform to the level mandated by the so-called 'Fiscal Compact', which has enshrined austerity across the EU. Whatever the case may be, the debate around immigration and demographics clearly cannot be dissociated from the question of the neo-liberal consensus that conditioned the response to the impact of the global financial crisis on the European Monetary System and has kept the European economy stagnant over the past ten years. More broadly, it cannot be dissociated from the combined impact on European societies of European economic integration and globalisation. As the Chatham House survey (2017) demonstrates, hostility towards Muslims thus mirrors a new fundamental divide that is evident in Europe: it is substantially less apparent among those who are younger, live in cities and have higher educational qualifications. Put differently, Muslim immigration is resisted by those that fear the economic and cultural challenges associated with globalisation in its current neo-liberal form.

The notions of Islamisation and Islamofascism that are invoked to justify hostility towards Muslim immigration have been gaining ground and intellectuals have often failed to bring clarity to the debate. A case in point is the contribution made by the German historian Egon Flaig (2012) to public debates about the place of Islam in Germany. Flaig establishes a dualistic contrast between Sharia Islam, by which he is obviously referring to the ideology of Islamic statehood, and forms of Islam presumably not following it, which he characterises as being compatible with what he defines, in the line of Enlightenment thought, as the three pillars of

European culture (republicanism, universal human rights and science). The dichotomy of Sharia Islam and tolerant Islam makes it difficult to distinguish the former from Jihadism, and the term Sharia is used to establish parallels with the racial hierarchy established by Nazism. The conclusion drawn is that Sharia Islam – that is, the Jihadist ideology – can be considered as a form of Fascism and the most dangerous threat to European liberal democracy. As Moshe Zuckermann (2012) has argued, Nazism and Islamism have, however, very little, if anything, in common in either origin or form, and the notion of Islamofascism, as it is used today, is an 'ideologeme'.

At the same time, the term 'Islamofascism', no matter how ill used, raises a valid question regarding the way the rise of politically militant Islamic fundamentalism has overlapped chronologically and ideologically with the European totalitarian ideologies defined by their belief in the possibility of producing a totally new society in the future. This then poses, at a theoretical level, the question of whether the notion of totalitarianism adequately accounts for Islamism. Gauchet (2015) argues that the countries that felt the attraction of totalitarianism and those affected by Islamic fundamentalism experienced a similar decay of the traditional autocratic state and the traditional hierarchy. They were similarly exposed to the attraction exercised by a new understanding of personal independence and, with it, of a new mode of social interaction and political power. In the countries that experienced totalitarianism, the push for modernisation came mostly from *endogenous* social forces, which encountered the resistance of remnants of the old order blocking their advance. This means that one can speak of an experience of internal dissolution, even if international dynamics were also involved, with the role of catalyst being played by World War I as the matrix of ideological radicalisation.

By contrast, the modernisation of those countries in which Islamic fundamentalism appeared was a form of social dislocation, predominantly driven by *exogenous* forces associated with domination by European culture, be it direct during the colonial era or indirect in the postcolonial world emerging from World War II (Gauchet 2015: 71–2). Whilst Islamism drew inspiration from European revolutionary ideologies, it explicitly pursued the reassertion of religious sacredness and traditional hierarchy as the ultimate organising principle of social life. At the same time, as first formulated by the Pakistani religious scholar Mawdudi (1903–79), it paradoxically integrated some aspects of modern culture, the personalisation of religious faith and the power of the people, engendering a new political ideal, that of 'theodemocracy' (Gauchet 2015: 72–3). If Islamic fundamentalism is bound with modern culture, the discussions of Islamofascism thus highlight the fact that the 'question of Islam', hotly debated in Europe today, is ultimately a debate about the meaning of European modernity.

The implicit target of Flaig's denunciation of Islamofascism can thus be said to be the postcolonial critique of European modernity, which has contributed to the notion of Islamophobia.[13] Contesting the entrenched universalistic claims first formulated by American modernisation theories in 1960 that became hegemonic in discussions of Western culture and their Eurocentricity, postcolonial theory has formulated a strong critique of the cultural bias behind European rationalism and the institutions to which it gave birth, such as the secular state. One strand of postcolonial theory, drawing on the work of Italian philosopher Roberto Esposito (2011), who has built on Foucault's notion of biopower and Derrida's deconstruction, has gone further, to argue that the very notion of secularity has always been culturally prejudiced and was conceptualised so as to 'immunise' European societies against foreign cultural influence, including that of Islam. Modern European culture is presumably predicated on a 'paradigm of immunity' from a threatening Other, a paradigm that gave birth to both a destructive form of biopolitics – that of Nazism – and to a life-affirming one – Social Democracy. With the contemporary crisis of the latter, there is now the prospect of a return to the destructive one, which designates Muslims living in Europe as constituting a foreign organism threatening the democratic identity of European societies (Mavelli 2012). Islamophobia is thus itself put implicitly on the same plane as Fascism.

Within the constraints of this chapter, it is not possible to examine in depth the blind spots in this postcolonial critique of European modernity derived from Foucault's exclusively epistemological conception of modernity. Suffice it to say that it reduces the significance of the modern liberal state to the notion of governmentality and its presumed liberal form, biopolitics; it ignores the emancipatory dimension of the modern idea of state sovereignty and its historical contribution to democratisation, choosing to see in it only a disciplinary, socially normative and irremediably ethnocentric principle. Whilst postcolonial theory has highlighted the undeniable, implicit cultural premises that shaped the genesis of European rationalism and secularism, it treats them as atemporal and immutable. In the process, rather than acknowledging the two sides of inclusive democratic citizenship, it indicts European

societies for a presumably structural Islamophobia, thus contributing, as Kepel (2016) argues, to legitimising the intolerance inherent in
the Islamist rejection of modern democratic culture in so far as it provides intellectual legitimacy to the mentality of victimisation fostered
by Islamism and the accusation of structural and institutional racism
against Muslims levelled at the West.

The postcolonial critique cannot promote a new vision of democratic
inclusion capable of defusing the spiral of mutual alienation described
above, which contains the seed of ideological co-radicalisation that the
confrontation of two extremisms, Islamism and neo-nationalism, can produce. This threat of co-radicalisation is fuelled by the fear of terrorism that
has encouraged politics reminiscent of the 1930s, thus suggesting parallels
between these new forms of ideological effervescence and the totalitarian
ideologies that came to challenge liberal democratic politics in the first
half of the twentieth century: the discourses of Islamofascism and Islamophobia invoke the same spectre of Fascism. There are, however, many crucial differences that make the parallel between the contemporary crisis of
party politics and that of the 1930s unsustainable. Neo-nationalism does
not offer a coherent ideology that can mobilise masses. It is the expression of profound disenchantment with centrist politics and yet it is also
a manifestation of a strong depoliticisation that is apparent in all Western countries but has been exacerbated in Europe through the authority
acquired by the technocratic governance of the institutions of the EU. By
contrast, the ideological radicalisation of the 1930s appeared in the context of a fundamental strengthening of the state and politicisation of European societies (Gauchet 2016: 315). The contemporary depoliticisation of
European societies is a complex and multifaceted phenomenon linked to
the liberalisation pursued in previous decades, not only in the economic
sphere but also in that of social norms, accompanied by the deconstruction of all traditional forms of hierarchy, including that of the nation-state
(Doyle 2018). This depoliticisation accompanied the emergence of a new
vision of collective life, a new social imaginary of human power that has
inspired a new form of capitalism and, through it, the pursuit of a novel
ideal: that of knowledge society, of a society presumably serving all the
needs of individuals and guaranteeing their complete autonomy through
the juridical arbitration of rights.

Whilst active in all Western societies, this vision found in the EU an
institutional embodiment. Through the economic liberalisation it pursued, the inner depoliticisation of European societies converged with
globalisation. Following the financial crisis, European societies were thus

plunged in a profound crisis of cultural identity, of which the discourse of Islamophobia and Islamofascism is a symptom. As we saw above, immigration and the recent refugee crisis became the symbols of a loss of political control, as well as of the encroachment of the external world, of the loss of cultural influence that has come with the provincialisation of Europe induced by globalisation. The economic success of the two first decades of the EU – largely illusory because it was mostly based on financialisation – boosted the confidence of European countries that they could maintain their influence in the world and even act as a model for a new regional rules-based mode of international governance, whilst maintaining their high living standards and level of social welfare. The 'lost decade' of economic stagnation in Europe has, however, made Europe's loss of civilisational status very visible. As Göle (2012: 665) points out, at the same time as Europe has become 'decentred', Islam has become an 'indigenous and central factor in shaping processes of change and self-understanding'. This is why it is now at the heart of Europe's current turmoil.

Notes

1. I use the term 'Islamism' as it was first coined in French in the 1970s and 1980s by a generation of scholars who conducted research on extremist social and political movements in the Middle East and Iran, including Gilles Kepel, Olivier Roy and François Burgat. The notion of Islamism is the subject of intense debates but these fall outside the scope of this chapter.
2. The notion of Islamofascism, if not the exact term, has been around since at least the Cold War, when Bernard Lewis spoke of the 'totalitarianism of the Islamic political tradition', and was used prominently as part of the neo-Conservative reaction to the 2001 terrorist attacks on the USA. For a genealogy of the term, see Wild (2012). For a scholarly argument supporting the notion, see Berman (2008).
3. Hostility to Islam assumes different forms across countries, depending on the framework within which collective identity is defined, from the salience of Enlightenment humanism in Northwestern Europe to the role that Catholicism plays in assertions of national identity in countries such as Poland, Greece, Italy or Ireland, the two not necessarily being mutually exclusive.
4. Despite its problematic character, the term has imposed itself in everyday language and the social sciences, and thus remains a convenient shortcut.
5. The participation of women in Islamist terrorist acts being extremely low, the use of masculine pronouns is justified, even if Islamic State at its height was successful in recruiting young women. See Khosrokhavar (2018: 127–51).
6. I use the term as John Gray (2002, 1995) first used it in his critique of how rights have acquired a foundational status in European contemporary political culture. This status has more recently been analysed by French political philosopher Marcel Gauchet (2017).

7. As part of its pursuit of a knowledge-based economy, first defined by the Lisbon strategy for growth and jobs established in 2001 (now the Europe 2020 programme), the European Commission pursued, for example, the project of a European blue card (inspired by the US green card) with a view to attracting highly skilled immigrants (Cerna 2013).
8. The adjective 'neo-liberal' was first used to refer to the 1980s economic ideology favouring globalised free trade and the deregulation of markets, especially financial, which became dominant in the subsequent decades. It has been explained primarily with reference to class domination. I draw on a broader understanding that stresses the success of this ideology with respect to its connection to a new social imaginary (Gauchet 2017). In Europe, the originally American ideology of economic liberalism became particularly influential because it offered the most plausible explanation of how postmodern and postnational European societies hold together, a convincing interpretation in so far as it echoes the individualism inherent in the contemporary imaginary.
9. See, for example, Fekete (2009). Hostility to Islam has, in some cases, been associated with neo-Nazi beliefs, as in the case of the so-called Döner murders in Germany, but the significance of German neo-Nazism is open to debate, and whether these murders are representative of all attacks against Muslims across Europe is also questionable.
10. On the appeal of Salafism in Europe and the diverse forms it assumes across countries, see Amghar (2008) and Olsson (2014). It is generally recognised that there are three different forms of Salafism that do not consider one another as equally legitimate: pietist, political and Jihadist (Wiktorowicz 2006).
11. This visibility is associated with both male and female appearance. With respect to women, this has led to the advent in Europe of the full body veil, which has been banned in a number of countries. Long before the niqab became a hotly debated issue, the re-Islamisation of a generation of young Muslim females had seen the headscarf banned in 2004 in French schools, with the question later becoming prominent in other countries too (Gould 2013). More recently, the burkini, a conservative form of swimwear designed in Australia with the express aim of bringing more Muslim females into the country's beach culture, was banned in the South of France until this was found unconstitutional. In March 2017, the European Court of Justice ruled that employers could also prohibit Muslim headscarves. The atmosphere of suspicion surrounding female clothing is encouraging confrontation.
12. Angela Merkel, for example, at the peak of her political leadership, stated that multiculturalism, the attempt to integrate immigrants into German society, had totally failed.
13. See Flaig (2017).

References

Adida V. L., D. D. Laitin and M.-A. Valfort (2016), *Why Muslim Integration Fails in Christian-Heritage Societies*, Cambridge, MA: Harvard University Press.

Amghar, S. (2008), 'Salafism and the Radicalisation of Young Muslims', in S. Amghar, A. Boubekeur and M. Emerson (eds), *European Islam: Challenges for Public Policy and Society*, Brussels: Centre for European Policy Studies (CEPS), pp. 38–51.

Berman, R. A. (2008), 'From Volk to *Ummah*: A Genealogy of Islamofascism', *Telos* 144: 82–8.

Castles, S. (2010), 'Understanding Global Migration: A Social Transformation Perspective', *Journal of Ethnic and Migration Studies* 36(1): 1565–86.

Castles, S., H. de Haas and M. J. Miller (2014), *The Age of Migration: International Population Movements in the Modern World*, Houndmills: Palgrave Macmillan.

Cerna, L. (2013), 'Understanding the Diversity of EU Migration Policy in Practice: The Implementation of the Blue Card Initiative', *Policy Studies* 34(2): 180–200.

Cesari, J. (2005), 'Introduction: Use of the Term "Islamophobia" In European Societies', in Cesari, *Securitization and Religious Divides in Europe: Muslims in Western Europe after 9/11 – Why the Term Islamophobia is More a Predicament than an Explanation*, Challenge Project Report: The Changing Landscape of Citizenship and Security, 6th PCRD of the European Commission 5–9. Available at: <http://www.euro-islam.info/wp-content/uploads/pdfs/securitization_and_religious_divides_in_europe.pdf> (last accessed 26 June 2019).

Chatham House (2017), 'What Do Europeans Think About Muslim Immigration?', 7 February. Available at: <https://www.chathamhouse.org/expert/comment/what-do-europeans-think-about-muslim-immigration> (last accessed 26 June 2019).

Doyle, N. J. (2013), 'Islam, Depoliticisation and the European Crisis of Democratic Legitimacy', *Politics, Religion and Ideology* 14(2): 265–83.

Doyle, N. J. (2014), 'The De-politicizing Logic of European Economic Integration', in N. J. Doyle and L. Sebesta (eds), *Regional Integration and Modernity: Cross-Atlantic Perspectives*, Lanham, MD: Lexington, pp. 213–40.

Doyle, N. J. (2018), *Marcel Gauchet and the Loss of Common Purpose*, Lanham, MD: Lexington.

Eger, M., and S. Valez (2015), 'Neo-Nationalism in Western Europe', *European Sociological Review* 31(1): 115–30.

Esposito, R. (2011), *Immunitas: The Protection and Negation of Life*, Cambridge: Polity Press.

European Union Agency for Fundamental Rights (2017), 'Muslims in the EU: High Levels of Trust Despite Pervasive Discrimination', 21 September. Available at: <https://fra.europa.eu/sites/default/files/fra_uploads/fra-2017-eu-minorities-survey-muslims-selected-findings_en.pdf> (last accessed 1 July 2019).

Fekete, L. (2009), *A Suitable Enemy: Racism, Migration and Islamophobia in Europe*, London and New York: Pluto.

Flaig, E. (2012), 'Der Scharia-Islam darf als Islamofaschismus bezeichnet werden, als der momentan gefährlichste Rechtsradikalismus', *Focus Magazin* 26. Available at: <https://www.focus.de/magazin/archiv/nur-ein-islam-ohne-scharia-kann-zu-europa-gehoeren-eine-klarstellung-von-egon-flaig_aid_771871.html> (last accessed 26 June 2019).

Flaig, E. (2017), *Die Niederlage der politischen Vernunft wie wir die Errungenschaften der Aufklärung verspielen*, Springe: zu Klampen.

Gauchet, M. (2015), 'Les Ressorts du fondamentalisme islamique', *Le Débat*, 3(185): 63–81.

Gauchet, M. (2016), *Comprendre le malheur français*, Paris: Stock.

Gauchet, M. (2017), *Le Nouveau Monde*, Paris: Gallimard.

Gingrich, A., and M. Banks (eds), (2006), *Neo-nationalism in Europe and Beyond: Perspectives from Social Anthropology*, New York: Berghahn.

Göle, N. (2012), 'Decentering Europe, Recentering Islam', *New Literary History* 43(4): 665–85.

Gould, R. ([2013] 2017), 'Alien Religiosity in Three Liberal European States', in N. J. Doyle and I. Ahmad (eds), *(I)liberal Europe: Islamophobia, Modernity and Radicalization*, London and New York: Routledge, pp. 6–25.

Gray, J. (1995), 'Agonistic Liberalism', *Social Philosophy and Policy* 12(1): 111–35.

Gray, J. (2002), *The Two Faces of Liberalism*, Cambridge: Polity Press.

Hadj Abdou, L. (2016), 'The Europeanization of Immigration Policies', in A. Amelina, K. Horvath and B. Meeus (eds), *An Anthology of Migration and Social Transformation*, Bern: Springer, pp. 105–19.

Haenni, P., and S. Amghar (2010), 'The Myth of Muslim Conquest', *Counterpunch*, 13 January. Available at: <https://www.counterpunch.org/2010/01/13/the-myth-of-muslim-conquest/> (last accessed 26 June 2019).

Hobsbawm, E. (1996), 'Identity Politics and the Left', *New Left Review* 1(217): 38–47.

Kepel, G. (2016), 'Il faut écouter les prêches du vendredi', *Libération*, 14 April. Available at: <http://www.liberation.fr/debats/2016/04/14/gilles-kepel-il-faut-ecouter-les-preches-du-vendredi_1446225> (last accessed 26 June 2019).

Khosrokhavar, F. (2009), *Inside Jihadism: Understanding Jihadi Movements Worldwide*, Boulder, CO, and London: Paradigm.

Khosrokhavar, F. (2018), *Le Nouveau Jihad en occident*, Paris: Robert Laffont.

Mavelli, L. (2012), *Europe's Encounter with Islam: The Secular and the Post-Secular*, London and New York: Routledge.

Mitchell, B. (2015), *Eurozone Dystopia, Groupthink and Denial on a Grand Scale*, London: Edward Elgar.

Offe, C. (2018), 'Germany: What Happens Next?', *Social Europe*, 3 October. Available at: <https://www.socialeurope.eu/germany-happens-next> (last accessed 26 June 2019).

Olsson, S. (2014), 'Proselytizing Islam – Problematizing "Salafism"', *The Muslim World* 104(2): 171–97.

Pew Research Centre (2017a), 'Europe's Growing Muslim Population: Muslims Are Projected to Increase as a Share of Europe's Population – Even with no Future Migration', 29 November. Available at: <http://www.pewforum.org/2017/11/29/europes-growing-muslim-population/> (last accessed 26 June 2019).

Pew Research Centre (2017b), 'Demographic Portrait of Muslim Americans', 26 July. Available at: <http://www.pewforum.org/2017/07/26/demographic-portrait-of-muslim-americans/> (last accessed 26 June 2019).

Rabasa, A., and C. Bernard (2014), *Eurojihad: Patterns of Islamist Radicalization and Terrorism in Europe* (Oxford: Oxford University Press.

Roex, I. (2014), 'Should We Be Scared of All Salafists in Europe? A Dutch Case Study', *Perspectives on Terrorism* 8(3): 51–63.

Roy, O. (2004), *Globalized Islam: The Search for a New Ummah*, New York: Columbia University Press.

Roy, O. (2015), 'Le Djihadisme est une révolte générationelle et nihiliste', *Le Monde*, 24 November. Available at: <https://www.lemonde.fr/idees/article/2015/11/24/le-djihadisme-une-revolte-generationnelle-et-nihiliste_4815992_3232.html> (last accessed 26 June 2019).

Sedgwick, M. (2010), 'The Concept of Radicalization as Source of Confusion', *Terrorism and Political Violence* 22(4): 479–94.

Turner, B., and J. Roos (2016), 'Islamophobia', in C. Çakmak (ed.), *Islam: A Worldwide Encyclopedia*, vol. 2, Santa Barbara, CA: ABC-CLIO, pp. 808–13.

van Spanje, J. (2010), 'Contagious Parties: Anti-Immigration Parties and Their Impact on Other Parties. Immigration Stances in Contemporary Western Europe', *Party Politics* 16(5): 563–86.

von Detlef, P., O. Müller, G. Tosta and A. Dieler (2016), 'Integration und Religion aus der Sicht von Türkeistämmigen in Deutschland', Münster: Westfälische Wilhelms Universität. Available at: <https://www.uni-muenster.de/imperia/md/content/religion_und_politik/aktuelles/2016/06_2016/studie_integration_und_religion_aus_sicht_t__rkeist__mmiger.pdf> (last accessed 26 June 2019).

Wiktorowicz, Q. (2006), 'Anatomy of the Salafi Movement', *Studies in Conflict & Terrorism* 29(3): 207–39.

Wild, S. (2012), 'Introduction', *Die Welt des Islams* 53(3–4): 351–69.

Zuckerman, M. (2012), 'Remarks on a Current Ideologeme', *Die Welt des Islams* 53(3–4): 225–41.

8

Central and Eastern Europe: The New Core or the Periphery of Europe?

Ireneusz Paweł Karolewski

IN DECEMBER 2018, the Polish Prime Minister, Mateusz Morawiecki, said during a PiS (Law and Justice) convention that Poland is 'the new heart of Europe': 'Today, it is we who inspire Europe, it is our successes, our effectiveness, our determination, our courage and our integrity that are a source of inspiration for Europe' (Barkiewicz 2018). However, this rather self-aggrandising assessment has little chance of being shared by other EU countries, especially since the multicrisis of the European Union has largely reshaped the internal constellation of conflict within the EU, with Central and Eastern European (CEE) countries drifting towards the new periphery, rather than representing the core of Europe. The likely consequence is a further internal differentiation of the EU, promoting conflict and limiting the EU's capacity to act.

This chapter will focus on CEE member states of the EU and how they positioned themselves in the new constellation of conflict within the EU in the aftermath of the multicrisis. It will deal mainly with the Visegrád Group (V4) and explore its 'repositioning' regarding two crisis-ridden policy fields of the EU: the rule of law controversies and the refugee/migration crisis. With regard to the rule of law controversies, I will focus on Poland as the most prominent case thereof in CEE countries. Against this background, the chapter will discuss two specific aspects of domestic politics in CEE countries that are related to the rule of law controversies and the refugee/migration crisis: the memory games that the V4 countries play with their past and the Euroscepticism of the countries in question. Here, too, I will focus on Poland but with references to other V4 countries.

As Kriesi at al. (2008) show, Euroscepticism represents a new and stable cleavage within the EU; to this, I add the argument that this cleavage also has a regionally fixed dimension, with CEE countries at the centre of it. I argue in this chapter that CEE countries are in the phase of neo-nationalism (Karolewski and Benedikter 2017b) that not only produces a number of conflicts with the EU, but also promotes disintegration tendencies within the bloc. In the process, neo-nationalism in CEE countries has become increasingly illiberal (mainly regarding the rule of law), Eurosceptic or even anti-European, where the EU is framed as a threat to national sovereignty and an alien power endangering the authenticity of societies in the region. As a result, CEE countries are seeking more cooperation in the V4 format and attempting to construct and strengthen alternative cooperation formats at the core of Europe. Such initiatives include the boycott of the EU refugee relocation scheme of 2015 and afterwards, and the Three Seas initiative aimed at increased collaboration between the countries neighbouring the Baltic, Adriatic and Black Seas as a counterbalance to France and Germany.

Rule of law controversies

The rule of law crisis started in Poland in 2015, when the newly elected PiS government decided to restructure the justice system of the country radically, as one element of a larger scheme of elite change at all levels of government. The justice system reforms were initiated in December 2015 with a new law on the functioning of the Constitutional Tribunal, which, after a period of domestic and international controversy also involving the European Commission and the Venice Commission of the Council of Europe, produced a Constitutional Tribunal consisting of party loyalists. As the aim of the PiS government had been to carry out a radical exchange of political elites, including the judges, the narrative for this radical change has focused on the alleged pathologies of the Third Republic (Poland after 1989), resulting from 'grey networks' of former functionaries of the Communist secret services and the liberal dissidents who, according to PiS, were their agents. In a sense, this is a Polish version of the 'deep state' narrative, in which the 'swamp' must be dried out using radical methods and without consideration for institutions such as the rule of law.

After PiS came to power in October 2015, the new government and the parliamentary majority introduced a law stipulating that the Constitutional Tribunal would need a two-thirds majority out of 15 judges, in the presence of at least 11 of them, and would be required to address constitutional issues chronologically, rather than based on their relevance, which would lead to paralysis of the Tribunal. Additionally, the newly elected President, Andrzej Duda, who won the presidential elections as a PiS candidate in May 2015, refused to swear in the judges elected in August 2015 by the then majority in parliament, but instead decided to accept the oaths of new judges elected by PiS. When the Tribunal itself rejected as unconstitutional the PiS amendments to the law regulating its work, the PiS government refused to recognise this decision. This amounted to there being two legal systems in Poland for a while: one backed by the Constitutional Tribunal – whose personnel structure was largely determined by today's parliamentary opposition – and the other supported by the PiS government (Karolewski and Benedikter 2017a). The PiS government persisted in its course, rejecting several rulings of the Tribunal, and arguing that the Tribunal could not make its own decisions about its personnel and the decision-making mode. In contrast, the critics of PiS argued that the PiS-backed changes were deliberately designed to paralyse the Tribunal.

The European Commission disapproved of the 2015 changes, its main thrust of criticism being that the ruling PiS had attempted to acquire power in a way that had no precedent in the country's recent history and that was very similar to what had happened in Hungary in 2010–14. By doing this, the PiS government had endangered the separation of powers and thus the functioning of democracy in Poland. In this way, Poland and Hungary contributed to the 'other democratic deficit' in the EU: that is, the democratic deficit in EU member states (Kelemen 2017).

The 2016 opinion statement of the Venice Commission pointed to an 'ongoing constitutional crisis in Poland [posing] a danger to the rule of law, democracy, and human rights' and criticised the changes to the law relating to the Constitutional Tribunal envisaged by PiS (Bilkova et al. 2016). Based on that, the European Commission intervened by formulating a number of recommendations, rejected by the PiS government as unjustified. In October 2016, the Commission received a response from the Polish government, refusing to implement the recommendations as being based on biased analysis and on misconceptions about the Polish legal system. It argued that the implementation of the recommendations would result in violation of the Polish Constitution.

After turning the Constitutional Tribunal into an appendix of the ruling party, PiS took on the restructuring of the ordinary courts, the National Council of the Judiciary and the Supreme Court. The central aspect of this law (very similar to Viktor Orbán's reform of the Constitutional Court in Hungary) was the lowering of the mandatory retirement age for Supreme Court judges from 70 to 65 years (and for female judges to 60 years), effective from 4 July 2018. As a result, 27 of the 72 Supreme Court judges have been forced to retire, including its First President, even though, according to the Polish Constitution, she should stay in office until 2020. All judges older than 65 wishing to continue their tenure were allowed to file an application with the President of Poland, who might or might not accept an 'extension'. The problem, however, was that the six-year tenure of Supreme Court judges is stipulated in Article 183 of the Polish Constitution, which, for critics of the controversial law, is further proof of the unconstitutional character of the PiS reforms (Grzeszczak and Karolewski 2018a).

In an attempt to halt the controversial reforms, the Supreme Court requested a preliminary ruling from the European Court of Justice and suspended implementation of the changes. The representatives of the PiS government criticised this suspension of the application of the law at hand, while the Presidential Office spoke about legal grounds for such a suspension being lacking. One of the Vice-Ministers of Justice, Michal Wojcik, argued that the Supreme Court was in revolt against the state, which fits the narrative of the ruling party by excluding the courts from the category of state institutions. The chairman of PiS, Jaroslaw Kaczyński, reaffirmed the will of the ruling party to carry on with 'cleansing' the courts, while government-controlled TV ran propaganda materials on the judges' alleged corruption and arrogance. The PiS loyalist judge of the Constitutional Tribunal, Julia Przylebska, said that the Supreme Court had violated the Constitution (TVPInfo 2018).

While the changes to the Supreme Court were eventually brought to a halt by the judgment of the European Court of Justice, which threatened to impose fines, PiS continued with other changes to the judiciary that it deemed essential (Grzeszczak and Karolewski 2018b). At the same time, Article 7 of the EU Treaty (stipulating sanctions for countries that violate the rule of law, to be decided unanimously by EU Member States minus the country in question) turned out to be self-defeating, as the EU knew that Poland would be supported by Hungary and possibly Slovakia.

The rule of law controversy became the most serious dispute between the PiS government and the EU, and developed into an ongoing controversy involving other countries in the region. This has promoted fears that the assumption about swift and final democratic consolidation in CEE countries was too optimistic and Eastern enlargement was premature, endangering the cohesion and democratic credibility of the entire EU.

The refugee/migration crisis

On 13 June 2017, the European Commission initiated legal action for infringement against three of its CEE members that belong to the so-called Visegrád Group: the Czech Republic, Hungary and Poland. The V4 has been a loose association of four CEE member states of the EU: Poland, Hungary, the Czech Republic and Slovakia. While the group was established in 1991, it was only in the aftermath of the 2015 EU refugee and migration crisis that it came to form a more visible interest group within the twenty-eight-member EU, aiming mainly to thwart the EU's refugee relocation scheme, adopted in 2015.

The EU frequently undertakes legal action against its own member states who drag their feet over implementation of EU law. However, the procedure against Hungary and the Czech Republic marks a conflict that is more than just a technical issue, as failure to implement the milk quota was, since the refugee/migration crisis in Europe has become one of the most politicised issues in CEE states, mobilising support for the nationalist and populist governments in V4 countries. The procedure was initiated because the V4 (including Slovakia, which later caved in and accepted only a symbolic number) have refused to take their share of asylum seekers from non-EU countries who entered the EU through Greece and Italy in 2015. The EU procedure against the V4 was a complex issue and revealed deep disagreements within the EU, with potential consequences for the bloc's coherence. Some V4 politicians and sections of the CEE population viewed the EU's migrant relocation agreement as a forced transformation of CEE societies towards multicultural societies. While the issue continues to polarise the EU even further, it is also generating strong anti-EU sentiment in the V4 countries.

The refugee crisis in Europe was an asymmetric one, there being a few destination countries (mainly Germany and Sweden but also Norway and Denmark), some transit countries on various migration routes (Greece, Italy, Hungary, Bulgaria, Croatia and Slovenia), some countries slightly affected (such as Poland, Ireland and Spain) and some countries not affected at all (such as Portugal, Estonia and Romania) (Karolewski and Benedikter 2018). However, this asymmetry has consequences for political conflict among EU member states, as the less affected countries (the 'fortunate' ones) and the more affected ones (the 'unfortunate' ones) have radically different interests within a common European solution (Genschel and Jachtenfuchs 2018). The V4 countries have criticised the repressive character of the EU's compulsory relocation scheme of September 2015. On 22 September 2015, the EU interior ministers decided to introduce compulsory quotas to resettle 120,000 migrants from Greece and Italy, the main coastal EU countries that had been subject to the greatest refugee pressure throughout 2015 and 2016. Poland initially accepted the EU resettlement decision, provoking criticism from the other V4 countries for undermining their unity, but the PiS government reversed the decision of the predecessor government and joined ranks with the V4.

Since then, the relocation plan has remained controversial, as almost all of the EU countries have failed to accept their share of refugees. The scheme is based on every participating country continuously pledging to receive a certain number of refugees and to resettle them, with the exception of Denmark, Ireland and the UK, who have so-called opt-outs from the EU's migration policy, negotiated as part of the EU Treaty. Examples of failed policy implementation abound. As of November 2018, Austria had accepted only forty-five refugees within the framework of the relocation plan, and Slovakia had accepted sixteen refugees from Greece. Both are migrant-sceptical countries and clearly acted thus to avoid an infringement procedure, while the EU has consistently criticised Vienna and Bratislava for their rather modest engagement. Whereas, in 2017, Austria had ranked among the nations of the Organisation for Economic Cooperation and Development (OECD) as one of the countries that was most accepting of migration, Slovakia's government considered its own country to be too small and ill prepared to become a migrant country of destination, thus subscribing to the exclusionary neo-nationalism of the region. By November 2018, the Czech Republic had accepted twelve refugees from Greece but had made no new pledges since May 2016. The Czech President, Miloš Zeman, has said on many occasions that the Czech Republic considers itself culturally Christian (even though the Czech Republic belongs to the most secular group of countries worldwide and Zeman himself is a self-confessed atheist), stirring up the populist political climate (Tait 2016). At the time of writing, Hungary and Poland remained the only countries not to have accepted any refugees within the relocation scheme (European Council 2018).

The V4 argue that, since the bulk of the refugees/migrants prefer the welfare-state countries of Germany, Italy and Sweden, who give them immediate financial support, they would, in any case, prefer to leave the poorer CEE states after resettlement, and so the latter would need to hold them against their will and thus violate the Geneva Convention. For example, many refugees to Poland leave just after they are granted refugee status (or subsidiary protection status) or even before the application procedure is finalised. Around 80,000 citizens of the Russian Federation (mainly from Chechnya) have claimed refugee status in Poland since 2010, but only 10 per cent have decided to stay in the country. The majority of refugees and migrants seem to respond, among various 'push' and 'pull' factors, to the different socioeconomic incentives offered by EU member states; these incentives are cultural on the one hand, as refugees often look to settle in areas with a high concentration of their compatriots, and financial on the other hand. For instance, in 2013, there was a surge in Poland in refugee applications from Chechens, due to the decision of the German Constitutional Court in 2012 to increase benefits for refugees to the same level as those enjoyed by the German unemployed. According to the Dublin conventions, Poland was the first EU country in which the refugees had to claim asylum; still, it was Germany that was the actual target country. Hungary has reacted to this fact by further disabling the Dublin pact and not taking back refugees from Austria and Germany who came from Hungary to these countries, but only such refugees who, according to the Hungarian authorities, first hit EU soil in Hungary. In 2015, the Hungarian authorities transported refugees en masse to the Austrian border, from where they would move to Austria and further to the north.

The EU has criticised Viktor Orbán for domestic politicisation of the migration crisis. While Hungary was the only V4 country on the migrants' route and was subject in 2015 to the highest number of asylum applications in the entire EU, many observers argued that the government under Orbán intentionally stirred up anti-migration xenophobia in order to boost its ailing popularity at home. In particular, the October 2016 referendum in Hungary on the EU relocation scheme was interpreted as an instrument for domestically exploiting the migration crisis (BBC 2015).

The PiS government has backed Budapest since October 2015. This is because the migration crisis has also become a central issue for political discourse in Poland, even though Poland is not located on the Balkan migration route. Warsaw has become an adamant critic of the relocation scheme, stressing its repressive nature, and pointing out that migration policy is a prerogative of the member states and that the redistribution mechanism is a way to attract more migrants. Moreover, the PiS government presented itself as a cultural bulwark against the Islamisation of Europe and a responsible government that fights threats to the country's cultural identity – in exactly the same way that Orbán has argued about

Hungary being the gatekeeper of Europe in the face of migration. But the physical threats posed by refugees were also invoked in the PiS discourse. Even during the election campaign of 2015, Jaroslaw Kaczyński argued that 'various parasites and protozoa in the bodies of those people, safe for them, can be dangerous to us' (Newsweek 2015). Kaczyński reiterated that the refugees were threatening 'others' in his speech at the PiS convention in July 2017. This time, he spoke of the danger of the 'radical lowering' of living standards in Poland, should refugees be accepted.

At the same time, the PiS government has been charming Orbán as Warsaw's natural ally against the EU. The Budapest–Warsaw axis has raised suspicion in Brussels that the two capitals are playing a blame game to mobilise their supporters at home and to support each other within the EU, mainly in the context of criticism concerning the rule of law. In this connection, the migration discourse in the V4 countries seems to be linked to the image of the EU as an alien oppressive power that not only violates the national sovereignty of V4 countries through unjustified pressure on legal issues but also forces them to change their national identity through alien migration.

Memory games

Apart from the institutional conflicts between the V4 and the EU, there is also an entire field of memory games that governments in the regions play with their own societies. They refer mostly to the past of these countries but also involve the EU as a point of reference. According to Mink and Neumayer, memory games 'generate public policies around political uses of memory'. Furthermore,

> the concept of memory games encompasses the various ways by which political and social actors perceive and relate to certain historical events, according to the identities they construct, the interests they defend and the strategies they devise to define, maintain or improve their position in society. (Mink and Neumayer 2013: 4)

The memory games in Poland and Hungary go beyond narrow electoral considerations; they are not just about processes of delegitimising political opponents to decrease their electoral chances, but should be viewed as an ideological instrument for legitimising the restructuring of the state that has been under way since 2010 in Hungary and since 2015 in Poland (Karolewski 2019). As early as 2015–16, PiS constructed a political discourse in which Poland was supposed to liberate itself from Western European dominance within the EU (meaning Germany and France mainly) and from treacherous liberal and pro-European elites that do not represent the true Poles and their interests (O'Neal 2017: 31).

In this vein, PiS argues that the renewal of Poland is necessary, as Poland's hidden and open enemies are in league with the liberal–Leftist elites in Europe and true Poles are marginalised. After October 2015, Poland under the PiS government has experienced a new surge of 'lustration' (political practices of dealing with the former employees and informants of the Communist security services), in contrast to, for instance, Slovakia under Robert Fico, where lustration and de-Communisation have not played any relevant role in the Slovak version of nationalism. However, the recent memory games in Poland seem to reflect key aspects of populism. They convey a binary image of society consisting of good ordinary people (who all were victims of Communism) and the corrupt elite consisting of former Communists and liberal sections of the anti-Communist opposition that were allied during the transformation processes of the 1990s and afterwards. In other words, the negotiated transition to democracy and capitalism is framed by PiS as having occurred largely due to bargaining between the security service informants from within the opposition and their Communist handlers. Both groups are accused of penetrating the Polish state at the expense of the ordinary people. As a radical restructuring of the state gets under way, the way of thinking about who are legitimate (and illegitimate) political actors is also being reframed to fit the new ideology of populist revolution (see Mudde and Kaltwasser 2017).

The critique of liberal 'traitors' goes hand in hand with rejection of the EU, which is accused of siding with the enemies of the government and plotting against PiS. In 2015–16, this type of discourse was directed against the KOD movement, which organised demonstrations against violations of the rule of law. The Committee for the Defence of Democracy (in Polish: KOD) – its name referring back to a Polish anti-Communist resistance movement of the 1970s, KOR (Committee for the Defence of the Workers) – has been critical of the changes to the legal system carried out by PiS. The head of PiS, Jaroslaw Kaczyński, said in an interview on 12 December 2015 that the protesters belong to 'the worst sort of Poles', who carry with them the gene of national treason (TVN24 2015). This very sentence has been picked up and used as a slogan by demonstrators at the January and February 2016 KOD rallies (Pytlakowski 2016).

An advisor to the President, Krzysztof Szczerski, also argued in March 2016 that the KOD demonstrations are a threat to democracy as they use hate speech (Gazeta Wyborcza 2016), while another presidential advisor, Andrzej Zybertowicz, pointed out that the KOD demonstrations might be an element of Russian hybrid war against Poland (that is, using domestic proxies combined with official denial of intervention, as Russia did in Eastern Ukraine) (Wilgocki 2016).

Since 2015, all radical reforms carried out by PiS have been accompanied by the discourse on 'lustration'. The main rationale for violations of the rule of law (such as the forced retirement of the Supreme Court judges) was that, due to insufficient lustration, post-Communist cronies and liberal traitors had hijacked various branches of the Polish government, including the courts. In particular, in the 2018 conflict over the Supreme Court, PiS representatives argued that some of the judges were involved in the Communist court system and collaborated with the Communist security service, which should disqualify them. From this perspective, the EU is siding with liberals in Poland because of ideological proximity and sympathy, rather than a proper understanding of the intricacies of Polish politics and history.

This is all the more striking as PiS itself seems to be a haven for a number of high-ranking Communist apparatchiks, including former prosecutors involved in the political trials of the 1980s. One of the more prominent examples is Stanislaw Piotrowicz, who played an active role in dismantling the Constitutional Court in 2016. Piotrowicz was a Communist prosecutor during the period of martial law in Poland (1981–3) and was actively involved in charging anti-Communist dissidents. In this sense, ideological consistency is secondary, since PiS is attempting to channel some of citizens' real grievances (in this case, the malfunctioning of the overburdened Polish courts) and to give politics an emotional twist of anger while constructing a new dividing line between the identity of real Poles and that of traitors. The cornerstone of these memory games is the narrative surrounding the security of the Polish state and its penetration by agents of influence (foreign agents who influence public discourse and political decisions, usually through propaganda, disinformation and manipulation) and former security service collaborators, in alliance with liberal–Leftist elites, who in turn collaborate with the EU to weaken the Polish nation. One of the PiS ideologues, sociology professor Andrzej Zybertowicz, argued in an interview that 'the splitting of the Polish national community has much to do with the conflict over the Constitutional Court' (Wilgocki 2016), indicating an EU conspiracy to divide the Polish nation.

A further element of the memory games refers to the 'Bolek Affair', the collaboration of Lech Walesa (secret codename 'Bolek'), Poland's legendary workers' leader and the country's first non-Communist President, with the Communist secret service in the early 1970s. Since PiS came to power in 2015, leading party politicians, as well as the PiS-controlled media, have been highlighting the 'Bolek Affair' by reducing Walesa's role to the activity of an informant and practically denying his role in combating the repressive Communist system. Walesa himself has become one of the most outspoken and candid critics of PiS, and for the latter he is a key enemy and symbol of the pathologies of the Polish state. As Szczerbiak (2018: 126) shows, the negative assessment of Walesa went hand in hand with the vision of Poland after 1989 – the Third Polish Republic – as a 'bastard child' of the Communist security services and a system of lies and manipulation. With regard to Walesa, Szczerbiak (2018: 126) quotes Zybertowicz, who has talked about the 'Bolek-isation' of the Third Republic: that is, the foundation of post-1989 Poland on 'a false myth of freedom' produced by a Communist agent. For many former opposition activists, the 'Bolek Affair' amounts to an attempt to replace Walesa as the hero of 'Solidarity' with Lech Kaczyński, the deceased brother of Jaroslaw Kaczyński (Harlukowicz 2016). Since the Smolensk catastrophe – a plane crash in 2010 in Russia, in which the then Polish President and further 96 people died – Lech Kaczyński has been the subject of vigorous politics of commemoration, including the building of monuments to him and the naming of streets after him. The PiS Vice-Minister of Culture, Jaroslaw Selin, has said in an interview that

> Lech Kaczynski is a legend and symbol of 'Solidarity'. He was second to Walesa at the time of the breakthrough. The difference is that Lech Kaczynski remained faithful to the ideals of 'Solidarity', while Walesa abandoned them in the 1990s and afterwards [. . .] and went over to the dark side [. . .]. (Nizinkiewicz 2016)

Similar to Fidesz in Hungary, the PiS government has been at pains to depict the EU (especially the European Commission) as a one-sided institution allied with Leftist groups in the EU and with the opposition to PiS. The former PiS Foreign Minister, Witold Waszczykowski, described the alleged Leftist leanings of the EU in his 2016 interview for the German tabloid *Bild*, in which he argued that the previous [Polish] government had a Leftist political program. It was like a Marxist ideology that views the world evolving in only one direction – the mix of cultures and races, a world of cyclists and vegetarians who accept only renewable energy and fight against any form of religious beliefs [. . .].

PiS supports 'what the majority of Poles represent – tradition, historical consciousness, patriotism, belief in God and a normal family between a man and a woman' (*Bild* 2016).

Against this backdrop, the PiS government (similar to Fidesz) depicts the traditional and patriotic Poles of the current state of Poland as being in ideological or even civilisational conflict with Left-leaning European elites. As a result, the conflict is framed as generating value incompatibility between Poland and the EU, with the EU being seen as a major threat to Polish society and a repressive organisation comparable to the Soviet Union. One of the consequences of this is Euroscepticism as the core of PiS nationalist ideology.

Euroscepticism

The rule of law controversy and the refugee/migrant crisis left the Polish and Hungarian governments and the EU in a state of conflict. The question remains as to how far these conflicts can be attributed to an inherent and genuine Euroscepticism on the part of PiS and Fidesz, or whether they are just a strategy for political mobilisation. While PiS is not a hard-Eurosceptic party comparable to the UK Independence Party (UKIP) or France's Front National (now Rassemblement National), both proclaiming the desirability of their respective countries exiting from the EU, it does espouse Eurosceptic positions (on soft and hard Euroscepticism, see, for example, Taggart and Szczerbiak 2004; Taggart and Szczerbiak 2013), which now centre on the areas of conflict with the EU. According to Szczerbiak and Taggart (2008: 2), soft Euroscepticism occurs

[w]here there is not a principled objection to European integration or EU membership, but where concerns on one (or a number) of policy areas leads to the expression of qualified opposition to the EU, or where there is a sense that 'national interest' is currently at odds with the EU trajectory.

While the PiS government is far from proposing the exit of Poland from the EU, it remains defiant concerning the EU's refugee policy. There are a number of arguments presented by Warsaw (and other CEE governments, with Austria and Romania often supporting these positions) in favour of their Eurosceptical policies. First, the dominant argument is that the EU relocation scheme remains illegal under EU law and lacks proper political legitimacy. Warsaw (along with Budapest, Bratislava and Prague) argues that the EU decision on forced refugee quotas from September 2015 was illegal in the first place, as, for instance, the Council applied a majority decision instead of unanimity, which was originally proposed by the Commission. Once the relocation scheme was decided upon, Warsaw and other CEE governments began speaking of the EU 'dictating' policy, as the majority bloc was pushing through a decision with limited legitimacy, and a large group of countries were to be forced to accept a decision to which they were adamantly opposed. For years now, the EU has applied a rule according to which, on highly controversial issues, unanimity is sought among member states, even though a majority decision is formally possible. If, however, a controversial majority decision is forced on others, it would mean a 'tyranny of the majority', given that the EU is not a democratic nation-state.

Recently, according to the V4, this type of tyranny came to the fore with Germany's 'open arms policy'. For the EU, Germany's migration policy amounted to legal infringement, as Berlin suspended the Dublin convention in September 2015, thus forcing the hand of other countries to reintroduce border controls and build fences. In this sense, the relocation scheme was unworkable due to its ill-conceived nature, and – more importantly – constituted a violation of EU regulations. Two further arguments are advanced to support this position. First, according to Warsaw, Budapest and Prague, the relocation plan actually represents a 'pull' factor, encouraging more migrants to come to Europe and thus contributing to the probable collapse of the entire Schengen zone, since many countries would start reintroducing border controls within the EU to prevent irregular mass migration. This narrative underlines the fact that the majority of the asylum seekers coming to Europe from the Middle East and North Africa in 2015 and 2016 were actually economic migrants. The Polish Foreign Minister, Witold Waszczykowski, has said, 'We think that in September 2015, the European Union made the wrong decision when it qualified all immigrants as refugees' (Radio Poland 2017b). Waszczykowski added that the majority of the people who came to Europe in 2015 and 2016 were targeting the wealthy welfare states of the EU, such as Germany and Sweden, rather than poorer ones, such as Poland and Hungary.

The V4 outlook on migration has also spread to other countries of the region. For instance, Romania asked, ahead of the informal EU summit in Bratislava on 14 September 2016, for a 'strong' position to secure Europe's borders and to fight against the origins of the migration wave. On that occasion, Romania's then Prime Minister, Dacian Ciolos, said that the EU must secure its outer borders in order to avoid any uncontrolled immigration – despite the fact that Romania is the second poorest country in the EU and thus is serving mainly as a transit ground for refugees on their way to Western Europe, therefore recording very few asylum applications (Siebenhaar 2016).

Second, Warsaw has stressed that the relocation scheme is doomed to fail, since the relocated refugees will leave CEE countries anyway and move to wealthier EU member states. On this view, the scheme would violate migrants' basic freedoms. Waszczykowski has argued on several occasions that most of the economic immigrants did not want to live in Poland. 'We would have [to relocate them] by force,' he said. 'Then in Poland, we would have to keep them in camps as well' (Foster and Day 2017).

Furthermore, the V4 governments and their supporters connect migration and relocation with an increased threat of terrorism and organised crime, as terrorist groups target refugees and try to recruit young males, many of whom come to Europe without being accompanied by their parents. This narrative points to the terrorist attacks in France, Belgium and Germany, and the failed integration of migrants who have become a serious threat for the nations in question. Viktor Orbán expressed this point of view in his famous statement: 'All terrorists are migrants' (Kaminski 2015). PiS politicians also point out that refugees pose a potential terrorist threat to the countries they reside in. As the Conservative Polish Member of the European Parliament Jacek Saryusz-Wolski has stressed:

If we are talking about the phenomena of migration and terrorism, there is a clear link between the first and the second. The fact is often denied in the name of political correctness, especially by the Western left-wing liberal elite, politicians, and media. At the same time, heads of intelligence services in Germany and other countries openly speak about it. They name the percentage of jihadists among of the flow of migrants. (UAWIRE 2017)

Similarly, Polish government officials have highlighted the security aspects of the migration crisis on many occasions. 'Until we have a mechanism to verify people who can settle in Poland, we will not accept them,' said Deputy Defence Minister Michał Dworczyk (Radio Poland 2017b). In the same vein, the Polish then Interior Minister, Mariusz Błaszczak, has stressed that the refugee crisis is to be seen as a security issue that has consequences for the division of competences between the EU and its member states, since 'security policy is a national, not European, competence' (Garcia 2017).

That even mainstream parties tend to toy with Euroscepticism to mobilise their political support is not a new insight, as there is plenty of research on Germany (Taggart and Szczerbiak 2013: 23–4), for example, or other long-standing member states. However, the question remains as to whether the V4 are part of a larger European trend or rather an exception in this regard. While popular support for Poland's EU membership is still high, amounting to about 70–75 per cent (see, for example, Radio Poland 2017a), the picture changes when it comes to the EU's refugee policy. The CBOS (Public Opinion Research Centre) polling agency conducted a survey in April 2017, which found that 70 per cent were against accepting refugees from Muslim countries and only 25 per cent were in favour; 65 per cent were still opposed, even if Poland was threatened with financial penalties (CBOS 2017).

According to an IBRIS opinion poll from July 2017, 57 per cent of Poles would give up EU financial support or even leave the bloc, should the EU enforce the relocation of Muslim refugees (Strzelecki 2017). On the one hand, the same author and some other observers argue that the dramatic drop in Poles' readiness to accept refugees since 2015 has been caused by the anti-refugee rhetoric of the PiS government, which has become the main element of the ruling party's Euroscepticism. On the other hand, there are arguments about the potential Euroscepticism in Polish society that cannot be reduced to political manipulation. It has often been argued that Poland, as a largely Catholic country with only a few historically established minorities, has produced a society that is quite sceptical regarding the large-scale immigration of Muslims. This is mainly seen as a matter of avoiding the cultural and security problems that many Poles believe West European countries have brought upon themselves by accepting large numbers of Muslim migrants. From this perspective, the newcomers are difficult to assimilate and their isolated communities generate violent extremists. Against this backdrop, the ruling PiS can rely on the anti-immigration sentiments in Polish society.

Should the latter hold true, this could also mean that any form of punishment of Poland by the EU is likely to produce a popular backlash against the EU, making things even worse: that is, potentially turning the current soft Euroscepticism into a hard version.

Conclusions

There are a number of possible conclusions, based on the variety of conflicts surrounding the V4 and the EU. First, the rule of law crisis and the refugee crisis have marked new cleavages within the EU that run between its core states and the CEE nations. Several countries in the region, including Poland, Hungary, Slovakia, Romania and Croatia, have been witnessing a revival of populist neo-nationalism. There is a difference here with the countries of Western Europe (to some extent with the exceptions of Italy and Austria), as populist parties run government business and are successful in mobilising their societies on the basis of Euroscepticism. Second, the EU turned out to be helpless when faced with violations of the rule of law and the rejection of refugee relocation. The EU does not have at its disposal any reliable political mechanism to protect the rule of law, despite the high ranking of this principle in the EU's normative system. The reason for this is probably a certain complacency on the EU's part, as it has been assumed that mere membership guarantees the consolidation of democracy and protection of citizens' rights. This leads to a gap between the political symbolism of the EU and its political practice. The protection of the rule of law functions only when there are violations of the EU's material law, as has been proven in the case of the reform of the Polish Supreme Court. Third, CEE countries have been attempting to strengthen regional groups within the EU such as the V4, which is increasingly based on illiberal ideas and practices, closely connected to ethnonationalism, and open to the inclusion of other countries such as Austria or Croatia. These ethnonationalist tendencies and the inability of the EU to deal effectively with them suggest a growing rift between old and new member states.

Even so, this does not mean that the V4 are a coherent group of countries successfully coordinating their policies against EU core members such as Germany and France. It appears that anti-migration policies are the main stable common feature of the V4 countries. There are a number of differences that make the V4 a rather loose bloc. While Hungary and Poland share a Eurosceptical and illiberal outlook, the

Czech Republic and Slovakia are different cases. Andrej Babiš, the Czech oligarch of Slovak origin turned politician and prime minister, leads a party that is very different from PiS and Fidesz. While both Kaczyński and Orbán use a heavy-handed and memory-laden nationalism to mobilise political support, this type of nationalism does not exist in the Czech Republic as a mainstream phenomenon. Prime Minister Babiš represents a more diffuse and opportunistic version of nationalism, also invoked by post-Communists like President Zeman and the neo-liberals (of the erstwhile Vaclav Klaus party).

However, this opportunistic nationalism does not morph into a broad nationalist ideology. As a consequence, the Czech government has been playing a rather successful game of staying on good terms with both Orbán's Hungary and Brussels. Slovakia appears to be an even more complicated case, which could be viewed as a mixture of the situations in the other three V4 countries. Slovakia is the only CEE country that has adopted the euro and declared that it wants to be part of a more tightly integrated eurozone, should there be a two-speed Europe. Against this background, the future coherence of the V4 will depend on EU reforms: in particular, whether the eurozone becomes the integrative core of the EU with its own budget, stricter rule of law regulations and new political institutions. With Brexit and with other EU countries joining the eurozone, Poland, Hungary and the Czech Republic are likely to drift towards the EU's periphery.

References

Barkiewicz, A. (2018), 'Morawiecki: Dziś Polska Inspiruje Europę', *Rzeczpospolita*, 15 December. Available at: <https://www.rp.pl/Prawo-i-Sprawiedliwosc/181219533-Morawiecki-Dzis-Polska-inspiruje-Europe.html> (last accessed 26 June 2019).

BBC (2015), 'Migrant Crisis "a German Problem" – Hungary's Orban', 3 September. Available at: <https://www.bbc.com/news/world-europe-34136823> (last accessed 26 June 2019).

Bild (2016), 'Polen-Minister Verteidigt Mediengesetz', 3 January. Available at: <https://www.bild.de/bildlive/2016/14-polen-minister-44000764.bild.html> (last accessed 26 June 2019).

Bilkova, V., S. Cleveland, M. Frendo, C. Grabenwarter, J.-C. Scholsem and K. Tuori (2016), 'Opinion on Amendments to the Act of 25 June 2015 on the Constitutional Tribunal of Poland, Adopted by the Venice Commission at its 106th Plenary Session', Council of Europe, Venice Commission, 11–12 March.

CBOS (2017), 'Stosunek do przyjmowania uchodźców. Research report.

European Council (2018), 'Member States' Support to Emergency Relocation Mechanism (as of 30 October 2018)'. Available at: <https://ec.europa.eu/home-affairs/

sites/homeaffairs/files/what-we-do/policies/european-agenda-migration/press-material/docs/state_of_play_-_relocation_en.pdf> (last accessed 26 June 2019).

Foster, P., and M. Day (2017), 'EU Migration Showdown: Divide Deepens After Brussels Launches Legal Action Against Hungary, Poland, and Czech Republic', *The Telegraph News*, 13 June.

Garcia, C. (2017), 'The EU Threatens Poland for Not Accepting Muslim Refugees: Here's How They Responded', *The Blaze*, 19 June.

Gazeta Wyborcza (2016). 'Krzysztof Szczerski o KOD: "Takie Demonstracje Zagrażają Demokracji"',2 March. Available at:<http://wyborcza.pl/1,75248,19706052,krzysztof-szczerski-o-kod-takie-demonstracje-zagrazaja-demokracji.html> (last accessed 26 June 2019).

Genschel, P., and M. Jachtenfuchs (2018), 'From Market Integration to Core State Powers: The Eurozone Crisis, the Refugee Crisis and Integration Theory', *JCMS: Journal of Common Market Studies* 56(1): 178–96.

Grzeszczak, R., and I. P. Karolewski (2018a), 'Die polnische Krise', *FAZ Einspruch Magazin*, 8 August. Available at: <https://einspruch.faz.net/einspruch-magazin/2018-08-08/4051d14a2597610af1ef063559b4282f/?GEPC=s5> (last accessed 26 June 2019).

Grzeszczak, R., and I. P. Karolewski (2018b), 'The Rule of Law Crisis in Poland: A New Chapter', *Verfassungsblog*, 8 August. Available at: <https://verfassungsblog.de/the-rule-of-law-crisis-in-poland-a-new-chapter> (last accessed 26 June 2019).

Harlukowicz, J. (2016), 'Pinior: Chcą zastąpić Wałęsę Lechem Kaczyńskim', 19 February. Available at: <http://wroclaw.wyborcza.pl/wroclaw/1,35771,19650606,pinior-chca-zastapic-walese-lechem-kaczynskim.html> (last accessed 1 July 2019).

Kaminski, M. (2015), 'All the Terrorists are Migrants', *Politico*, 23 November. Available at: <https://www.politico.eu/article/viktor-orban-interview-terrorists-migrants-eu-russia-putin-borders-schengen/> (last accessed 26 June 2019).

Karolewski, I. P. (2019, forthcoming), 'Memory Games and Populism in Postcommunist Poland', in C. de Cesari and A. Kaya (eds), *Memory and Populism in Europe and Beyond*, London: Routledge.

Karolewski, I. P., and R. Benedikter (2017a), 'Poland's Conservative Turn and the Role of the European Union', *European Political Science* 16(4): 515–34.

Karolewski, I. P., and R. Benedikter (2017b), 'Neo-Nationalism in Central and Eastern Europe', *Global-E* 10(18), 16 March. Available at: <https://www.21global.ucsb.edu/global-e/march-2017/neo-nationalism-central-and-eastern-europe> (last accessed 26 June 2019).

Karolewski, I. P., and R. Benedikter (2018), 'Europe's Refugee and Migrant Crisis', *Politique européenne* 2: 98–132.

Kelemen, R. D. (2017), 'Europe's Other Democratic Deficit: National Authoritarianism in Europe's Democratic Union', *Government and Opposition* 52(2): 211–38.

Kriesi, H., E. Grande, R. Lachat, M. Dolezal, S. Bornschier and T. Frey (2008), *West European Politics in the Age of Globalization*, vol. 6, Cambridge: Cambridge University Press.

Mink, G., and L. Neumayer (eds) (2013), *History, Memory and Politics in Central and Eastern Europe: Memory Games*, Basingstoke: Palgrave Macmillan.

Mudde, C., and C. R. Kaltwasser (2017), *Populism: A Very Short Introduction*, Oxford, Oxford University Press.

Newsweek (2015), 'Kaczyński: Pasożyty i Pierwotniaki w Organizmach Uchodźców Groźne dla Polaków', 13 October. Available at: <https://www.newsweek.pl/polska/jaroslaw-kaczynski-o-uchodzcach/89mwbx3> (last accessed 26 June 2019).

Nizinkiewicz, J. (2016), 'Lech Wałęsa przeszedł na ciemną stronę', 26 February. Available at: <http://www.rp.pl/Archiwum-Kiszczaka/302249890-Lech-Walesa-przeszedl-na-ciemna-strone.html> (last accessed 8 July 2019).

O'Neal, M. (2017), 'The European "Other" in Poland's Conservative Identity Project', *The International Spectator* 52(1): 28–45.

Pytlakowski, P. (2016), 'Komitet Gorszego Sortu', 9 February. Available at: <https://www.polityka.pl/tygodnikpolityka/kraj/1650166,1,kod-przeswietlony.read> (last accessed 26 June 2019).

Radio Poland (2017a), 'Poles Support EU Membership: Survey', 14 March.

Radio Poland (2017b), 'EU "Made Wrong Decision" in Refugee Policy: Polish FM', 14 June.

Siebenhaar, H.-P. (2016), 'Romanian PM: Secure Borders, Then Resettle Refugees', *Handelsblatt Exclusive*, 14 September. Available at: <https://www.handelsblatt.com/today/politics/handelsblatt-exclusive-romanian-pm-secure-borders-then-resettle-refugees/23540828.html?ticket=ST-472535-uoZ7D9Zus5E1jgzfUoas-ap3> (last accessed 26 June 2019).

Strzelecki, M. (2017), 'Poles Value Denying Muslim Refugees Over Being in EU, Poll Shows', *Bloomberg Politics*, 5 July.

Szczerbiak, A. (2018), *Politicising the Communist Past: The Politics of Truth Revelation in Post-Communist Poland*, London: Routledge.

Szczerbiak, A., and P. Taggart (2008), 'Introduction: Researching Euroscepticism in European Party Systems: A Comparative and Theoretical Research Agenda', in A. Szczerbiak and P. Taggart (eds), *Opposing Europe? The Comparative Party Politics of Euroscepticism*, vol. 2: *Comparative and Theoretical Perspectives*, Oxford: Oxford University Press, pp. 1–27.

Taggart, P., and A. Szczerbiak (2004), 'Contemporary Euroscepticism in the Party Systems of the European Union Candidate States of Central and Eastern Europe', *European Journal of Political Research* 43: 1–27.

Taggart, P., and A. Szczerbiak (2013), 'Coming in from the Cold? Euroscepticism, Government Participation and Party Positions on Europe', *Journal of Common Market Studies* 51(1): 17–37.

Tait, R. (2016), 'Miloš Zeman: The Hardline Czech Leader Fanning Hostility to Refugees', *The Guardian*, 14 September. Available at: <https://www.theguardian.com/world/2016/sep/14/milos-zeman-czech-leader-refugees> (last accessed 26 June 2019).

TVN24 (2015), 'Kaczynskim Mówi o "Najgorszym Sorcie Polaków"'. Available at: <http://www.tvn24.pl/wiadomosci-z-kraju,3/jaroslaw-kaczynski-w-tv-republika-gen-zdradynajgorszy-sort-polakow,602334.html> (last accessed 26 June 2019).

TVPInfo (2018), 'Sąd Najwyższy Postawił się Ponad Konstytucją: Takie Zachowanie Prowadzi do Anarchii', 3 August. Available at: <https://www.tvp.info/38365412/

sad-najwyzszy-postawil-sie-ponad-konstytucja-takie-zachowanie-prowadzi-do-anarchii> (last accessed 26 June 2019).

UAWIRE (2017), 'Warsaw: Poland Cannot Take Any More Refugees Since it Already Accepted More Than 1.4 Million Migrants from Ukraine', 28 June.

Wilgocki, M. (2016), 'Prof. Andrzej Zybertowicz Patrzy na Marsz KOD. I Widzi Wojnę Hybrydową z Rosją', 1 March. Available at: <http://wyborcza.pl/1,75398, 19699456,prof-andrzej-zybertowicz-patrzy-na-marsz-kod-i-widzi-wojne.html> (last accessed 26 June 2019).

9

Scandinavia Within and Without Europe

Bo Stråth

Scandinavia and Europe: the historical legacy

BEFORE 1500, IT is difficult to discern a clear boundary between continental Europe and the North. It was much more a matter of a boundary zone where the Baltic increasingly emerged as both a demarcation and a communicative bridge for the conveyance of political, economic and religious power. Today's Russia, Finland and the Baltic states, together with the three Scandinavian states of Denmark, Norway and Sweden, were ever more exposed to these influences and seen as a part of Northern Europe.[1] The Catholic mission (Orthodox in Russia), together with commerce and warfare, Europeanised the North and blurred the boundary zone. In the sixteenth century, Lutheran Protestantism reinforced connections across the Baltic.

The seventeenth century brought a counter-movement to this trend. In the North, Protestantism contributed to the centralisation and militarisation of monarchic states; these states then intervened in the Catholic–Protestant conflict south of the Baltic. This confrontation, added to the shift towards transatlantic trade around 1500, broke Hanseatic commercial power. The conflict culminated in the Thirty Years War (1618–48), which went beyond religion and pitted new forms of centralised state power against the Habsburg empire and the Catholic establishment, but resulted in entanglements of throne and altar on both sides of the religious divide.

The demarcation between the North and continental Europe became more distinct in some ways but not in others. Centralised states brought clear and militarily defended border lines. The boundary nevertheless remained, in many respects, a vague zone. Protestantism, for example, united the territories to the north and the south of the Baltic, the Scandinavian- and Finnish-speaking cultures with the German-speaking ones. The consolidation and centralisation of monarchical state power resulted in two competing composite Scandinavian states with territories beyond the Fenno-Scandinavian peninsula in today's Baltic states and Germany: Denmark–Norway and Sweden including Finland. Schleswig–Holstein was not understood as German in the sense these names would come to bear in nineteenth-century nationalism. They were simply two duchies under the Danish Crown, where a large part of the population happened to be German. Through conquest of the eastern shores of the Baltic, Sweden built a zone that prevented Russian access to the sea (Stråth 2015).

The Great Nordic War (1700–21) was a conflict in which a coalition led by Russia confronted Swedish supremacy in the Baltic. Continuing military coalitions and cabinet wars involved the Scandinavian states in a fluctuating European network of power, transcending the Baltic as a border and connecting them to the continent. However, the struggle between Sweden and Russia during the first decades of the eighteenth century was decisive for a new understanding of the border. Peter I put an end to the Baltic as a Swedish *mare nostrum* and the sea again became a dividing line, although acting as an East–West divide as opposed to the previous separation between North and South. Until then, for some two centuries, Russia, together with Denmark, had been the sworn hereditary enemy of Sweden, with frequent wars and shifting border lines. The three powers struggled for control over the Baltic region. They were seen by others and saw themselves as Northern European powers on the periphery, confronting each other in a quest for hegemony in that area. After its definitive triumph over Sweden around 1720, the Russian empire emerged ever more as the dominant power. The diffuse imaginary of a Northern Europe, from Russia in the east via Finland and Sweden to Denmark with Norway, Iceland and Greenland in the west, shifted to the imaginary of Russia as an East European power demarcated from the Nordic countries, which thus became a kind of annex to Western Europe.

In cultural terms, Enlightenment philosophy spread from its French, British, German, Italian and Dutch centres to the universities in Northern Europe, involving them in an emerging European *république des lettres* that transcended the old Catholic–Protestant religious division. The North was certainly more taking than giving in this spread of Enlightenment thought but, as was the case with Nordic involvement in European military conflicts, it was more a matter of a continuum with, rather than a separation from, continental Europe. The Nordic countries were, in this respect, within Europe. On the other hand, Enlightenment discourse reinforced the dividing line between Eastern and Western Europe.

The Industrial Revolution reinforced this trend, but before that the French Revolution and the Napoleonic wars, which heavily involved the Nordic countries in European turbulence and rapidly shifting border lines, changed their relationship to the continental powers. The British naval bombardment of Copenhagen in 1807 projected Denmark, from its status as neutral, into the Napoleonic camp, whereas Sweden under its new Crown Prince, Napoleon's field marshal, Jean-Baptiste Bernadotte, sided with the coalition against France and struck a deal with the Russian Tsar in 1812. In return for this, Sweden was allowed to conquer Norway from Denmark but had to confirm the Russian conquest of Finland in 1809, which was part of the deal between Tsar Alexander I and Napoleon in Tilsit in 1807. Finland became an autonomous Russian grand duchy on the new mental map, more of an Eastern country, whereas the United Kingdoms of Sweden–Norway (in the plural, as opposed to the British UK) and Denmark consolidated their statehood while de-escalating their martial heritage; this was accompanied by an emerging pan-Scandinavianist ideology. In the North, the spread of nationalism after 1815 did more to unify than to divide.

One issue at stake was the role of Finland. The language of *Nordism* emphasised Finland as part of Nordic unification, challenging the Russian conquest. Scandinavianism emphasised the unification of the three Scandinavian countries of Sweden, Norway and Denmark, including Iceland and Greenland. In Finland, the main trend was forward-looking recognition of its new status as a grand duchy under the Russian Tsar with the possibility of state-building of its own, rather than backward-looking Nordic unity under Swedish supremacy. The main trend was Scandinavianism. However, those Swedes who believed in a Finnish *reconquista* – not very many but influential – preferred to talk about Nordism.

The European revolutions in 1830 and 1848 highlighted the national question. National liberals in Denmark confronted national liberals in Prussia on the question of where the two Danish bilingual duchies of Schleswig and Holstein belonged. In 1864, Bismarck put an end to the national–liberal conflict by conquering Holstein and the German-speaking part of Schleswig, thus putting a damper on Scandinavianist rhetoric. The establishment of a German empire on the ruins of the French one in 1871 reinforced Scandinavian feelings of being on the periphery, potentially squeezed between the new great power of Germany in the south and the old consolidated Russian empire in the east. The third major actor in European politics was the British empire, more liberal and parliamentary than the conservative and authoritarian Russian and German empires. This geopolitical context brought political tensions to Scandinavia, in particular to the United Kingdoms of Sweden and Norway, and especially during the great European conflict between free trade and protectionism in the 1880s, when the commercially orientated, liberal Norwegian leadership gravitated towards Britain, and the conservative Swedish landlords and industrial interests towards Germany. This was not the main reason behind the breakdown of the Swedish–Norwegian union in 1905 but it was a contributing factor. Not only political and economic but also cultural orientations confirmed and reinforced this shifting map, where Scandinavian public opinion saw itself as ever more differentially connected to and separated from Europe, and drew a distinction between Britain and continental Europe.

There was a growing awareness of increasing tensions between Germany and Russia in the Baltic, and also between Germany and Britain. A neo-Scandinavianist movement that existed for a few years around the turn of the nineteenth century failed to get off the ground. When World War I broke out in 1914, the three Scandinavian governments issued declarations of neutrality and intensified their political cooperation, at least on a symbolic level.

At the same time, and in connection with these developments, the Social Democrats in Scandinavia gained strength during the 1920s in the wake of industrialisation and the struggle for universal suffrage. They established positions of parliamentary power and became ever more involved in the formation of governments. In the prevailing postwar mood of growing confidence and optimistic expectations for a better future, Social Democratic leaders invested great hope in the League of Nations. The socially orientated liberal parties in the three Scandinavian countries shared many of the ideas of the Social Democrats in this respect, and also as regards universal suffrage, modern parliamentarianism and social justice.

Throughout the decade, the Social Democratic and Liberal leaderships in Sweden, Norway and Denmark were made up of true internationalists, in contrast to the more inward-looking Conservatives, who argued for national politics based upon a strong army. The Social Democrats and the Liberals believed that they could obtain peace and

follow progressive policies of social justice through international cooperation and disarmament. The League of Nations was their political
instrument. Social Democratic and Liberal leaders – such as Hjalmar
Branting, Arthur Engberg and Richard Sandler in Sweden, Halvdan
Koht in Norway and Peter Munch in Denmark – were true internationalists. Many of them spoke English, French and German fluently
and went on frequent party political and government missions to 'the
Continent'. The train to Geneva became a true bridge to Europe. They
were part of and active participants in a new Europe, perceived as
being politically progressive. As a matter of fact, the Social Democrats
invested much more political energy and expectations in international
cooperation at that stage than they had done during the Second International prior to 1914. They did so in the same spirit that underpinned
the pan-European movement and caused the German Social Democrats
(SPD) to speak about a United States of Europe in their Heidelberg programme of 1925, and that drove Aristide Briand and Edouard Herriot
to express their federalist visions.[2]

The 1930s again brought development towards more intensified
Nordic rather than Scandinavian cooperation. After Hitler's triumph
in 1933, the Danish Prime Minister, Thorvald Stauning, suggested a
Nordic defence treaty, while in 1934, the Finnish Prime Minister, Toivo
Mikael Kivimäki, stated that his government favoured a Nordic neutrality policy. Deliberations began over a combined Finnish–Swedish
defence of the demilitarised Åland Islands only a decade after the two
countries had clashed, after Finnish independence, over the question
of which of them the islands should belong to; international arbitration had settled the issue in favour of Finland. The Nordic orientation
was an attempt to avoid being squeezed in the case of a German–
Russian conflict. But as external factors had driven the Nordic countries together, so external forces, growing in intensity, split them apart
again. Neither Hitler nor Stalin wanted Nordic cooperation. In 1937,
Stauning abandoned his earlier view and stated that Denmark was no
longer prepared to be a watchdog at the southern border of the Nordic
countries. When the Soviet Union vetoed the Åland Plan in 1939, the
plan was dropped.

Europe in the 1930s was perceived more and more as the dangerous
Other in Social Democratic strategic thinking. The friendly world of the
1920s was, at least from 1933 onwards, seen from a much less optimistic
perspective. The feelings of crisis gradually emerged as a dark sideshow,
which rejected the glossy language of the 1920s and promoted national

consolidation for political stability. One of the key instruments in the appeal for national conciliation was the demarcation from Europe by means of mental projections around oppositions like Protestant–Catholic and Social Democratic–Conservative. The autostereotype of a Protestant, progressive and labour-orientated Scandinavia emerged, juxtaposed against the xenostereotype of a Catholic, Conservative and capital-orientated Europe ('the Continent').

In Sweden, the main architect of the Social Democratic image of a Catholic threat was Arthur Engberg, who, in the 1920s, had been such a devoted adherent of European cooperation, although this did not exclude negative views on certain European phenomena. Early on in that decade, he had already developed a Social Democratic Church policy that, instead of crushing the state Church, aimed at taking it over. A key instrument was political control over the teaching of theology at the universities and the guarantee of a liberal theology through this authority. In this environment, the idea of a Catholic threat was developed and, in fact, was contradictorily used in parallel with the international commitment during the 1920s. Europe contained a progressive potential, in which the Social Democratic commitments were invested, as well as a Conservative threat, and Catholic was, from that point of view, a byword for Conservative. The threat became in the 1930s an active instrument – indeed, the key instrument – in the reorientation of Scandinavian politics towards the demarcation from Europe. Engberg warned of an expansive and greedy Catholicism that was beyond every form of political control. A Lutheran state Church, under political control, was a guarantee against this 'Catholic lust for power' and an instrument in making 'the nation invulnerable against the weapons of Papism' (Beltzen and Beltzen 1973).

The expectations of the Social Democratic leaders with regard to the League and to collective security were pronounced. Engberg, editor-in-chief of the party organ *Arbetet* and several times Swedish delegate to meetings in Geneva, returned repeatedly in the columns of his newspaper to the League of Nations. The very idea of the League was, according to him, to 'stretch a state organism over the international relationships, an international state', which would gradually expand and strengthen its authority vis-à-vis the member states in order to 'bring the anarchic conditions of international society under state order'. In this formulation, Engberg comes close to Jean Monnet's vision and the creation of the High Authority of the European Coal and Steel Community (ECSC) more than twenty years later – but the latter took shape only after another world war. The League of Nations, according to Engberg, should be an organisation with 'power and authority to guarantee the observance of international law'. Engberg also drew on one aspect of Swedish political culture that had links to its historical heritage – that which emphasised state authority.

The picture of the attempts at Nordic cooperation is one of an oscillating movement, with developments in the surrounding world as an impelling force. There does not seem to be any independent impetus inside the Nordic countries themselves towards Nordic cooperation. The pressures towards cooperation have come from without. When the force of the wind from the east and the south has increased, the incentives for cooperation have broken down. In the storm, each nation has preferred to look for protection alone rather than risk becoming involved in a conflict in defence of a neighbour. Interest politics and pragmatism, rather than idealism as in the 1830s and 1840s, have promoted Nordic cooperation or prevented it. The imagery of slyness, attached to a peasant mentality, rather than heroic hubris derived from past achievements as warriors, has underpinned the self-understanding of the Nordic countries. The relative lack of hubris has not excluded pride in welfare, neutrality, compromise and arbitration capability, or understandings of themselves as development aid protagonists and peace promoters. These are all values attributed to the imaginary of *Norden*. To this observation, one must add that the distinction between pride and hubris is not always very clear.

The Scandinavianism of the 1830s and 1840s emerged as a parallel to the German, Italian and Slavic unification movements of that time, as a positioning within a European framework. However, when, in the 1850s, the Bernadotte dynasty hijacked the intellectual movement for Scandinavian or Nordic (including Finland) unification, and the conflict between Denmark and Prussia accelerated, perceptions of a threat grew. The Swedish and Norwegian King, hoping to acquire the Danish Crown, became a foreign-policy activist who made the governments intervene in order to cool down Scandinavianist rhetoric. Prussia's victory over Denmark in 1864 put a sudden end to Scandinavianism, when the governments of the United Kingdoms of Sweden and Norway refused to come to Denmark's assistance.

During World War I, on the other hand, outside pressure gave impetus to Scandinavian unity. The main line of conflict was south of the Baltic. There was a threat of war for Scandinavia too, but it was not overwhelming. The aim of Scandinavian cooperation was to support neutrality in the war. During the war, the Kings and Prime Ministers met several times to consider the situation in the three countries and to underpin their declaration of neutrality. As a grand duchy under the Russian Tsar, Finland could not, of course, participate in the politics of neutrality.

With the Soviet Union and Germany weakened as a result of World War I, the stimulus towards Scandinavian cooperation – or, more correctly, Nordic cooperation, as Finland now gained its independence – again disappeared, and new expectations were invested in the internationalism of the League of Nations. In the early 1930s, when the future looked more dangerous, Nordic cooperation gained new strength, only to evaporate when external pressures and threats became more urgent at the end of the decade.

Developments after World War II confirm this pattern. The plans for a Scandinavian defence union in 1948–9, the negotiations concerning a Nordic customs union in 1947–59, and the Nordek Plan for a Nordic common market around 1970 are three Cold War examples of how attempts to achieve Nordic cooperation in more organised forms have failed. The defence union talks broke down when Sweden could not accept a link with Western military cooperation. Instead of joining a Nordic customs union, which was thought of as an alternative to the European integration project around the ECSC in 1951 and the European Economic Community (EEC) in 1957, the Nordic countries became members of the European Free Trade Association (EFTA), headed by Great Britain. The Nordic countries were afraid of being absorbed by continental Europe, and at the same time – against the backdrop of the Cold War – interested in a connection to Western Europe. This interest they shared with Britain. The Nordek Plan collapsed when Finland, because of pressure from the Soviet Union, could not accept it as a link in one form or another with the European Community (Ström 1980).

This pattern is relevant not only in the area of military cooperation and foreign politics, but also for economic and trade relationships; softer policy areas, like culture and ideology production, also follow and underpin the pattern. The politics of Scandinavian or Nordic cooperation have generally been about alternatives to European cooperation projects or threats. However, Scandinavian/Nordic cooperation plans have sometimes served, in some form, as bridges to Europe in attempts to reinforce bargaining power. There has historically, since the Napoleonic wars, been a sort of *Berührungsangst* of coming too close to the European power game, a feeling of basically being without Europe. The Social Democratic

189

and Social Liberal 1920s in Scandinavia saw a rupture on this point, whereas the Conservatives stood for continuity. However, in a contradictory way, there has also been angst around becoming isolated from Europe and having to rely fully on oneself. The therapy for this angst has been Scandinavian or Nordic cooperation, but when the angst grew in intensity the preferred treatment was national isolation.

The Scandinavian experiences in the 1930s and during World War II brought a heavy historical mortgage when the new postwar world was formed after 1945. Denmark and Norway had been occupied by Nazi Germany since 1940, whereas Sweden managed to remain neutral through opportunistic politics and adjustments to the power situation. Finland in the east experienced a strong Soviet intrusion into its relationships with the Nordic countries, which were seen in the Kremlin as a bridge to Western Europe and therefore opposed. In cultural terms, the Scandinavian orientation towards the USA and Great Britain after 1945 replaced the prewar German orientation, which had been strong in Sweden and, to a certain extent, also in Denmark, but less so in Norway, where the Atlantic point of reference had been strong ever since 1814. However, military experiences during the war provoked different policy choices. Denmark and Norway did not consider the neutral Scandinavian defence union proposed by Sweden to be sufficient in the emerging Cold War but joined NATO instead, whereas Sweden proclaimed its neutrality. Swedish neutrality, however, was more West-orientated or biased than Finnish neutrality.

Cultural orientations separating *Norden* from Europe

There is one specific dimension of the Scandinavian historical legacy that provided an important framework for Social Democratic and Social Liberal politics: *Folkrörelserna* (Swedish), *folkbevegelserna* (Norwegian), the popular (rather than populist) or people's movements that emerged in the nineteenth century to protest against the old society and to express specific educational ideals. The message they mediated declared an individual-orientated pietistic Protestant ethic of responsibility rather than holistic collectivism. This individualist orientation constitutes an important element of Nordic culture. The welfare-state projects that came out of this were a kind of emancipation of the individual from the family, where the state instead of the family provided social security. These people's movements were crucial in a chain of events that ran from the Enlightenment, as a reaction to Lutheran state Church orthodoxy.

This specific Protestant ethic in the North – that is, the individualisation and institutional dehierarchisation of religious experiences – preserved a principle that was not only different from Catholic cultures, but openly hostile to them: this was the principle of unconditional personal freedom and the supreme value of the individual. The pietistic Enlightenment tradition emerged in confrontation with the Lutheran state Church orthodoxy. This confrontation influenced the state Churches and low-Church tendencies developed within them. Religion was a field of tensions where various approaches were moulded together into a kind of cultural Protestantism. The degree of pietism and moralism varied between the Nordic countries and so did the profile of the Lutheran state Churches; in Denmark and Norway, these had a higher degree of lay influence and are perhaps better described as people's Churches (*folkekirker*), whereas the Swedish and Finnish Lutheran Churches were marked by a higher level of authoritarian statism. The Lutheran outlook and the popular chain of events in political culture merged within civil society and formed a parish community that, during the second half of the nineteenth century, became the nucleus of the secular communes. Here, Kantian self-realisation took on a popular and pragmatic dimension. The central state and the local community confronted one another in pragmatic bargaining (Sørensen and Stråth 1997).

The outcome was a peculiar merger of images of individual freedom with those of state authority. The Enlightenment's permeation in *Norden* must be seen in the context of the capacity for social communication developed through the people's movements. Education (*bildning, dannelse*) was a key instrument in emancipation and self-realisation, and was created from below, in contrast to, for example, the German *Bildungsbürgertum* (a mandarin-like social formation of educated bourgeoisie and civil servants). Here, attention must be drawn to the Scandinavian peasantry's communicative skills, developed in parish meetings, which paved the way for communication between Social Democracy and Liberalism with a social, rather than an economic, emphasis.

This cultural and political imaginary constituted the sounding-board of the Social Democratic demarcation to Europe in the 1930s. It did not suddenly disappear with the end of the war in 1945. The demarcation built in the 1930s had a long-lasting impact, not least in the influential puritan and moralistic free Church movements in Scandinavia where the Catholic threat made an impression – in particular in

Norway and Sweden, but much less so in the less moralistic and puritan Denmark. After 1945, the mental–cultural barrier was, of course, formulated much less bluntly than Engberg had done. Democratic governments now ruled in the western part of the continent, and there was a shared threat in the east to consider. The barrier prevailed more as a subcurrent, implicit rather than explicit. Social Democratic Scandinavia had, for example, no difficulty in identifying with the warning about the 'four dangerous Cs' that came from the German Social Democratic leader Kurt Schumacher after the war (Catholicism, clergy, conservatism, capitalism) (Huldt and Misgeld 1990).

The Nordic countries and European integration during the Cold War

Against the cultural backdrop of Scandinavian doubts about continental Europe, the scepticism vis-à-vis the ECSC in 1951 and the EEC in 1957 was as strong as in Great Britain. The imaginary of a Conservative and Catholic threat created in the 1930s remained, certainly implicitly rather than explicitly, and was reinforced by the fact that all six signatories of the Paris and Rome Treaties were Christian Democrats. The EEC was seen by many leading politicians in Scandinavia as a 'black international' (an international of Conservative and Christian Democratic parties). With Great Britain and the neutral Austria and Switzerland, they established the European Free Trade Association (EFTA) in 1959. How Portugal under Salazar could become the seventh member of this allegedly progressive association remains an enigmatic and under-researched issue. From 1947, parallel negotiations on a Nordic free trade area or customs union were an instrument in the search for alternatives to the continental European scheme. From 1956 on, these talks also served to help Finland build bridges to Western Europe via *Norden*.

The Nordek Plan negotiations on a Nordic customs union between 1968 and 1971 should be seen in this Finnish–Western European context but also against the backdrop of growing Danish interest in the EEC after the repeated British applications for membership since 1961. The sceptical Danish view on the EEC persisted, but the prospect of a European customs union with both Britain and Germany, the two most important markets for Danish agricultural products, alerted political leaders. The Nordic alternative as a bridge to Western Europe for Finland resulted in strong centrifugal pressures when it became clear that Denmark wanted to use Nordek as a bridge to the EEC. The Finnish government cancelled its participation when an elaborated treaty was ready for signing. In 1971, Danish and Norwegian negotiations for entry to the EEC buried once and for all the draft Nordek treaty, which had, nevertheless, come close to a successful conclusion after twenty-five years of discussions on a Nordic free trade and customs union. Denmark decided to apply for membership of the EEC despite the failure to agree on a Nordic bridge to Europe, and the Norwegian government followed suit. Just as they had done in 1961 and 1967, Ireland, Denmark and Norway followed closely behind the UK from the very moment that the latter submitted its request for membership of the EEC. In Ireland, there were few problems since both the government and the people were unreservedly in favour of accepting accession to the Community. This was not the case in Denmark, however, and even less so in Norway. There were problems for the governments of both the applicant countries and the member states. Indeed, Danish agriculture, being highly efficient, could have threatened the interests of small farmers in other countries in the Community. Norwegian fishing rights, for their part, soured negotiations on Norway's entry.

The Danish and Norwegian membership applications and the collapse of the Nordic integration project occurred in a situation where Charles de Gaulle had just resigned from the French presidency and the prospect of British accession to the EEC was growing. The Swedish government applied for a tighter connection but left the issue of membership open. Swedish neutrality in response to the experiences of World War II, not exclusively linked to military policy issues but also related to their uneasiness over the fate of Social Democratic welfare policies inside the EEC, established a higher European threshold in Sweden than in NATO members Denmark and Norway. The Werner Plan for a European monetary and economic policy union and the Davignon Plan for a European security policy union frightened the Swedish Social Democrats and restrained the margin of manœuvre of Prime Minister Olof Palme, who wanted closer relations with the EEC, and eventually membership (Stråth 1993). In Norway, a 'no' in the referendum on the treaty for EEC membership, signed by the government after the negotiations, was approved by 53.5 per cent in September 1972. As for the Danes, in October of the same year and in spite of the Norwegian refusal, 63 per cent voted 'yes'.

The Cold War, in particular its phase of relative détente from the 1970s, split unification plans in the North, which now included Finland and Iceland, with Iceland closely following Norway. Unification now had to do with the integration of trade policies. The issue at stake was how Nordic economic integration could be combined with European economic integration in the market expansion provoked by the postwar boom. The interwar European threat was diluted and the EEC had, by the 1970s, become more attractive, at least for the Danish government, which simultaneously made the Nordic option less interesting. In turn, the Finnish trade policy situation became more difficult. The demarcation from Europe eroded and so did Nordic cohesion. One factor to consider was the Soviet Union. The years around 1970 were certainly no longer haunted by Stalinism, nor by the Berlin Wall and the Cuban Missile Crisis, but expectations of Soviet reactions nevertheless continued to be a crucial factor in the shaping of Nordic relationships with the EEC, in particular in Finland and Sweden, if rather less so in Denmark, Norway and Iceland. A new issue to consider around 1970 was the prospect of British membership of the EEC after de Gaulle. Whether Britain was within or without the integration of continental Europe was a crucial question, and conclusions drawn from the case for being within went in different directions. Evaluation of the risks and the possibilities, disadvantages and advantages, split Nordic views on Europe, both within and between countries. As the referenda in Denmark and Norway and the Swedish 'no' to membership in 1972 showed, these disagreements had a strong impact on domestic politics.

After the Cold War

The Soviet Union was a crucial divisive factor in Nordic evaluations of risks and possibilities regarding Europe. The collapse of the Soviet Union in 1989–91 altered the preconditions of the debate fundamentally. The European integration project as such also changed at this time, with the internal market and the Single European Act, which attracted public attention in the Nordic countries. Without the fall of the Soviet Union, the Nordic countries would probably have taken less interest in the acceleration of the integrative process.

In October 1990, the Swedish currency came under severe speculative pressure. Swedish political tradition saw the solution to such problems in the form of forcible devaluation, through which the problems were then exported. This had been the solution used extensively from the 1930s on, but it was not applied in 1990. The government was impressed by the neo-liberal end-of-history rhetoric about a seamless global market and a narrowing scope for political management of the economy in a national framework. This rhetoric was effective during the ongoing flight of investment capital. The political debate centred on whether Sweden risked de-industrialisation. The solution of promoting economic growth through the provision of positive conditions for industry, generally favoured by the Social Democrats, appeared irrelevant. The solution to the Swedish Crown crisis – and the crisis of the Social Democrats' shrinking confidence in a manageable and benevolent capitalism – was to apply for membership of the European Community.

In January 1989, the President of the European Commission, Jacques Delors, responded to the appeals of the EFTA governments for intensified cooperation by suggesting the establishment of a European Economic Area; this was soon deemed insufficient by several of the EFTA governments. In July 1989, Austria, for instance, applied for membership of the European Community. The Swedish government realised that there was an obvious risk of Sweden becoming isolated. The fall of the Berlin Wall in November 1989 changed the preconditions of the neutrality rhetoric even further and, in the spring of 1990, a cautious redefinition of the concept began among the Social Democrats. One line of thought that emerged was a narrowing of the concept to security politics in the strict sense, with the suppression of welfare policy connotations; the European Community was no longer described as a threat to welfare policies.

From this point, things moved quickly: a dike had burst. Everybody in the political elite convinced one another about how right this historical decision was and the media sang from the same song-sheet. What had been wrong up until a few years ago was suddenly right. Swedish political leaders competed with one another regarding who was most European. The political conflict was directed towards this competition. The Conservative leader, Carl Bildt, demanded a referendum on Sweden's membership of the European Community. While he had no doubts about the outcome, convinced as he was that a vast majority of the people would accept Swedish entrance into the European Community, he considered that Swedish membership would bring an end to more than fifty years of Social Democratic power. Thus, he wanted solemn and formal confirmation of this change by the people through a free referendum. Bildt and the Social Democratic Prime Minister, Ingvar Carlsson, quarrelled over who was to submit the Swedish application to Brussels. Bildt wanted this to take place only after the parliamentary elections in September 1991, hoping that his party would win and he would succeed Carlsson as head of government. However,

Carlsson submitted the application to the European Community on 1 July 1991, himself hoping to profit from this act in the elections. It is difficult to discern the various meanings or interpretations of others' actions during this European euphoria, other than from the small Communist and environmental parties.

However, things changed quickly when Carlsson's party lost the election. Carl Bildt became the leader of a coalition government, and this gave many Swedish Social Democrats cause for concern. The Conservative–Liberal appeal was to 'europeanise Sweden' after too many years of Social Democratic rule and demarcation from Europe. The Social Democratic counter-appeal was the missionary task of 'swedenising Europe', to translate and transfer the Swedish welfare model to Europe.

Discussion about these two alternatives became ever more vociferous, at the same time as popular feeling on membership was changing. Initial popular passivity shifted to activity through resistance. A popular movement against the European Community was formed and enjoyed a great deal of success, making deep inroads into the Social Democratic party. As a matter of fact, it paralysed both the party and the trade unions confederation (LO); whereas the male-dominated unions in the manufacturing industry were for Swedish membership, the female-dominated unions in the public sector were massively against because they feared that Swedish membership would mean neo-liberal budget politics and lost job opportunities. The party told its members that it did not have any position on the European issue; the members and party adherents could vote for what they wanted in the referendum and still be good Social Democrats, irrespective of how they voted. Neither did the LO give its members any voting recommendations.

The outcome of the referendum was relatively clear: 52.3 per cent of the voters were for Swedish membership, while 46.8 per cent vote were against. The figures could be interpreted as a severe polarisation of the population. However, rather than being a polarisation, the outcome was the fruit of general confusion. A considerable proportion of voters determined how they would vote only very late in the day and were very uncertain about their choice. Paralysis of the Social Democratic party and the LO is another expression of this confusion. The people had disarmed their leaders and imposed a general political passivity in dealings with Europe. In this divided atmosphere, the Swedish government decided to stay outside of the Economic and Monetary Union.

Finland developed a more determined European approach from 1985, with the ascendance of Mikhail Gorbachev in the Soviet Union.

With him at the Soviet helm, the shadow from the East became less ominous and the Finnish political elite perceived increasing possibilities for action. Finnish historical experiences, within the country's geopolitical position between East and West, had led to a political culture of faster decisions and less open debate about controversial issues in foreign politics. The Finnish government applied for membership of the EU in March 1992, nine months after Sweden. The Swedish decision was obviously crucial for the Finnish one. It came as a great surprise in Finland and required some time to digest and consider. In this situation, the Norwegian government also applied for membership in November 1992, despite memories of the agonising 1972 referendum campaign. Simultaneously with this Nordic knock on the door of European institutions, Danish reservations about the European framework were growing. In 1986, a referendum had said yes to the European Single Act with a majority of 56 per cent. In June 1992, however, between the Finnish and the Norwegian membership applications, a Danish referendum rejected the Maastricht Treaty with 52 per cent against. After renegotiations resulted in the granting to Denmark of considerable opt-outs, relating to the euro among others, 56 per cent approved the treaty in a second referendum. Nordic–European relationships were as contradictory in the early 1990s as they had been in the 1970s, although the without/within positions of the separate states had shifted considerably.

The enlargement negotiations with Austria, Finland, Norway and Sweden ended in March 1994. After 66.6 per cent of Austrians had approved EU membership in a referendum in June 1995, 56.9 per cent of Finnish voters did the same in October and 52.8 of Swedes in November. The referendum in Norway took place two weeks after the Swedish one: even against a backdrop of membership majorities in the other three candidate countries, it resulted in 52.2 per cent against. The campaign, however, was less inflamed than in 1972. Referenda on the euro in Denmark in 2000 and in Sweden in 2003 rejected entry into the monetary union, with 53 and 56 per cent respectively. The fact that Iceland never voted on a membership application emphasises Nordic split loyalties and allegiances vis-à-vis Europe, with some states in and some out, but all having considerable sections of their populations sceptical or negative about the integration project. The sentiments are not necessarily polarised. It is maybe better to describe these European sentiments in terms of alienation or lack of interest.

After the first market euphoria, in the wake of the collapse of the Soviet empire and the rapid spread of the globalisation rhetoric, the social question has made a comeback. It had been historically strong since the 1930s in Nordic political debates, and connoted national self-images of welfare-providing communities of destiny. The response to the Great Depression was seen as the beginning of the proud project of progressive welfare politics. It was on this point that the rhetoric demarcation in the 1930s between a progressive, Protestant, Social Democratic *Norden* and a Conservative, Catholic and capitalist Europe served as a mobilising intellectual tool. The recent return of the social issue, following twenty years of globalisation and market rhetoric that left no place for this question, has reactivated the old demarcation between *Norden* and Europe. The vision of Europe as a market project directly challenges Nordic models of societies centred on social welfare.

Some labour market verdicts by the European Court of Justice – the Viking and the Laval cases – have reinforced interpretation of the EU as being against historical achievements in labour relations (Joerges and Rödl 2008). The Nordic trade unions have historically given priority in their labour market strategies to collective agreements with employers, estimating that this strategy has given them better outcomes than state-guaranteed minimum wages would have done. Therefore, they are much more sensitive than trade unions in countries with minimum wage legislation to any sign of erosion of the collective bargaining order through the dictates of the internal European labour market.

The enlargement from EU 15 to EU 25 and 27 in 2004 and 2007, respectively, and, in particular, the collapse of the global financial markets in 2008 and the subsequent euro crisis, brought the question of social solidarities back on to the agenda in a way that has decreased general commitment for the European project all over Europe. The refugee crisis of 2015 reinforced the European North–South divide provoked by the euro crisis at the same time as giving added strength to the old historical East–West divide, which did not cease with EU enlargement in 2004. These developments made an impression on Nordic opinion, as they did on opinion in Europe in general. Nordic scepticism has changed from being an exceptional case to becoming a European standard. The social issue, which was at the core of the Nordic response to developments in the 1930s and, of course, also at the heart of the European collapse then, seems once again to be the pivot of the xenophobic nationalism eroding European integration.

Notes

1. Today *Norden*, the Scandinavian word for the North, meaning Northern Europe, consists, in political and administrative terms, of five countries (Denmark, Finland, Iceland, Norway and Sweden) and three areas with a degree of local autonomy (the Faeroe Islands and Greenland under Denmark, and the Åland Islands under Finland). The term 'Scandinavia' refers to Denmark, Norway and Sweden, although the distinction between *Norden* and Scandinavia is increasingly getting blurred and Scandinavia is used to mean *Norden*. During the Middle Ages, the aristocracy in Sweden, Denmark and Norway, which possessed properties across the borders, created a union against the economic pressures exerted by the Hanseatic League, called the Kalmar Union (1397–1523). When Sweden, with its province Finland, broke away from the union in 1523, Denmark became the competing state in the North, with Norway as an integrated part. Norway's colonies – Greenland, Iceland and the Faeroes – became Danish colonies. In the turmoil of the Napoleonic wars, Russia conquered Finland from Sweden in 1809 and made Finland an autonomous Grand Duchy. The conquest was part of the Tilsit agreement between Napoleon and Alexander I in 1807. In a next step, after the break between Alexander and Napoleon, Denmark ceded Norway to Sweden in 1814; as a result, Norway achieved independent status in a personal union with Sweden, which lasted until the peaceful separation of the two countries in 1905. The former Norwegian colonies remained Danish, however. Iceland became an independent state in 1918 in an Act of Union with Denmark, and then a formally recognised independent republic in 1944. In the upheavals of the Russian Revolution, the Finns declared their independence in December 1917, which was recognised by the Soviet Union, but the declaration threw the country into a bloody civil war in 1918.
2. For pan-Europe, see Orluc (2005).

References

Beltzen, N., and A. Beltzen (1973), *Arthur Engberg – Publicist och Politiker*, Stockholm: Prisma.

Huldt, B., and K. Misgeld (eds), (1990), *Socialdemokratin och Svensk Utrikespolitik: Från Branting till Palme*, Stockholm: Utrikespolitiska Institutet.

Joerges, C., and F. Rödl (2008), 'On the "Social Deficit" of the European Integration Project and its Perpetuation Through the ECJ Judgements in Viking and Laval', *RECON Online Working Paper*, Oslo University: ARENA Project.

Orluc, K. (2005), *Europe Between Past and Future: Transnational Networks and the Transformation of the Pan-European Idea in the Interwar Years*, Florence: European University Institute.

Sørensen, Ø., and B. Stråth (1997), *The Cultural Construction of Norden*, Oslo: Scandinavian University Press.

Stråth, B. (1980), 'The Illusory Nordic Alternative to Europe', *Cooperation and Conflict* XV: 103–14.

Stråth, B. (1993), *Folkhemmet mot Europa*, Stockholm: Tiden.

Stråth, B. (2015), 'The Conquest of the North', in P. Rossi (ed.), *The Boundaries of Europe: From the Fall of the Ancient World to the Age of Decolonisation*, Berlin: De Gruyter, pp. 95–109.

10

Conceit and Deceit in the European Union: Imaginaries of Europe and a Pan-Eurasian Alternative

Chris Hann

Introduction

FOLLOWING THE DECISIONS of British voters (by a narrow majority) to leave the European Union and of US voters (albeit a minority of the popular vote) to send Donald Trump to the White House, 2016 has been widely hailed as a turning point in modern history. Most analysts of global politics see these events as manifestations of 'populist' or 'neo-nationalist' trends that are evident in numerous other Western countries, including both old and new member states of the EU. There is much bewilderment and wringing of hands: the stable polarities of the Cold War era have been replaced by a climate of pervasive 'fake news', in which liberal values and the established institutions of representative democracy are threatened as never before. Many citizens of European states bemoan a coarsening of *Realpolitik* as the rest of the Eurasian landmass becomes increasingly authoritarian, from the Turkey of Recep Tayyip Erdoğan (still a NATO member) to the Russia of Vladimir Putin and the China of Xi Jinping.

But Europe is itself deeply divided. In the first part of this chapter, I consider two competing ideal constructions. Both lay much stress on values, but while one puts the main emphasis on liberal notions of rights, the other privileges conservative sentiments of culture. The former is institutionalised in Western capital cities, including the epicentre of the Union in Brussels. Acknowledging the resilient power tandem of the old EU, we might call this the Berlin–Brussels–Paris model (BBP). The latter model is particularly strong in parts of the new, post-socialist EU, where populist forces that were historically strongest in rural areas nowadays form governments in the capitals. Let us call this the Hungary–Poland model (HP). For Viktor Orbán and Jarosław Kaczyński, Europe is not (at least not primarily) a political community based on human rights and the rule of law. It is a Christian civilisation that must be defended by its sovereign member states against external threats. For adherents of the BBP model, the HP vision replicates the nastiness of anti-pluralist nationalism at a higher, civilisational level. Liberal cosmopolitan elites tend to see themselves as the rational secular heirs to the Enlightenment, which they view as a uniquely European breakthrough to the modern world.

These are models or ideal types. They can also be analysed as social imaginaries. Of course, their geographical distribution is more complex than this schema would suggest. Adherents of the BBP imaginary are thick on the ground in Budapest and Warsaw, while the HP imaginary has deep roots even in founder members of the Union. Nevertheless the patterns are there and in need of explanation. They have become clear in the long-running rhetorical skirmishes prompted by the 'migrant crisis' that erupted in summer 2015, in which both sides claim the moral high ground. Proponents of the BBP imaginary invoke human rights and humanitarian ethics, while their opponents stress the imperative to protect evolved solidarities, spiritual as well as material. I argue that these competing models of Europe are equally illusory. Yet they have already produced a significant rift within the EU, which is likely to be deepened in the parliamentary elections of 2019. The division of Western Eurasia in the Cold War decades has been replaced by a new binary division within the EU.[1]

The second section of the chapter addresses the causes of these political phenomena in the global political economy of the neo-liberal decades. Xenophobia in post-socialist Eastern Europe has complex historical roots that differ from country to country, but it is triggered by a common peripheral status vis-à-vis the core powers of the EU. Austerity policies have vitiated earlier commitments to economic harmonisation. The most insightful analyses have come from German scholars. For Wolfgang Streeck and Fritz Scharpf, the institutions of the EU, above all those charged with managing the eurozone, have no credibility and it is necessary to rebuild democratic legitimation in the member states. For Jürgen Habermas and Claus Offe, by contrast, it is neither economically feasible nor ethically desirable to move in this retrograde direction. They argue that only a deepening of the EU in the direction of a federal superstate can provide an escape from the present impasse. This would require more responsible policies on the part of Germany, the dominant economic power and major 'winner' of the eurozone. German leaders pay lip service to European solidarity but their policies have wrecked entire economies and are clearly unsustainable.[2] I call this the great Berlin *deceit*.

But this German debate is too narrow. The North–South optic needs extending to take account of Brexit and the processes currently under way as BBP elites seek to sanction the HP populists they despise. During protracted negotiations before and after the UK referendum, the British were treated similarly: as the petty-minded nationalists of an offshore island. But those opinions were triggered by the fact that the EU today really is a very different body from that in which the British electorate opted to remain (by a large majority) in 1975. Moreover, Brexit would not have been carried in the referendum of 2016 without the votes of those who believe strongly in supranational solutions, but who feel unrepresented and betrayed by the institutions of the EU in their present form. Yet there has been no rethinking on the BBP side, no recognition of the damage caused by problematic rates of immigration from east to west and the complete failure of west to east redistribution. I call this BBP myopia the great *conceit*: that the (neo-)liberal EU remains a beacon of freedom and moral light in a darkening world.

It is instructive to probe beyond the imaginaries of old EU versus new EU and address a more insidious binary: that which opposes Europe to Asia as a separate continent. After providing some examples of how this absurd equivalence is currently operationalised by the EU, the final section of this chapter will set out a Eurasian 'big history' perspective on the crisis currently besetting the macro-region Europe (which, in my usage, is a synonym for Western Eurasia). Following social anthropologist Jack Goody, I reject ethnocentric claims that 'modernity' is the product of a unique concatenation of conditions in one relatively small subregion of Europe. Building on foundations laid by the theoreticians of the Axial Age, I suggest we need to attend to the long-term expansion of collective social responsibilities in ever larger, more complex political formations.

The Trump presidency has opened up unprecedented opportunities to forge new, historically warranted partnerships across Eurasia understood in this frame. To reverse the economic and moral irresponsibility of neo-liberalism, liberals in Europe need to overcome the occlusions of recent centuries of Euro-American domination and instead recognise commonalities across the world's largest landmass. For all the differences between the major civilisations that have defined the last few millennia of Eurasian history, all have contributed to expanding solidarities on the basis of social inclusion. But how large can society become? Can it be stretched to embrace the whole of humanity, as generous liberal–rationalist thinkers might urge? Unfortunately, the recent evidence from Western Eurasia is disappointing in this regard.

In a world where identitarian loyalties remain powerful (subjective consciousness of belonging), the construction of polities on principles of 'post-identity' rational redistribution is hardly possible. The current divisions within the EU that pit BBP liberal cosmopolitanism against HP nationalist–civilisational discourses reflect this fundamental tension. The solution I propose is to move up the scale to Eurasia, a level at which emotional identitarian issues do not arise. This is not only warranted historically: it is the logical way to transcend the conceit and deceit that mark European politics today.

Two rival imaginaries of Europe

The Berlin–Brussels–Paris imaginary of Europe is the dominant one in the old EU. Great weight is laid here on Europe as a *Wertegemeinschaft*, a community based in common values. This has been amplified in formal amendments to treaties over the years, notably when the Preamble to the Treaty on European Union was amended in Lisbon in 2007 to declare that inspiration is drawn from 'the cultural, religious and humanist inheritance of Europe, from which have developed the universal values of the inviolable and inalienable rights of the human person, freedom, democracy, equality and the rule of law'. The language has become more grandiose during the years in which inequalities within and between European societies have increased. Youth unemployment was already a major problem in the Iberian peninsula when the Treaty of Lisbon was signed. Thereafter, the situation deteriorated rapidly. In the decades of austerity, significant resources have been allocated to the domain of culture, including the production of new history textbooks, the creation of a House of European History in Brussels, and a Museum of European Cultures in Berlin. The bias towards Western Christianity is strong in such initiatives and the basic narrative is one of progress. It is one that has little to say to those who evidently did not belong to this fortunate stream: not only the new members of the EU, but also large regions still excluded from the EU altogether. The catastrophes of a violent past are acknowledged but the optimistic message is that Europe has learned its lessons. Its people(s) are now successfully forging ahead with the construction of peaceful, tolerant, multicultural societies. This imaginary is not one that I have researched as a social anthropologist but, as a resident of Germany (since 1997) and a daily consumer of its mass media, I feel very familiar with it. The historical reasons why Germans across a broad political spectrum have invested so much in the European project are obvious. Quite apart from the volume of budgetary contributions, no country has done more to bring Europe into the everyday life-worlds of its citizens (Johler 2013).

The concern with values has become more salient since the arrival in the EU in summer 2015 of large numbers of refugees and other migrants. Angela Merkel has consistently justified her dramatic gesture to open Germany's borders in late August in terms of a moral obligation to alleviate suffering. She states that this sympathy with others lies at the heart of Christian European identity. It so happens that I was doing field research near the Serbian border during the weeks when Germany astonished the Hungarian authorities with unprecedented action that the latter considered to fly in the face of existing law (the 'Dublin convention'). Viktor Orbán proceeded to whip up emotional opposition to 'illegal migrants' and to construct a fence along Hungary's southern border to close the so-called 'Balkan route' to Western Europe (in particular, Germany). Along with later measures, notably the construction of container-camps in so-called 'transit zones', his actions have been repeatedly condemned by organs of the EU. In this context, it has suited Orbán's political purposes to cast 'Brussels' as an enemy of the Hungarian people. Fully conscious of his international reputation, he revels in the role of populist ogre. His Fidesz party triumphed in the Hungarian parliamentary elections of April 2018 with allegations that the European Commission, together with financier–philanthropist George Soros, is plotting to undermine national identity in Hungary and the traditional Christian identity of Europe as a whole. Similar rhetoric is used by the Law and Justice (PiS) party in Poland. In these Hungarian–Polish discourses, liberal cosmopolitan notions of what Europe is and should be are comprehensively rejected. Thirty years after the end of the Cold War, when Eastern Europeans were told by their new elites (among them the young Viktor Orbán himself) that they would be 'rejoining Europe', this rejection of the West (in the form of the BBP model) is remarkable.

How far do the discourses of elites reflect the opinions of larger populations? In Germany, the rapid emergence of the nationalist Alternative für Deutschland as the leading opposition party in the Bundestag suggests that many voters do not share the vision of their Chancellor as far as the meaning of Europe and European values is concerned. The situation in the Visegrád states is more complex. Among English-speaking non-governmental organisation (NGO) activists in the major cities one finds enthusiastic variations on the BBP imaginary. These liberals deplore what they consider to be the undermining of the rule of law by their own elected leaders. They point to endemic corruption and in particular to the fact that much of the financial support provided by the EU to its new members only serves to increase the cronyism of a 'mafia state' (Magyar 2016). While most of these critical voices are secular, some clergy (especially Protestants) have joined in the criticism of their governments' inhumane stance on refugee-migration issues.

Unlike the Western journalists who report plaintively on these developments from the capital cities, I spend several weeks a year in the provinces. In rural and small-town Hungary, I detect subtle changes in the associations of 'Europe' in recent years. Before accession to the EU in 2004, the most common usage was a generic one that equated Europe with 'the West'. Even before labour markets became legally accessible following accession, many went to work seasonally in Germany. The emphasis was on the disparity of living standards rather than liberal values. To Europeanise meant to emulate the technologies and lifestyles of the wealthy countries to the West.

The westward exodus intensified after EU accession, but people are nowadays more likely to state their exact destination (most commonly Britain) rather than cite a generic 'Europe'. They refer to 'Brussels' and 'the Union' to identify the BBP imaginary that they do not share. This precision reflects the success of their own authorities in filling 'Europe' with new meaning. For Viktor Orbán (as for Angela Merkel but in a quite different sense), Europe refers to the Christian continent. The protection of Hungary's 'Christian culture' is written into the new Constitution introduced by his government in 2011. Orbán considers the humanitarianism of Merkel to be misguided and even hypocritical, a gesture to disguise Germany's need to alleviate demographic shortfall and satisfy the needs of big business. Orbán's Europe is geographically larger than the EU. He is more ready to embrace the eastern, Christian half of the continent than Merkel or other EU leaders (for example, in supporting the membership aspirations of states such as Moldova). To counter allegations of lingering antisemitism in his party (blatant in the campaign against the 'Soros plan'), Orbán goes out of his way to emphasise the Judaic component in Europe's traditions. His 'other' is unambiguously Islam, the religion of most of the 'illegal migrants' that he is determined to exclude. The main result of saturation news coverage in this vein since early 2015 (before the eruption of the crisis in August) is Magyar xenophobia. But a secondary result is the promotion of a local model of Europe as a Christian civilisation that needs to maintain its 'spiritual' (*szellemi*) integrity. This message is strongly reinforced by most clergy. It is making steady inroads into school text-books in the context of what Orbán terms 'cultural struggles' against those liberal–cosmopolitan forces that threaten traditional identities at both the national and the civilisational levels.

For example, Hungarians celebrate 20 August as their Constitution Day. In a folk register it is also the day of 'new bread', but the prime signifier of this public holiday is King/Saint Stephen, who, over 1,000 years ago, committed his pagan nomadic people, originating beyond the Urals, to new sedentary ways of life in Christian Europe. Sovereign state-hood is therefore a leitmotiv on this holiday, the rituals of which open with a military ceremony (oath-taking by newly commissioned officers) outside the parliament. But, at a higher level, in 2018 speeches by leading politicians included numerous references to Europe. Thus László Kövér declared in a radio interview that 'to defend Hungarian national culture is, in a broader sense, to defend the civilisation and culture of the entire European continent'. According to the President of the parliament, Saint Stephen had understood that Hungary could never afford to be in a posi-tion of subordination to other European powers. Hungary had 'lost the twentieth century' but it could win the twenty-first if it preserved its inde-pendence, language and faith. Kövér's message was that 'Brussels' and pro-migration forces elsewhere in Western Europe, together with NGOs such as 'Migration Aid' at home, were the greatest threat of the age, because they were betraying civilisational values.[3] Viktor Orbán did not deliver a speech himself on King Stephen's Day in 2018 but his position is well known: Europe is a family of Christian nations whose sovereignty and values are gravely threatened by unrepresentative BBP elites.

Increasingly fierce criticism of the BBP axis, and the cultivation of closer links to right-wing populist parties than to the mainstream Conservatives with which his Fidesz party is formally aligned in the European Parliament, have led some analysts to conclude that Viktor Orbán is out to force a split in the EU. But it is probably more accu-rate to conclude that his goal is not so much to destroy the EU as to change its ideological profile by substituting one imaginary of Europe for another. Sceptics ask: why would Orbán wish to break up a system of Brussels-based redistribution that has proved so lucrative for mem-bers of his family and many personal friends? The next section of this chapter will consider the perverse logic of the political economy that leads nominally socialist parties to express support for the neo-liberal EU and which, in the guise of regional harmonisation, in fact serves to reproduce structural inequalities and corrupt regimes.

Exploring the political economy

The models or imaginaries of Europe discussed in the preceding section must be analysed in the light of neo-liberal political economy. In a powerful contribution to *Kapitalismuskritik*, first delivered in the form of the 2012 Adorno Lectures in Frankfurt, Wolfgang Streeck showed how postwar capitalist market economies, based on progressive taxation and redistribution to promote equity and social inclusion, have given way to economies based on sovereign debt that favour the rich and promote social fragmentation (Streeck 2017). The institutions of the EU and especially the eurozone have sacrificed social goals to the logic of markets. The countries that signed up to join the eurozone in 1999 were far too diverse to be able to adapt to its discipline. The clear winner is export-orientated Germany, while the main losers are the Mediterranean members who cannot compete economically but who no longer have the option of adjusting their national currency through devaluation. Streeck calls for a renationalisation of fundamental political and economic decision-taking, since, in his view, only national parliaments are capable of sustaining the liberal democracies that matter so much to Germans of his generation. Streeck draws upon the work of his Cologne colleague, political scientist Fritz Scharpf, who has long highlighted the contradictions between the aspirations of technocrats in Brussels (epitomised in the euro) and the realities of sustaining democratic government (see Scharpf 2013).

Streeck's work has attracted criticism from other distinguished German scholars who, while sympathising with his analysis of capitalist crisis, cannot accept his rejection of the EU. Jürgen Habermas himself has weighed in heavily with familiar normative arguments. If there are problems to be addressed in the realm of political economy, for the philosopher the solution can only be more Europe rather than less. The continent should be equipped with a constitution and a parliament capable of playing the legitimating role currently performed at the level of nation-states. Habermas concedes that there is no such thing as an *europäisches Volk*, but he believes that rational liberal individuals are ready to subscribe to a federal model and that this is the only way forward (Habermas 2013). This position can be summed up as *Verfassungspatriotismus* at the continental level. It is shared by more empirical social scientists. In an elegant comprehensive analysis, Claus Offe (2014) questions whether the renationalisation urged by Streeck is remotely conceivable, given the extent to which economic and political integration has already been implemented. Even if the eurozone were to be abandoned forthwith, its consequences cannot be wished away. The measures urgently needed to help the victims of the neo-liberal 'negative' integration that has taken place so far can be envisaged only if the political community sticks together and faces up to the challenges. According to Offe, it is not difficult to specify the 'positive' forms of integration that are needed if Europe is to emerge from the 'trap' in which it presently finds itself. The problem is how to rally political support for these measures. Offe is scathing of the way in which German politicians have found it convenient to hide behind the embarrassments of German history in order to evade their responsibility as the major beneficiaries of European integration to date. But neither he nor Habermas is able to suggest how these dilemmas can be *democratically* overcome.

Offe notes some interesting data from the World Value Survey (2008), which indicate 'a noticeable *dis*-identification of Germans with *both* their nationhood and their Europeanness' (2016: 74n). The former is readily attributable to those historical calamities but what is one to make of the latter? The fact is that large elements of the German public are profoundly suspicious of President Macron's proposals for EU reform, believing them to be skewed in the national interests of France. The attitudes are more deeply sceptical when it comes to measures such as writing off Greek debt. According to powerful representations, Greeks and other southern European states are simply not deserving of German largesse. It is pointed out that most Greeks own more assets than the mean in Germany (due mainly to high rates of home ownership), and that pension conditions are similarly more favourable for large sections of the Greek population. Even if this were not the case, it seems unlikely that the radical degree of redistribution across nation-state boundaries proposed by Claus Offe could ever enjoy mass support. This is exactly Streeck's point.

Following Habermas, Offe also considers more normative arguments. In his longest chapter (curiously entitled *Finalitées*, pp. 61–80) he considers a range of 'bases of identification with European integration as a political project'.[4] These include 'Europe as the globally unique scene of intrinsically valuable diversity of cultures, historical traditions, artistic styles, languages, patterns of settlement, and urban structures, all of which stand in a relationship of mutual exchange and influence' (p. 63). He also salutes what he terms 'auto-paternalism', a uniquely European self-critique amounting to a '*mission civilisatrice interne*' that enables the supranational entity Europe to counter the malignant tendencies so abundantly present in the history of all its national units. To be fair, Claus Offe also takes note of the arguments to be made from the other side, including the demise of social agendas, threats to the independence of the judiciary, and the persistence of violent conflict in immediately adjacent regions. He concludes that 'the EU depends on receiving more loyalty and support from its citizens than it has been able to generate' (p. 72). Here, Offe touches on the commonplace that, due to its origins as a customs union, for decades rather little attention was paid to the cultural and what might be termed 'symbolic' dimensions of European unity. When it was eventually realised that ever closer economic and political union did not automatically lead to greater awareness of European identity, new initiatives were taken to promote European 'cultural integration'. The effects, however, have been limited (Shore 2000). The massive expansion of student mobility has surely contributed to expanding the mental horizons of young people. Yet social scientific investigations have also drawn attention to the limitations of such programmes. In some instances, such as German–Greek relations in recent years, more intensive contacts seem to have generated misunderstanding and frustration (see Miller 2012).

There are underlying affinities between the protagonists in this debate, all of them German intellectuals, conscious of German responsibilities, and optimistic that tinkering with EU institutions in one direction or another can save the day. If the national-democratic agendas of Streeck and Scharpf are hardly viable in view of the economic and political processes that have already unfolded in the EU, which can hardly be reversed, the project of Offe and Habermas is technocratic and elitist. It exemplifies the German current of Left–liberal 'Old Europe'. Offe actually defines 'the Europeans' as being 'the citizens of the EU', thus excluding large populations living outside the fortress but traditionally considered to be European.

It is increasingly obvious that large majorities in many member states do not conform to the Habermasian norm of individualist rationalism. The post-socialist states have not been prominent in the German intellectual debates. In the previous section I have described how Viktor Orbán merges nationalist rhetoric with the manipulation of identity sentiments at other, higher levels. My field research in southern Hungary suggests that his civilisational rhetoric has increasing resonance. The dislocation caused by economic collapse and the polarising impact of privatisation policies create fertile soil for xenophobia. Families whose own children have migrated to London in search of better-paid work are among the most bitter critics of 'illegal migration' from outside Europe. Rather than condemn these Hungarians as irredeemably xenophobic and repugnant, one needs to appreciate their sense of helplessness in the present conjuncture. The only significant alternative to Viktor Orbán in the Hungarian parliamentary elections of 2018 was Jobbik, a party that had, since its foundation, positioned itself even further to the nationalist right.

In short, the current political economy of the EU reinforces the polarised imaginaries of Europe outlined above. The free movement of labour has caused huge problems in many regions of the UK and contributed to pro-Brexit sentiment, while there is no evidence that migrants' exposure to more cosmopolitan conditions changes their political attitudes and voting behaviour (it is significant that Viktor Orbán goes to great trouble to ensure that Hungarians resident outside their country take part in parliamentary elections). At the same time, the free movement of capital is intensifying regional and social inequalities. In a sop to the legacies of enlightened redistribution (which began to wane in 1985–95 when the Commission was headed by Jacques Delors), economic integration through the market is still ostensibly accompanied by policies intended to promote 'coherence'. The sums transferred look large (especially when distorted by Brexiteers). But in countries such as Hungary, which use the funds they receive from Brussels to oil the wheels of the mafia state and to attract transnational corporations with subsidies and sweeteners, this form of redistribution has become farcical. The corporations benefit from low labour costs and far lower taxation. According to some calculations, the sums that they transfer abroad in the form of profits from their operations in the new member states *exceed* the sums received by those states from Brussels under the rubric of cohesion (Piketty 2018).

Europe and Asia: two great continents?

In the previous section, I suggested that the most incisive analysts of the structural problems of the EU have paid insufficient attention to the East–West tensions that have led to high levels of xenophobia both in post-socialist Eastern Europe and in Britain. But the East–West optic needs to be extended much further eastwards. It is interesting to observe how the BBP elites imagine their relation to Asia, as materialised in the 'Asia–Europe Meeting'. This institutional cooperation was launched

in 1996 and can be considered another example of highfalutin political rhetoric that conceals ugly processes of debasement in the course
of accelerating globalisation. Thus the representatives of the fifty-three
members who met in Brussels in September 2019 agreed on the need
to promote further 'sustainable, rules based cooperation'. It was striking that Asia, despite its vastly greater size, had fewer representatives
at the table. In addition to all twenty-eight member states of the EU,
Switzerland and Norway also took part. Russia participated too, but in
this forum the largest state of the landmass has always been classified
as Asian. In his Twitter review of the meeting, Donald Tusk wrote that
'we want our two great continents to be ever more connected'. Many
platitudes about connectivity can be found at the web pages of the
Commission. One of five concrete examples of how the EU is promoting Europe–Asia connectivity is the investment of 35 million euros in
the construction of the Žeželj Bridge in Novi Sad, Serbia. This is the
bridge that was built by socialist Yugoslavia in 1961 and destroyed by
NATO in 1999. It is part of the Trans-European Transport Network,
but how this reconstruction contributes to connecting Europe with
Asia is not explained on the factsheet.[5]

The present EU Commissioner for Education, Culture, Youth
and Sport is a Hungarian called Tibor Navracsics. He is on record as
asserting that 'Connectivity inside Europe and inside Asia is currently
five times stronger than connectivity between Europe and Asia.'[6] The
appointment of Navracsics, a member of the dominant Fidesz party, in
Brussels is considered in Budapest to be a form of political exile after he
had experienced some problems with his party leader.[7] Viktor Orbán's
own views about Europe and Asia are not without interest. Just two
weeks after the celebrations of King/Saint Stephen, in early September
2018, the Hungarian Prime Minister visited Kyrgyzstan to participate
in the Sixth Summit of the Cooperation Council of Turkic-speaking
States. The member states of this body are overwhelmingly Muslim but
this did not hinder the Hungarian Prime Minister from asserting that
Hungarians continue to feel kinship with other peoples who share Attila
the Hun as a common ancestor.[8] These sympathies have shaped government policy since 2010, but Orbán expressed the hope that his 2018
visit would open 'a new chapter in Hungarian–Turkic cooperation'. He
further ruminated on how strange it was to be an 'eastern people' within
the EU, lacking close cultural ties to any neighbours in Europe. This led
the opposition Hungarian Socialist Party to react by presenting itself as
assertively pro-Western and pro-EU. When one recalls that, within the

memory of many voters, this party was called the Hungarian Socialist Workers' Party and widely perceived as an instrument of domination by an Eastern power, the ironies are complete.

We can see here how 'Eurasian' elements figure prominently as a *mythomoteur*, an imaginary that enables Hungarians to distinguish themselves from their culturally and linguistically different neighbours in Central Europe (Armstrong 1982; see also Kürti 2015). The option to emphasise Eastern, non-Christian roots clearly has resonance not only for geopolitical relations but also in many domains of popular culture and counter-culture, where nowadays many people find it cool to be a pagan. It would seem that the Hungarian social imaginary is sufficiently flexible to include multiple levels of collective identity: the ethnically defined nation, Christian Europe, and pan-Turkic Eurasia. This third level is sometimes labelled Eurasian. However, Viktor Orbán appears to use this word not to mean a vaguely defined space at the interface of two continents, but rather to refer to a much larger territory that extends eastwards from Hungary to embrace the whole of Asia. This is the sense in which he speaks of building 'a truly unitary Eurasia', primarily through new infrastructural developments.[9]

Admittedly, the Hungarian case is a distinctive one. Let us probe further. By the end of the twentieth century, scholars in various disciplines had critiqued the very notion of continent (Lewis and Wigen 1997). They also dealt severe blows to received narratives of world history that privileged European imperialism and focused almost entirely on the last half-millennium. The contributions of social anthropologist Jack Goody are fundamental for the case to be made here (Goody 1996, 2006, 2010). Building upon classical works by prehistorian Gordon Childe, Goody argued that it was misconceived to posit a 'European miracle' as the breakthrough to a modern world. From his point of view, as a scholar who had previously specialised in sub-Saharan Africa, the *similarities* between East and West in Eurasia were much greater than the *differences* on which Eurocentric historians had lavished excessive attention. The East was not to be dismissed as stagnant, as it had been by the most influential founding fathers of the social sciences. Starting from what Childe termed the 'urban revolution' of the Bronze Age, Goody argued that Eurasian civilisations diverged from what he knew from first-hand observation in Africa. The plough enabled more intensive agricultural production than the digging stick. The emergence of literacy enabled new forms of abstract thought and more systematic knowledge production. Differentiated urban societies enabled the emergence of taste discrimination and 'connoisseurship' in consumption. Social stratification was perpetuated across generations by new forms of kinship and inheritance. For example, the emergence of the dowry as a form of pre-mortem inheritance reflected the high value of women in Eurasian societies, where their role in production came to differ significantly from their typical role in African divisions of labour. These developments, first documented by archaeologists for Mesopotamia, spread widely across the landmass and the southern shores of the Mediterranean. While much that we know about ancient Egypt and China appears to be attributable to independent invention, Goody places considerable emphasis on the connectivity effected by 'merchant cultures' through which people, goods of many kinds, and also technologies and ideas were transported along both terrestrial and maritime routes.

On the basis of this wide-ranging analysis, Goody rebuts many of the assumptions most dear to Western historians. The basic features of capitalism are not a unique product of the Mediterranean and/or Northwest Europe, but are abundantly displayed in earlier periods in China, which, for centuries, also led the way in science and technology. Far from being stagnant and despotic, many parts of Asia witnessed great dynamism and forms of responsible government comparable to the 'democracy' of ancient Athens. Wage labour and factory organisation, far from originating with the Industrial Revolution, as postulated by Marx, were widespread in East Asia in much earlier periods. And so on. Goody does not seek to counter triumphalist Western narratives with an equivalent narrative prioritising the East. He has no truck with Chinese nationalist narratives that assert the primordial superiority of the Middle Kingdom. Rather, he develops a model of 'alternating leadership' (Goody 2010), in which the West obtained a decisive advantage only when the East was comprehensively subordinated economically, politically and militarily in the nineteenth century. China's astonishing rise in the early twenty-first century would suggest that it was unnecessary to concede such a decisive moment or 'great divergence' (Pomeranz 2000). The leadership exercised in recent centuries by Western Eurasia appears now to be passing again to the East.

Wide-ranging and ambitious though it is, Goody's account of the Eurasian landmass is not immune to criticism. I have argued elsewhere that he is mistaken in paying little attention to religion and to *ideas* more generally (Hann 2017). New technologies of communication (writing) were vital not only for the development of science and technology but also for philosophy and morals. From this point of view, it is profitable to combine Goody's materialist macro-history with the concerns of the Axial Age literature (for a recent discussion see Bellah and Joas 2012). In the course of the first millennium BCE we find in various regions of Eurasia the development of new, universalist ethical codes grounded in ideas of transcendence. These took various forms, of which Abrahamic monotheism was one. One common element was the moralising of punishment. What earlier scholars referred to as a 'moral revolution' is seen by contemporary anthropologists as the expansion of 'prosocial behavior' (Mullins et al. 2018). Some of these claims are clearly exaggerated, as similar elements occur in earlier societies. But the main thrust of the claims submitted by the Axial Age theorists has not been refuted.

The moral–religious component needs to be combined with politics, another sphere that Goody tends to neglect as a consequence of his bias toward commerce and consumption (Hann 2017). The connectivities of long-distance trade, not to mention local markets, were always subject to sociopolitical constraints. The polities of the Axial Age ranged from city states to large empires, which makes generalisation difficult. But it is possible to detect an evolutionary tendency to modify increased social inequality with new forms of inclusion and responsible rule. In most places, most of the time, these early forms of what we nowadays term social citizenship, often grounded in religious notions of charity, did not amount to much. But the long-term trend was to ratchet care for society's weaker members upwards.

The socialist movements that emerged in the course of the uneven expansion of industrial capitalism were a radical attempt to implement principles of care and redistribution in the cause of equality and inclusion. They took many forms, from the Lutheran restraint of bureaucratic Social Democracy in Scandinavia to the charismatic excesses of Mao Zedong. By the end of the twentieth century, socialism had retreated everywhere, even in China, Vietnam and most other one-party states that still claimed loyalty to the tradition. In Western Eurasia, too, only the label seemed to survive. The Social Democracy of the postwar decades was severely weakened by the 1980s. The end of the Cold War and Soviet-type state socialism coincided with an acceleration of globalisation and the triumph of neo-liberalism. Across Eurasia, the institutions of central planning were dismantled in favour of the market principle. In the EU, welfare states were forced into retreat by pressures to remain competitive in a cut-throat global economic order. This was the inauspicious context in which ten former socialist states were admitted to full membership of the EU in

2004–7. Although the rhetoric of 'rejoining Europe' was still heard, the EU was by now a very different creature from the 'social Europe' envisaged by the younger Jacques Delors. For the new members, a shift from Marxist–Leninist principles of redistribution to Social Democratic, 'guided market' principles might have been manageable, but sudden exposure to the imperatives of neo-liberal markets proved to be catastrophic for large swathes of these populations.

These are the people whose children have flocked to the UK and who cast their votes for parties such as Fidesz, Jobbik and PiS. They are the human victims of macro-level processes. They can also be seen as the agents of what Karl Polanyi, with reference to *laissez-faire* in the nineteenth century, referred to as the double movement (Polanyi 1944). The expansion of the market principle prompts all manner of self-defence mechanisms on the part of society, not all of them benign. Abstractly, one might fuse the analyses of Polanyi and Goody, and envisage Eurasian history since the Axial Age as a long succession of double movements: commercial (capitalist) interests were always locked in tension with the imperative to protect the cohesion of communities and their evolved identities. The question is how this dialectic will continue in the Age of the Anthropocene, when planet Earth has become small and vulnerable.

Conclusion: the case for a new cooperation across the landmass

The brief narrative outlined above is put forward as an objective or 'etic' outline – of course, one that is open to contestation – of the history of the Eurasian landmass, viewed analytically from the perspective of world or universal history. In earlier sections of the chapter, I was concerned with localised or 'emic' models of Europe, for which we might equally use the term 'imaginary'. There exist emic models of Eurasia too. Viktor Orbán has promoted a Eurasian imaginary for his own Hungarian people (sometimes with a slippage that allows him to extend Eurasia to the Pacific). For significant intellectual communities, originally in Central Europe and Russia, and nowadays more widely, Eurasia refers in similar fashion to a vast space at the *interface* between Europe and Asia (see Hann 2016). This usage has spread among wider publics in recent years, such that Western journalists and academics commonly contrast the Eurasian (always valued negatively) with the European. This is a continuation of the distortions critiqued by Jack

Goody. Obviously, neither Orbán's imaginary for the Magyars, nor Russian nationalist usage, nor derivative Anglo-Saxon adaptations have anything in common with Goody's deployment of Eurasia to denote the entire landmass (and North Africa).

Social imaginaries of Europe and Eurasia can have significant effects in the real world but they remain illusory and incompatible with an etic model that privileges Eurasian commonalities over a much longer period of history. We need to be suspicious of all imaginaries. The most edifying value-based BBP Europeanist narratives may have crude materialist rationales. Behind the rhetoric of humanitarianism deployed by the German Chancellor, we may detect demographic anxieties and the interests of German capital. Many Eastern Europeans cannot grasp why those needs cannot be met through more creative mechanisms that would help *them*, rather than Muslim others, to occupy desirable positions in wealthier countries. But perhaps they would expect higher wages than the new underclass of non-European immigrants. In a neo-liberal world, the long-term costs of integration do not figure in corporations' calculations. What is more remarkable is that BBP elites line up behind them. The much vilified Visegrád states have a more exclusionary, civilisational model of Christian Europe. Though territorially closer to congruence with the etic perspective that views Europe as a macro-region of Eurasia, the HP model is repugnant to BBP liberals. The tragic migration spectacles of recent years have highlighted this opposition within the EU. I have argued that it has deep, systemic causes, and that it is insufficient to concentrate on the North–South cleavages.

Solutions might be found in new forms of cooperation across Eurasia. We should start by recognising the obvious differences in scale between the macro-region Western Eurasia (Europe) and the landmass or super-continent (Eurasia). The former has been touted as a level for subjective identifications. While understandable in the light of tragic nationalist legacies, attempts to promote a European identity are evidently futile. Europe cannot generate emotional loyalties and it is a mistake to manipulate past and present to this end. The attraction of Eurasia is that it cannot possibly lend itself to such a chimera. The task of implementing a political project might (however paradoxical it may sound) be easier when this project is *not* confused with emotional loyalty to a 'we group'. In a hypothetical Eurasian alternative, progressive redistribution (rational enough to satisfy even Jürgen Habermas) would unfold without any attempt to create a parliament and public sphere as we have known them in a world of sovereign states. Rather, it would be enough to secure agreement on a limited set of rules. The most important might be that not more than 1 per cent of a country's GDP could be allocated to the military budget. Strict limits might also be agreed to the intergenerational transfer of wealth. A currency union might be conceivable in a later phase, but participation should remain optional. There would be discussion, perhaps heated, about political pluralism and the time limits on individual office-holding. But, whether through multiparty competition or through new channels to promote pluralism within a single ruling party, the distasteful features of many contemporary authoritarian regimes could be expected to diminish in a transparent Eurasian cooperation. The main axes of democratic political debate in reinvigorated national parliaments would probably revolve around the scope of markets (broadly interpreted). Some societies might wish to extend commoditisation further than others, to make greater use of wage differentials in the interests of economic efficiency, and to accept the social consequences in terms of inequalities. Some will devote more resources than others to localised elaboration of the symbolic dimension, in the form of inculcating national(ist) narratives. But all would be obliged to accept the fundamental tenets of the Eurasian Constitution and to contribute to the Eurasian Social Justice Fund.

For the time being, this Eurasian alternative is fantasy. I advance it as an imaginary that, given other emic models currently available, might have much to commend it, not least to liberals of the BBP persuasion. It is important to resist both sides of that debate in Germany in which the protagonists concur that beleaguered European ideals and values can be saved by reform of the eurozone and tinkering with other EU institutions. This, too, is a conceit that continues centuries of Eurocentric thinking, while concealing the deceit of the politicians who impose austerity to serve the interests of capital. Europe has little coherence in sociocultural or political terms and there are no ideals and values that are uniquely European. That Western Eurasia has played a crucial role in planetary history is indisputable but there are no grounds for placing this region on a moral pedestal. The first move of those who wish to re-establish the *sozialer Rechtsstaat* and to secure a peaceful, sustainable future for this planet should be to look beyond the macro-region Europe to a comprehensive Eurasian frame.

Notes

1. Since the greater part of the former East has not been incorporated into the EU, the configuration nowadays is better seen as tripartite; but this third component will not figure in the analysis of this chapter.
2. At the time of writing in November 2018, it seems increasingly likely that Italy will follow the path of Greece, but it will be even harder to administer the medicine of austerity in this case.
3. As reported in *Magyar Hírlap*, 21 August 2018, p. 2. According to Kövér, the Hungarian population had confirmed its wish to preserve its Christian heritage in a recent national consultation. This was not a question of regular church attendance but of everyday life: 'everything that we take for granted is bound up with our Christian cultural roots, our system of norms based on the Ten Commandments'.
4. Like Jürgen Habermas, Claus Offe is careful to distinguish 'identification with a political project' from a collective identity with an ethnic community or nation. He agrees with those intellectuals who scoff at notions such as the Christian Occident ('a plain non-starter if suggested as a self-description of the most secularized region of the globe', p. 61).
5. Available at: <https://eeas.europa.eu/sites/eeas/files/europe_asia_connectivity_fact-sheet_1.pdf> (last accessed 8 July 2019).
6. This statement was made in the context of the meeting noted above, following which the Commissioner launched an 'online tool offering a wealth of data on the political, economic and social relationship between the two continents'. See: <https://composite-indicators.jrc.ec.europa.eu/asem-sustainable-connectivity/> (last accessed 26 June 2019).
7. Navracsics also experienced problems with the European Parliament, which initially rejected his nomination by the Hungarian government in 2014 due to his role in implementing judicial reforms that were heavily criticised by BBP elites.
8. While serious linguists and historians classify Magyar as a member of the Finno-Ugric language family, Orbán declared Hungarian to be 'a unique and strange language, which is related to the Turkic languages . . . the Hungarians see themselves as the late descendants of Attila' (Prime Minister Viktor Orbán's speech at the Sixth Summit of the Cooperation Council of Turkic-speaking States, 6 September 2018. Available at: <https://www.kormany.hu> (last accessed 26 June 2019)).
9. See his speech on 9 November 2018. Available at: <www.miniszterelnok.hu/prime-minister-viktor-orbans-address-at-the-meeting-of-the-central-bank-governors-of-china-and-central-and-eastern-european-countries/> (last accessed 26 June 2019). The chief guest at this meeting was the Chairman of China's Central Bank, a man with heavy responsibilities for the implementation of President Xi Jinping's 'one belt one road' policy to bring the Eurasian landmass under Chinese hegemony. At my field site near the Serbian border, many people are pinning their hopes for the future on investments from China rather than from the EU (in particular to finance an upgrading of the Budapest–Belgrade railway link). Hungary has enthusiastically embraced China's '16 + 1' initiative to engage with the countries of Central and Eastern Europe (at least rhetorically).

References

Armstrong, J. A. (1982), *Nations Before Nationalism*, Chapel Hill: University of North Carolina Press.

Bellah, R., and H. Joas (eds) (2012), *The Axial Age and its Consequences*, Cambridge, MA: Harvard University Press.

Goody, J. (1996), *The East in the West*, Cambridge: Cambridge University Press.

Goody, J. (2006), *The Theft of History*, Cambridge: Cambridge University Press.

Goody, J. (2010), *The Eurasian Miracle*, Cambridge: Polity.

Habermas, J. (2013), 'Demokratie oder Kapitalismus?', *Blätter für deutsche und internationale Politik* 13(5): 59–70.

Hann, C. (2016), 'A Concept of Eurasia', *Current Anthropology* 57(1): 1–27.

Hann, C. (2017), 'Long Live Eurasian Civ! Towards a New Confluence of Anthropology and World History', *Zeitschrift für Ethnologie* 142(2): 225–44.

Johler, R. (ed.) (2013), *Where is Europe?/Wo ist Europa?/Où est l'Europe? Dimensionen und Erfahrungen des neuen Europa*, Tübingen: Tübinger Verein für Volkskunde (Studien & Materialien des Ludwig-Uhland-Instituts der Universität Tübingen, 46).

Kürti, L. (2015), 'Neoshamanism, National Identity and the Holy Crown of Hungary', *Journal of Religion in Europe* 8: 1–26.

Lewis, M. W., and K. Wigen (1997), *The Myth of Continents: A Critique of Metageography*, Berkeley: University of California Press.

Magyar, B. (2016), *Post-Communist Mafia-State: The Hungarian Case*, Budapest: Central European University Press.

Miller, R. (with G. Day) (eds) (2012), *The Evolution of European Identities: Biographical Approaches*, Houndmills: Palgrave Macmillan.

Mullins, D. A., D. Hoyer, C. Collins, T. Currie, K. Feeney, P. François, P. E. Savage, H. Whitehouse and P. Turchin (2018), 'A Systematic Assessment of "Axial Age" Proposals Using Global Comparative Historical Evidence', *American Sociological Review* 83(2): 596–626.

Offe, C. (2014), *Europe Entrapped*, Cambridge: Polity.

Piketty, T. (2018), '2018, l'année de l'Europe', *Le Blog de Thomas Piketty*, 16 January. Available at: <http://piketty.blog.lemonde.fr/2018/01/16/2018-lannee-de-leurope/> (last accessed 26 June 2019).

Polanyi, K. (1944), *The Great Transformation: The Political and Economic Origins of Our Time*, New York: Rinehart.

Pomeranz, K. (2000), *The Great Divergence: China, Europe, and the Making of the Modern World Economy*, Princeton: Princeton University Press.

Scharpf, F. (2013), 'Monetary Union, Fiscal Crisis and the Disabling of Democratic Accountability', in A. Schäfer and W. Streeck (eds), *Politics in the Age of Austerity*, Cambridge: Polity Press.

Shore, C. (2000), *Building Europe: The Cultural Politics of European Integration*, London: Routledge.

Streeck, W. (2017), *Buying Time: The Delayed Crisis of Democratic Capitalism*, 2nd Edn, London: Verso.

Index

EU representative:
Easy Access System Europe
Mustamäe tee 50, 10621 Tallinn, Estonia
Gpsr.requests@easproject.com

www.ingramcontent.com/pod-product-compliance
Lightning Source LLC
Chambersburg PA
CBHW052002270326
41929CB00015B/2753